Hertfordshire
COUNTY COUNCIL
Community Information

940.548

23 OCT 2000

– 2 DEC 2000

– 5 DEC 2000

2 2 DEC 20~~

– 7 MAR

2 5 MAY 2002

Norfolk

7 | 6 | n i

z

Please renew/return this item by the last date shown.

So that your telephone call is charged at local rate, please call the numbers as set out below:

	From Area codes 01923 or 0208:	From the rest of Herts:
Renewals:	01923 471373	01438 737373
Enquiries:	01923 471333	01438 737333
Minicom:	01923 471599	01438 737599

L32b

ARGUMENT OF KINGS

ARGUMENT OF KINGS

Vernon Scannell

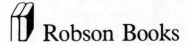 Robson Books

First published in Great Britain in 1987 by Robson Books Ltd.,
Bolsover House, 5–6 Clipstone Street, London W1P 7EB.

British Library Cataloguing in Publication Data

Scannell, Vernon
    Argument of Kings.
    1. World War, 1939-1945 – Personal narrative, British
    I. Title
    940 . 54'81'41   D811.A2

ISBN 0-86051-444-9

Typesetting by concept, Crayford, Kent
Printed in Great Britain by Redwood Burn Limited,
Trowbridge, Wiltshire.
Bound by Dorstel Press, Harlow, Essex.

Ultima Ratio Regum

(inscription on the cannon of Louis XIV)

The Final Argument of Kings, viz. Cannon, or War.

War never, with good will,
Doth choose the evil man, or leave the good.
Sophocles: *Philoctetes*

The common soldier must fear his officer
more than the enemy.   Frederick the Great

Contents

PREFATORY NOTE

IN THE EARLY autumn of 1985 BBC Television transmitted a documentary series called *Soldiers, A History of Men in Battle* which attempted to explore the nature of warfare and the responses of the individual soldier in combat from ancient times to the wars of the 20th Century. One of the production team had evidently read the short description I had written in my autobiographical *The Tiger and the Rose* of a few personal impressions of aspects of the Second World War and he asked me if I would speak about these on the series. I agreed to do so but after the recorded interview I realised that all that I had said was – while factually accurate as far as it went – essentially untruthful because of what was omitted. I spoke of certain experiences in the desert war and in Normandy. What I did not mention was something that would probably have interested my interlocutor a great deal more than the events I was describing: I failed to say that in the later stages of the war in North Africa I had 'deserted in a forward area' and been sentenced to three years' imprisonment. My concealment of this fact was caused, at least in part, by shame. The curious thing to me is that I did not experience this sense of shame at the time of my flight, court martial and sentence nor immediately after when I was prematurely released on a suspended sentence to take part in the invasion of Normandy. This feeling of shame seems to have been born some years later and it has steadily grown as the years have passed and, accompanying this growth, the need to record the circumstances of the desertion and subsequent events as honestly as I can has become steadily more pressing. This book, I suppose, is a kind of confession.

Before I set myself to the task of writing *Argument of Kings* I had to decide upon what form it would have to take in order to accommodate the honesty that I have just mentioned. I realised at once that I could not write an orthodox autobiographical narrative using the first person pronoun. In the forty or so years that have elapsed since the actions I deal with I have become someone quite other than the twenty-one-year-old who was the protagonist, though the slight family resemblance remains to cause me occasional embarrassment. I naturally think of that young man as 'him', not as 'I'. So I decided that I would write in the third person employing some of the conventions and techniques of fiction which would permit me a degree of the objectivity available to the novelist. But *Argument of Kings* is not a novel, nor, I hope, will anyone attach that barbaric journalistic solecism, 'faction', to it. The book is autobiography. It is a record of what happened to the 'me' of over forty years ago, a record which avails itself of some fictive techniques – notably direct speech and dramatisation, though not falsification, of incident – but there is no invention. The people and the events in which they figure are portrayed as I recall them. I may have misremembered some of the details of time and place. I do not think that this possibility is an important one. At the risk of sounding pretentious I should say that my aims in writing this book are less concerned with the facts of history than with the truth of art.

The problem of naming my young self was very easily solved. I have simply used the name which appears on my birth certificate, John Vernon Bain, which is the name I was known by during my army service. I changed my name to Vernon Scannell when I was on the run from the army from 1945 to 1947, an experience recounted in some detail in *The Tiger and the Rose*, a more orthodox autobiography which oddly makes no reference to this change of name, though I expect I had my reasons, now forgotten, for the omission.

I hope that *Argument of Kings* will offer the reader the pleasure of brisk, eventful narrative. If a book does not give enjoyment it is not worth reading or writing. But if a book has any claim to seriousness it must offer more than the ephemeral pleasure of a beguiling tale and I hope that this one will tell readers something about the Second World War – and perhaps all wars – that is not to be found in other accounts of military life. I hope, too, that it might throw a little light on the nature of human courage and its lack and the terrible uses to which the young are put when the last argument of kings pursues its loud and murderous course.

Otley, January 1987

Part I

ON THE RUN

THE RIDGE OF hills was a dull grey dusty shade like the hide of an elephant. After the sun had set, the surface darkened to a smoky blue which gradually melted into the gathering darkness. But, although the ridge was not physically discernible, there was not a man in the battalion who was not aware of its menacing bulk as they moved as quietly as they could to the area at the foot of the hills where they were to dig in and wait for the dawn when the other battalions in the brigade would pass through their positions and attack the enemy in the hills. Private John Bain was glad that his unit for once was not going to be in the assault, though 'glad' is too positive, too lively a word to describe the superstitious tentativeness of his sense of relief, superstitious because to be ebulliently thankful would be to invite disaster. When the news had reached them only an hour before moving forward that they were to be support battalion he had watched and listened bleakly to the exuberant expressions of joy and reprieve among the other men. If he had learnt anything in the past few months it had been mistrust, mistrust of authority, of fortune, of the capricious ways of chance. Of course he was relieved not to be taking part in the attack, but he wasn't going to crow about his luck. He knew about the tricks that fate liked to play; he knew about the trip-wires, the booby-traps, the malevolence of the stray shell, the sniper's bullet, the dive-bomber screaming down at you from what had, moments before, been a clear sky; he was resolved that he would not be wrong-footed by the feints of chance.

He was in B Company and they were leading the march, each platoon moving in single file, section after section. Occasionally he heard someone's boots scrabble on the small stones on the rough track. There was the sound of uneven breathing, now and again a grunt or cough, but no speaking. They had been forbidden to talk, not that the enemy could hear from their positions on the ridge, but it was possible that forward listening-posts had been established.

John was sweating though the night air was becoming quite cold. The straps of his small pack were too tight and his shoulders ached. He could see the silhouette of the man in front of him, the small dome of tin hat, the distorted hump of pack and entrenching-tool, but little else. They were wearing khaki drill. They had changed out of winter battle-dress after the forced march from Mareth when they had bivouacked near Gabès. Mobile showers had been brought up and they had got rid of their lice-infested, filthy uniforms and for the first time in many weeks they had been able to soak their grimed and verminous bodies and put on clean shirts and shorts. The Germans were on the run. There were rumours that once the fighting in North Africa was over the division would be sent home. But the fighting was not over. The enemy was there in the Roumana Hills above Wadi Akarit and many men would be killed and maimed before those positions were taken.

John Bain could smell and taste in the night air the faintly sweet breath of corruption and fear. It was the odour of North Africa, of exile, war and mortality. The night was unusually quiet but the silence was not reassuring. It was like a great fist in the sleeve of darkness and it might at any second unfold to release the terrifying, lethal secrets it held.

He did not think of the seductive and treacherous past. He knew men who thought and talked and dreamed of an idyllic existence which they believed they had once led in that illusory place they called 'civvy street'. He believed this to be dangerous, debilitating and, again superstitiously, he felt that it was to challenge the limitless and vicious resources of providence. He tried not to think of the past nor did he look beyond the next step into the future. For him this was the only way to survive, second by second, breath by breath, step by step, refusing to be wooed by regret or duped by expectation.

He heard the aeroplane a few moments before Hughie Black, who was marching behind him, whispered, 'Hear that fuckin' plane, Johnny? Sounds like a Jerry.'

John grunted. The throbbing hum in the sky grew louder. Someone ahead, probably the platoon commander, Lieutenant Fergusson, had given the signal to halt. The men came untidily to rest, many, who had been unaware of the order, bumping into the man in front. The whispered instruction was hissed and muttered from front to rear of the column: 'Still! Don't move!' The plane was overhead now and seemed, from the noise of its engine, to be flying quite low. Then it dropped the parachute flares, three of them, hanging in the sky like drifting chandeliers, lighting the earth below with a theatrical brilliance. John could see the men ahead of him: some were crouching down, close to the ground, waiting for the bombs; others stood upright, faces lifted to the sky.

'Fucky Nell,' Hughie muttered, 'the bastard must've seen us.'

The sound of the plane's engine was now growing fainter and from the front of the column the signal came to continue the march. The battalion seemed to creak and clank jerkily into motion, like a shunting goods train until it slipped back into its slow, plodding rhythm. John moved his slung rifle from one shoulder to the other in the unfulfilled hope of easing the discomfort caused by his pack-straps. He let the slow and steady pace of their marching exercise its dulling effect on his responses, blunting the points of perception, until he was in a state not far removed from somnambulation. And this was a good, if not the best state to be in when facing the unpredictable events of the coming night and the following day.

The battalion had been moving for perhaps another two hours or so when they were again halted. This time they had reached their objective, the area close to the foot of the hills where they were to dig in. Captain Walker, the company commander, self-important and, John suspected, desperately afraid, was instructing his platoon officers as to where they should place their sections. Lieutenant Fergusson, a thin worried ex-schoolmaster, relayed his orders to his platoon. 'Black,' he said in a loud whisper, 'I want you and your Bren-gun over here. Right? . . . Who's your number two? Oh yes, Bain . . . Okay. Get digging you two. Sooner your heads are down the better. We've been lucky so far.'

He had only just moved off into the darkness when the first mortars began to come over. John heard the thin wail of the bomb as it passed overhead and burst about thirty yards behind where he and Hughie had already begun to dig. The next three came in quick succession, the third of them exploding close enough to prompt John and Hughie to drop their tools and nose-dive into the sand and rubble. Then they both began again to dig with frenetic speed as the mortar barrage continued and increased its intensity. The noise of the bombs' passage through the air was now almost continuous and the bitter-sweet pungency of cordite was strong in the darkness. From one of the positions on the right flank came a scream and then the shout of 'Stretcher-bearers!' Neither John nor Hughie paused in his digging and soon they had scooped out enough earth to have formed a trench of about four feet in depth and just long and wide enough for them both to crouch foetally, face to face, knees to chin, helmeted heads fractionally below the parapet.

The mortars continued firing steadily for about twenty minutes. Then the intervals between each bomb grew longer and at last the bombardment stopped. John and Hughie remained in their trench for some minutes, neither daring to suggest that the barrage was over. Then Hughie said, 'Come on, Johnny. Let's get down deeper before the bastards open up again,' and they returned to their digging until they were satisfied that the trench afforded them all the protection it was able to. Back in the trench Hughie said, 'You want a smoke?'

'What are they? Victory Vees?'

'Aye. Worse luck.'

'No thanks. I'm too dry anyway. You'd better be careful lighting it.'

'Don't worry.'

Hughie had forced himself deep down in the trench, his face quite close to the bottom as he struck the match, held it for a moment in cupped hands, lit the cigarette and blew out the flame. He drew the smoke into his lungs and expelled it with a long sigh. Then he straightened up, hiding the glowing tip of the cigarette in an expertly concealing fist.

He said, 'You have first kip Johnny. I'm okay. I'll give you a shake in a couple of hours. Right?'

He fixed the Bren-gun on the parapet pointing towards the hidden ridge of hills.

'Sweet dreams,' he said.

John slept sitting on the bottom of the trench, knees up, chin on chest. Sleeping was not difficult. He was used to this kind of rest. He had slept like this in cold and in heat, when great shit-beetles were crawling over him, even during a barrage when the heavy stuff was shrieking and booming and ripping great chunks out of the earth and the white-hot shrapnel was chirring through the air inches above his head. He slept until he felt Hughie shaking him quite gently by the shoulder. 'Come on Johnny. You've had nearly three hours – I'm buggered. My bloody head's just about falling off.'

'Okay.'

John struggled against the dark warmth that threatened to drag him back into oblivion. He forced himself into wakefulness with resentment and regret. He straightened his painfully stiff limbs and slowly heaved himself upright. The air was cold and he badly needed to piss. He climbed out of the trench and, in a crouching walk, moved a few yards away, emptied his bladder and returned to find Hughie already asleep. He detached his water-bottle from his belt and took a small drink of the water that tasted of chemicals. A cigarette would have been welcome, if only as a tiny distraction from present misery; even one of Hughie's Victory Vees, the free-issue smokes that were allegedly made with dried camel shit, would have been better than nothing, but he did not want to awaken his companion. He stared out into the night and remembered his early days in the army when he had first stood guard at Duff House in Banff in the cruel winter of 1941. He had thought then that he had reached the Ultima Thule of human misery but now he would give his right arm to be there, protecting the old mansion against imaginary German parachutists dressed as nuns. Would he literally sacrifice his right arm? Given half a chance he would.

He thought of the summer which had at last routed that terrible winter. In the evening, off duty, walking into Macduff and having a couple of pints in the Fife Arms and, maybe, if the fishermen had enjoyed a good catch, being treated to a dram or two. At least once a week the Alexanders, who kept the chemist's shop in Banff, would invite him and his friend Tommy McGuire to a fine meal, high tea of fish or chicken and fried potatoes, followed by baps, scones, jam, and Mrs Alexander's own rich and seductive chocolate cake. Then he and Tommy would sit with their kind and tolerant hosts drinking Mr Alexander's whisky and smoking his cigarettes until the time came for them to get back to billets, stomachs bulging with rich food and drink and heads muzzy with malt. There was a sadness, too, in those days, the melancholy of deprivation, loss, wasted time, erotic frustration. He had believed himself to be unhappy yet now, less than two years later, the stay in Banff had become in his memory an idyll of peace, safety and human kindness.

Hughie grunted and his helmeted head raised and rolled on his shoulders then fell forward again but he did not wake. John thought that the darkness was beginning to fade just a little. Twice, flares lit the sky but a long way from the battalion's positions and once he heard the distant iron chatter of a machine-gun and saw tracers gliding through the night from the direction of the ridge but these, too, were not close enough to cause alarm. Occasionally he heard a faint noise from one of the other slit-trenches, a cough or low voices, a faint metallic clink but apart from those he might have been alone in this barren landscape of sand and rock and darkness.

He knew that the brigade was to attack without artillery support. This, he supposed, was intended to preserve the element of surprise. In any case artillery barrages never seemed to have much effect on defensive positions. When the infantry moved in there was always a hot reception awaiting them. Quite early in the campaign he had learned that, of the tons of high explosive hurled over in a barrage, only a tiny proportion caused casualties. He had even tried to comfort himself with that knowledge when it was he who was under bombardment, but terror was always deaf to reason.

The dragging weight of drowsiness had left him now and he decided to let Hughie sleep on, at least for another hour or so. He leaned on the trench parapet and stared sightlessly ahead and very, very gradually the darkness was diluted to a bluish-grey twilight. Then he saw, crawling towards him from an adjoining slit-trench, an accoutred figure which he recognised as it drew close as his section leader, Corporal Jamieson.

'You all right Bain?' Jamieson said in a whispered growl. 'Wake your mate up. We're standing-to'.

The corporal crawled away to the next trench.

John tapped on Hughie's tin hat. There was no response.

'Hughie!' John said sharply. 'Wake up!' He took his friend by the shoulder and shook him.

Hughie's head jerked upwards. He scowled and blinked and rubbed his eyes.

'Thanks a million, china,' he said. 'I was just getting stuck into a smashing big blonde. Lovely she was.'

'I'm glad I rescued her.'

'Jealous. That's what you was. Jealous!'

Hughie hauled himself upright. He felt in his pockets and brought out his cigarettes.

'Want one?'

John nodded. 'I will, thanks.'

Hughie ducked down low in the trench and struck a match. 'Get down here and light up.'

They lit their cigarettes and stood erect again, shielding the glowing tips in the palms of their hands.

'It's getting lighter,' John said.

'Aye . . . Christ these fucking fags are horrible.'

John agreed, but they smoked them to the finish.

A few minutes later Hughie, who had turned his back on the Bren-gun to face away from the hills, exclaimed suddenly, 'They're coming Johnny. Here they come. Poor bastards!'

John peered in the direction that Hughie was facing and saw, only a few dozen yards away, the leading sections of the attacking force moving slowly, with almost no sound, towards them. As the first of them reached the slit-trench John saw they belonged to the Seaforth Highlanders.

Hughie called softly, 'All the best mate!'

One of the Seaforths answered 'It's all right for you Jimmy . . . Lucky bastard!' but the tone of his voice did not carry true resentment: it was rueful, resigned.

Spectrally in the half-light, the Seaforths moved with almost no sound through the support positions and moved towards the hills. Farther away on the left and right flanks, unseen in the dimness, other Highlanders would be advancing towards their objectives on the ridge. John felt immense relief that he was not one of them but the relief was tainted with guilt.

'It's going to be daylight by the time they get up there. They'll be sitting ducks.'

Hughie nodded. 'Sooner them than me. But let's hope they chase the bastards out. 'Cos you know what'll happen if they don't? It'll be us in there with the bayonet. And I can't say I fancy that one little bit.'

A few minutes later the Seaforths were out of sight and John heard the first yammer of German machine-guns from the direction of the hills.

'Spandaus,' Hughie said. 'Jerry must have spotted them.'

The firing increased, now augmented by small-arms and some mortar bursts. In the east the sky was smeared with red. Soon it would be fully daylight.

'Better check the magazines, in case we have to go and help out up there,' Hughie said.

John shrugged. 'They're all right. I cleaned them yesterday. Maybe you'd better fire a few rounds. Make sure the one on the gun's all right.

'I'll wait till I get the order.'

'Think we'll get any breakfast?'

'No . . . rations won't come up while this is going on . . . Christ I could do with a mug o' tea.'

The fighting in the hills seemed to be intensifying. Twilight was sharpening into the metallic, clearer greyness of early morning but you could not see much of what was happening in the hills. Human figures moved insectile and anonymous in little clusters, forming irregular patterns that kept breaking and coming together again. Some of the small individual fragments were left motionless on the hillside. The noise of the machine-guns was irregular, too, coming in quick jabbering bursts which gradually grew less and less frequent. At times John thought he heard voices shouting orders or perhaps crying out in fear and pain, but he could not be sure that they existed outside his own head. Later the noises stopped and no movement could be seen.

Corporal Jamieson came trotting over in a crouching posture, more from habit than any real fear of enemy fire, and told them they were to get ready to move.

'What's happened?' Hughie said. 'They chased the fuckers out?'

'Dunno. Fergusson's gone over to HQ Company for an O. Group. We'll get the gen bah-deen.'

Jamieson moved off to the next slit-trench.

Hughie called after him, 'We going to get any char?' but the corporal did not answer.

'Fucking cooks. They could've brewed-up easy. You bet your nelly they're no' going without their fucking char, the bastards.'

Hughie detached his water-bottle, uncorked it and took a mouthful of its contents. He swilled the water round his mouth and spat it out. 'Camel's piss!'

The sun was now brightening and, just perceptibly, warming the air. All sound of the battle had died into a waiting silence. Lieutenant Fergusson came back from Headquarters Company and ordered Jamieson to get the platoon on the move. B Company began to advance, marching as on the night before, each platoon's sections in single file. John found that the steady rhythmic plodding, lack of sleep and too much unrelieved anxiety induced a physical and mental state with which he had become familiar during the past six months, a condition of almost trance-like indifference to, or unawareness of, his immediate circumstances. It was not that he was mentally elsewhere; rather that his mind was nowhere at all. He had become a kind of automaton.

The battalion soon reached the foot of the hills and began to climb up to where the fighting had been going on. They had been marching for about twenty minutes when the first dead Seaforths were seen.

John was nudged into awareness when Hughie said, 'There's one poor bastard's finished with fuckin'-an'-fightin'.'

The soldier was lying on his stomach, his head turned away from John's regard so his face could not be seen. There was no sign of a wound. He might have been asleep except that his stillness was that absolute, immovable stillness of the dead, that total cancellation of any possibility of movement. Yet the dead were not inanimate things. They were not like stones or burntout vehicles or discarded equipment. They remained human and vulnerable and pathetic.

Soon more dead were seen, scattered on the hillside like big broken dolls and when John's platoon reached the now deserted enemy slit-trenches the area was littered with corpses. The rocks and sand had lost their earlier greyness and were now a pale yellowish brown in the morning sun. Already the flesh of the dead soldiers, British and enemy, was assuming a waxy theatrical look, transformed by the maquillage of dust and sand and the sly beginnings of decay.

B Company was ordered to halt and stand easy.

'Can't see any wounded,' Hughie said. 'The meat-wagons must've got them away down one of them tracks on the left flank.'

John did not answer. He thought he could already smell the sweet feculence of the dead.

'You all right, Johnny?'

He nodded. 'Yeah, I'm okay.' But he was feeling strange and Hughie must have seen some outward sign of the sick, slightly feverish condition that seemed to generate an inward shivering and veil his surroundings with a transparent yet elusively transforming tegument of, not so much unreality, as a changed, harder and sharper reality. Then he saw that the other men in his section and from the other platoons must have been given the order to fall out because they were moving among the dead bodies, the Seaforths' corpses as well as the German, and they were bending over them, sometimes turning them with an indifferent boot, before they removed watches, rings and what valuables they could find. They seemed to be moving with unnatural slowness, proceeding from one body to another, stooping, reaching out, methodical and absorbed. Hughie had gone. He must have joined the scavengers.

John Bain watched this scene for a few moments. Then he turned away and started to walk back down the slope towards the foot of the hills where they had dug in on the previous night. No one attempted to stop him. No voice called out, peremptory and outraged. He walked unhurriedly but quite steadily, not looking back, his rifle slung on his right shoulder. And still no one shouted. It was as if he had become invisible. He plodded onwards and downwards. The sun was strong now and he felt the heat biting through his KD shirt. Sweat was soaking his hair under the steel helmet. He did not look back but kept his eyes down, seeing no more than a few yards in front of him. If there were any sounds his ears did not register them. He moved without any sense of physical exertion as if he had been relieved of a great burden and could enjoy an easy, almost floating sense of effortlessness as he walked onwards, down to the level ground and on to a rough track.

He did not know for how long he had been walking when his sense of almost total insulation from his surroundings was penetrated by the noise of a motor-engine coming from some-where behind him. But even then he did not bother to look round and when a jeep driven by a lieutenant wearing the peaked cap of an English regiment, or perhaps some service corps, came to a halt at his side, John felt unalarmed.

The officer said, 'Hullo. You heading for B Echelon?'

John said that he was.

'Hop aboard then. That's where I'm going.'

John climbed into the passenger seat and the jeep moved forward.

The lieutenant said, 'I see you're in the Jocks. What regiment?'

'Gordons.'

'Ah, the Gay Gordons, eh.' The officer had a small, pale moustache. 'They've kept you chaps pretty busy since Alamein, you and the Fifty Div.' His voice was a parody of the upper-class young subaltern's manner of speech, with its unfocused enthusiasm, its slight staginess. Then supplying the explanation for his passenger's solitary trek that John would not, in his bemused state, have been able to furnish on his own behalf, the lieutenant added, 'You've got a dispatch or something from your CO?'

'That's right,' John said. 'For Brigade Intelligence. I'm Company Runner.'

The officer seemed to accept this improbability without question. 'You're not a Scot, are you? How did you get into the Gordons?'

'Transferred from the London Scottish.'

'Oh yes. They're the chaps with the funny-coloured kilts. Sort of pink.'

'Hodden grey.'

'That's what they call it, is it? I remember we were stationed near some of them in Hampshire, near Winchester. Under canvas they were. Some of the officers used to come over to our mess for drinks. Nice chaps. Some of them.'

The lieutenant went on speaking. It seemed that he did not require any response. John was dimly aware of the sound of the officer's voice but not of the meaning, such as it was, of the words. The jeep bumped and shuddered along the track and the sun drummed down on the dusty rocks and sand. Then they came in sight of the cluster of tents and parked trucks, jeeps and Bren-carriers that comprised B Echelon. The lieutenant brought the jeep to a standstill outside a tent which had a crude signboard stuck in the ground close to its entrance with the words 'Brigade Signals' painted on it.

'Here we are,' the lieutenant said. 'You know where you've got to go?' They both climbed out of the jeep.

John said that he did know and he thanked the officer, who acknowledged his salute and went into the signals tent.

There were a few men of various ranks moving about the

camp but no one paid the least attention to John. He walked along the track which led through the centre of the camp and still no one spoke to him. In a few minutes he had left the tents and vehicles behind him and was tramping in what he believed was the direction of Gabès. Not that he had any plans for what he might do if he reached there. All he cared about was moving back, away from the front, away from where the dead Seaforths were disposed on the sand and rocks in their last abandonment, in their terrible cancellations, their sad mockery of the living. And he saw again the living themselves, his comrades, moving among the corpses, settling on their prey like vultures or jackals.

John's earlier sense of effortless motion had faded but, though walking was now quite hard work, he still felt that he could go on for a long time. And his sense of unreality persisted. If his situation seemed dream-like it was also real, like one of those dreams which are not furnished with the surrealistic events and objects of fantasy but are versions of a sharper, more intense experience of the familiar world, those dreams which are only unreal because choices are simplified and the dreamer is liberated from the conventional restraints of his waking existence.

Twice, trucks passed him travelling towards the front-line and towards Sfax; the second vehicle was carrying troops who shouted and gesticulated at him. He decided to move away from the track and he found, in the sand and scrub, a wadi that ran parallel to the crude thoroughfare and concealed him from its view. He stopped and took off his helmet and wiped the sweat from his forehead and neck. There was little water left in his bottle. He took a very small drink. It was warm and, with the chemical taste of its sterilising agents, it did nothing to assuage his thirst. He tramped on.

The regular, mechanical rhythm of his plodding feet, which seemed to vibrate in his skull like a distant drumbeat, deepened his already trance-like state. If there were noises of traffic from the rough road he did not hear them. He did not think about the men in his section or about the possible consequences of his actions. His mind had ceased to function as an instrument of

ratiocination, even of consequential or simple narrative recollection. The images that did drift in and out of his consciousness
were repetitive and apparently unrelated: the slopes of Wadi
Akarit, the early sun rinsing the rocks and the dead Highlanders
in their repose. For they were truly in repose. Even those whose
wounds were blatantly on display, the ones whose limbs had
been shattered or whose faces had been smashed out of human
resemblance, were immodest yet childlike in their complete
surrender to insentience and stillness. From some dark place in
the depths of his memory a few words almost surfaced, showing
themselves for a moment but not clearly. *Not dead but
sleeping . . . but sleepeth.* 'Bollocks,' he said aloud, surprising
the still, clammy silence. 'They were dead all right.'

He had been walking for a long time for the sun was now
staining the skies in the west when he came to a clump of palm
trees which had clearly been occupied fairly recently by German
or, as was more probable, Italian troops. It must have been a
small detachment for there were only a few slit-trenches, less
than a dozen, and in one of these he found three tins of meat. Of
less interest were half-a-dozen red-devils, those little hand-
grenades the Italians carried, brightly painted, deceptively
unthreatening, like toys. John took his bayonet and hacked open
one of the tins of meat. The heat of the sun had melted the
gelatinous part of the contents so that not very much gristly meat
floated in a warm and oily bath. John swallowed some of the
mixture and threw away the tin. Suddenly he felt very tired. It
seemed that the strength which had kept him moving for so long
had drained away in a few seconds and left him incapable of
walking even another few yards. Laboriously he took off his
helmet and small pack, belt and ammunition pouches and lay
down beneath one of the palm trees with his head pillowed on
the valise. Then he slept.

He was awakened by someone shaking him by the shoulder
and a voice exhorting him to get up. Briefly he was utterly
confused, forgetting for a moment his circumstances and
wondering why the soldier bending over him was dark-skinned
and speaking English with a strange accent. Then he sat upright,

shook his head and rubbed his eyes. He saw that the man who had disturbed his sleep was a Gurkha private.

John did not know how long he had slept though he guessed from the disappearance of the sun and the coolness of the air that it was now fairly late evening.

He said, 'What time is it?'

The Gurkha grinned. 'About nine o'clock. Maybe bit more. Maybe less. You come with me. I get you tea and chapati. Okay?'

Had the Gurkha been a white British soldier John would almost certainly have felt alarmed and unwilling to accept the invitation but, although he had seen Indian soldiers of the Fourth Division passing in trucks on the march, he had never spoken or even been close to one. The man's foreignness as well as his friendly smile were somehow reassuring and John's earlier sense of unreality returned.

'Bring your things,' the Gurkha said.

John stood up, picked up his steel helmet and put it on. He slung his webbing over one shoulder, carrying the valise in one hand and his rifle in the other, and followed the Gurkha through the trees to a clearing where tents had been erected and Bren-carriers and trucks were parked. He was led to a fairly large bell-tent and inside were three more Gurkhas sitting on ammunition boxes and each holding an enamel mug of tea. They smiled at him, friendly and only just a little curious. His escort said something to them and one rose and filled a mug from the tea-pail that stood near the tent-pole and handed it to John. He indicated that John should sit down and the soldier who had brought him there went away.

John thanked them and drank some of the tea. It was warm and very sweet.

One of the Indian soldiers said, 'He gone to fetch chapatis.' The other two sat with their mugs of tea, smiling, pleased, it seemed, that he should be enjoying his tea.

John had heard many of the stories about the Gurkhas, legends that had become part of the mythology of camp and barrack-room, tales of their ferocity in action when they would not attack with the support of an artillery barrage but chose to swoop on the enemy in silence and darkness, inflicting dreadful carnage with their glinting kukris. And there was the common belief, true or false John did not know, that the Gurkha would not unsheathe his kukri except to kill, and killing meant the decapitation of his foe. The tale was told of Gurkha fighting-patrols which would infiltrate the enemy positions at night, creep upon a slit-trench and cut off the head of only one of its occupants so that the daylight would reveal to the other his headless comrade. Oddly, the cheerful amiability of the little men did not rob those tales of credibility but increased their power to disturb.

The Gurkha who had said that chapatis were being fetched spoke again: 'You are only one? Alone? Where your people? Your regiment? How is it you alone?' He did not seem suspicious, merely curious, in a wondering almost childlike way.

'I got lost,' John said.

His interlocutor smiled more broadly and said something to his companions and all three laughed quietly.

John said, 'I was on patrol. Get-away man. I got cut off from the others and couldn't find my way back to the battalion. I'm trying to get to Gabès. Divisional HQ.' It did not sound very convincing, he thought, hoping that their ignorance or imperfect command of the English language might somehow make it seem less implausible.

The Gurkha who had awakened him returned to the tent with a tin platter of chapatis. He extended them first to John and then to his comrades. The one who had questioned John spoke to the chapati-bearer who looked quickly at John and laughed quietly as the others had done.

John ate his chapati and drank the strong sweet tea.

Then he said, 'Thank you for the tea and everything. I'd better be going.' He stood up and began to put his equipment on properly.

They watched him, still smiling. Their eyes were bright and their teeth gleamed in the deepening darkness of the tent into which their coppery faces were beginning to merge. He ducked out of the tent and began to walk back to the palm trees. He half expected them to follow him or to call out but they did neither. Back at the old enemy positions he stopped to urinate. Then he returned to the track and began walking again. Darkness was thickening in the air which grew colder. He tramped on for about an hour when the rough track joined a broader and better kept road which he guessed was the main route to Gabès. Now that it was growing dark he thought he would be safe to follow it. The distant lights of any traffic would give sufficient warning for him to hide before he could be seen.

It was now quite dark, the high, cloudless sky of a blue so deep that it was almost black, sprinkled with minute stars like grains of sugar. His marching was becoming mechanical and the weight of sleepiness seemed to hood his mind so that it was scarcely functioning at all. Occasionally he stumbled and the jolt of sudden wakefulness was like an unexpected blow, disconcerting and painful, but each time this happened he continued onwards, the regular tempo of his tramping feet restoring him to the state of near somnambulation. And then he fell. He hit the ground as if he had been thrown from a ledge and for a few seconds he struggled to get air into his lungs as explosions of weightless and soundless shrapnel corruscated inside his skull.

When he was able to breathe more easily he was aware of pain and a warm saltiness in his mouth and he realised that he had bitten his tongue. He heaved himself on all fours and felt about in the darkness for his fallen rifle. His hand soon encountered it and he used it as a crutch to push himself to his feet. Momentary dizziness made him take a backward step and his boot struck something metallic. He stood quite still. Many booby-traps and mines littered the terrain which had until recently been in the possession of the Germans or Italians. Slowly he bent his knees until he was in a squatting position and then he reached out, his hand patrolling in a slowly widening arc. Involuntarily he snatched it back as it touched metal; then he extended it again and began to investigate the object he had touched. It was too big for a mine. His hand made further explorations and was rewarded by recognition. He was touching a jerry-can and he had obviously wandered off the road into the sandy scrub-land through which it ran. An intolerable weariness again came down upon him like a dark, falling canopy and from his squatting position he simply keeled over on to his left side, stretched out his legs, pulled off his helmet and cradled his head in his arms and fell into a deep sleep.

When he awoke it was daylight and he was shivering with cold and the dampness of the slight dewfall. He could feel the soreness on his tongue where he had bitten the tip when he fell. He heaved himself upright, grimacing at the pain of stiffened joints as limbs were straightened and circulation restored. The ground inclined towards the road and he had apparently slithered or rolled down the bank to this place where the enemy had stopped, perhaps to brew up, in their retreat from Mareth. He picked up the jerry-can, shook it and found that it was empty. There were a few crumpled and empty tins that had contained meat or jam, some scraps of paper and a field-grey forage-cap. John shifted some of the pieces of paper with his toe, saw that they seemed to be unsoiled, then picked a few up. There was a printed handbill of some kind and a couple of letters written on thin airmail paper. He took them with him and, with the absurd and mindlessly puritanical modesty of the British, found a place of concealment in a hollow sheltered by scrub where he took off his equipment, lowered his KD shorts and crouched to empty his bowels. When he had completed this operation and readjusted his clothes and equipment he felt slightly dizzy and sick. But the feeling passed and he put on his helmet, slung his rifle on to his right shoulder and climbed up to the road.

He was soon warmed by the climbing sun and the exertion of walking and after a while he became unconscious of the effort of movement, the weight of his rifle and equipment and the increasing heat as he moved forward mechanically, his mind a screen on which fitful and indistinct images came and went. For a few seconds he saw quite clearly the face of a dead soldier turned upwards, eyes wide open, staring undazzled into the sun. The soldier was not a Seaforth. He was darkly bearded and lay on the lip of a trench. Perhaps the image was not of the Wadi

Akarit battle at all but from some earlier memory of action in the desert. The soldier, most likely an Italian, lay there, handsome with his dark-curling beard, outstaring the sun. A large fly crawled down his forehead on to his nose and from there it stepped delicately on to his eye where it stayed, moving a little, but not leaving the glassy surface of the cornea . . . Then it flew away. The image faded and others, vaguer, sometimes hardly recognisable, came and went until all but the merest dregs of consciousness were drained away by the heat and the automatic thumping of his marching feet.

The truck was almost upon him before the sound of its engine penetrated his somnolence and he jumped back as the vehicle pulled up a few yards ahead of where he now stood. It was an RAF three-tonner.

The driver stuck his head out of the cab and shouted, 'Want a lift, mate?'

John approached the cab. 'Where you heading for?'

'Tripoli.'

'Okay.'

The driver looked surprised. 'You mean you're going to Tripoli?'

John, trusting to what he hoped would be the ignorance of the RAF about infantry matters, said, 'I got taken prisoner. Then escaped. I got lost and couldn't find where my mob had got to. So I managed to find my way to Brigade and they said I'd better make my own way back to Tripoli. Report to Transit Camp. I'd get posted from there.'

The RAF man looked more puzzled than persuaded. He said, 'You look like the Unknown Warrior. A couple of weeks after they dug him up. Come on. Chuck your stuff in the back and get up in here with me.'

John threw his rifle, helmet and webbing into the back of the truck and joined the airman in the cab.

'My name's Frank Jarvis,' the airman said. 'What they call you?'

'John Bain.'

Frank Jarvis moved the truck forward and, as he changed

gear, he said, 'If you're hungry or thirsty look behind the seat there. You'll find a jerry-can of good water and some hard tack and bully. You'd have to be bloody hungry to eat that. If you can wait we'll stop and brew up in an hour or so.'

John said he could wait.

They drove on for a couple of minutes before Frank spoke again: 'You on the run, John? You can trust me, mate. I wouldn't shop you.'

'I told you what happened,' John said.

'Yeah. I heard you. Sounds like a load of bullshit to me.'

John hesitated. Then he said, 'Okay. I'm on the run.'

'Thought you was.' Frank nodded. He looked older than John, perhaps approaching thirty, very sure of himself, knowing, undeceivable. His dark hair was glossy with a sweet-smelling unguent and a small neat moustache gave him a dashing but untrustworthy look. He would be a skilful exponent of the slow foxtrot and tango, John thought, a knock-out at the Hammersmith Palais.

'What happened? How d'you manage to get away?'

'I walked.'

'Yeah. Sure. I know. But how come nobody stopped you? Where was you, anyway?'

'A place called Wadi Akarit. North of Gabès. In the hills. I just turned round and walked away.'

'Was there – you know – like a battle going on?'

'No. There had been. We were in support. We went up to consolidate and that was it.'

'What you mean that was it?'

'I don't know. The dead. There were dozens of our blokes, Seaforths. All lying there. They looked like big dolls or dummies or something. As if they'd never been alive. But they'd passed through our positions only two or three hours before. Now they were dead. And our lot – my own mates – were going round taking their rings and watches and stuff. That's what sickened me. I think. I don't know. Maybe I'd have fucked off anyway.'

'Yeah. Well. I don't blame you. Listen. We'll stop soon for a brew-up. You'd better have a shave. You look fucking terrible.

And get rid of that tin hat. Haven't you got your what-you-call-it? Funny hat with the pompom?'

'Balmoral . . . It's in my small pack.'

'Well, wear the fucking thing.'

They drove on for a while without conversing then Frank said, 'It'll take us about five hours to get to Tripoli. That's allowing for a stop or two. I'll drop you off a couple of miles outside the town. I'm on your side, mate, but I don't want to get done for aiding and abetting or whatever they'd call it. I don't know what the fuck's going to happen when you do get there. You might be able to scrounge some grub at the Transit Camp but you'll get picked up sooner or later. Unless you dress up as a wog or something. Kip up with an Arab bint.'

John's head was weighted with tiredness. The moving landscape of sand and rock began to blur. The smell of petrol was quite strong in the warm air. Frank continued talking but the words melted into a long slur of meaningless sound; then silence and darkness as John's head dropped forward and he slept.

When Frank woke him up the truck had been pulled off the road and the tea had already been brewed.

'Here you are, mate. Get this down you.'

John climbed down from the cabin and took the mug of tea. It was hot and sweet and, at first, it was painful on his bitten tongue, but when it had cooled a little he enjoyed it and was refreshed by it. Frank had spread some apricot jam on hard-tack biscuits and they both ate as they sipped their tea. When he had finished eating and drinking John took his shaving-kit and towel out of his pack and, using his mess-tin as a shaving-mug, he scraped away at his bristles until his face was sore but relatively smooth.

'You look a bit more like it now,' Frank said as he heaved the petrol-can on which they had brewed up into the back of the truck then lit a cigarette. 'Want one of these?' he said.

He held out a cylindrical tin of English cigarettes.

John stared. 'Christ! How the hell did you get hold of those?'

'I go back and forward from the docks. Fetch supplies for the

airfield at Wadi Zigzaou. Plenty of good stuff that's not meant
for the likes of us.' He winked. 'These are the real McCoy. Navy
issue.'

He lit John's cigarette with a lighter made from a small
cartridge case. The scent of the tobacco was strong and sweet
and for a moment stirred dormant feelings of regret and loss
because it carried faint, unfocused memories of another time
and another world. But John was quick to stamp on these
for he knew instinctively how treacherous and debilitating
they could be.

'We'd better have a slash before we hit the trail. Then maybe
we'll get there without stopping,' Frank said.

John said he did not need one and climbed into the truck. A
few minutes later they were back on the road.

'You know you don't stand a chance, don't you?' Frank said
after they had been travelling for a mile or two. 'They're bound
to pick you up.'

John did not answer.

'You scared? I'd be fucking scared I don't mind telling you.
They reckon the glasshouses out here are bloody terrible. Worse
than in Blighty. And that's saying something.'

John said, with slight but quite authentic surprise, 'I never
thought about it.' Then he added, 'Nothing could be worse than
action.'

'Yeah. Well, let's hope you're right . . . You married?'

'No.'

'Nor me. A mug's game. Why make one woman unhappy
when you can make a hundred happy, eh? That's my motto.'
When John did not speak Frank said, 'You had any crumpet out
here? Since you been overseas like?'

'Plenty of crump. No crumpet.'

'Well you should've known better than letting the army get
hold of you. Tell you what I did. I volunteered for fucking Air-
Crew. You know why? 'Cos I knew I'd fail the medical. Got
asthma, see. Then they said, "What you do in civvy-street?" and
I said, "I'm a bus-driver." So I was. Green Line. And they says,
"Okay we'll put you in transport. You can drive a truck instead

of a bomber." And that's what I did – what I'm doing in the war, Daddy.'

John nodded. He was beginning to feel sleepy again.

'But getting back to crumpet. I must admit I've not had all that much lately. Won't touch them brothel bints, mate. You see the swaddies lined up in Tripoli. Some of them bints'll take sixty, seventy blokes in a day. I'm not kidding. One of the red caps on brothel-duty told me. He counted. I mean that's disgusting. Like animals. But I tell you what. When we was back in Egypt I had a smashing bint in Cairo. She wasn't a wog. She was a Greek. And she wasn't on the game. Not really. She never charged me nothing. Do anything for me she would. 'Course I used to keep her in fags and that and I used to have a mate in the cook-house so I took her plenty of grub. You know that film star, what's-her-name? Dark one. French name. Was in a picture with Gary Cooper. Smashing looking bit of stuff. Well my Greek bint was a dead ringer for her. I'm not kidding. A dead ringer . . . hey, listen! You going to sleep? Fucking good company you are!'

John's head jerked up and he tried to blink the weight of sleepiness from his eyelids. 'I was listening,' he said.

'Yeah. Well, I was telling you about this Greek bint. Penelope her name was. I called her Penny. Funny she had an English name like that. But she was Greek all right. Anyway she was a lovely bit of stuff, had her own flat and everything. Classy she was, too. Educated. Worked in an office. Secretary or something to some wog businessman. I used to go up there when I was off duty and she'd treat me like a bloody prince. I'd have a shower, we both would. Then we'd have a smashing meal. She was a terrific cook. We'd sit there in her flat, eating and drinking. Plenty of booze. We'd sit there well nigh bollock-naked in the hot weather. And then we'd go to bed. Oh Christ, she was a beauty! Honest, you could use her shit for toothpaste.'

John said, 'You keep in touch with her?'

'No point really. I mean I'm not likely to go back down there. And I'm not much of a one for writing letters. She cried when I told her I'd been posted. We had a terrific last night though. She

couldn't get enough of it. I'm not kidding. I fucked her all ways.
I give her something to remember. Yeah. She was a smashing
bint.'

The brown and ochre landscape slid past and the sun
hammered down on the cab roof. Once they were passed by a
convoy of troop-carrying trucks travelling in the other direction.
Frank's voice went on, soft, persuasive, sometimes marvelling a
little at the events it narrated. John tried to stay awake but the
heat, the truck's motion and Frank's indefatigable voice together
proved irresistibly sedative and he slept, occasionally being jolted
into semi-consciousness by the truck's uneven progress on the
cratered road. Twice Frank, who must have resigned himself to
an unappreciative audience, woke John to ask him to light
cigarettes for each of them and after the second time John did
not go back to sleep.

Frank looked at his watch. 'We ain't doing too bad,' he said. 'I
reckon we'll be in the outskirts in about three-quarters of an
hour. That'll be about six o'clock. I'll drop you off then. If I was
you I'd keep off the main road. Redcaps are always pissing up
and down there. They'll be sure to stop you. If they do pick you
up don't mention getting a lift. Or if you do, tell 'em it was an
army truck. Okay?'

'Don't worry,' John said. 'I won't tell them anything.'

The sun was beginning to lose a little of its strength when
Frank stopped the lorry.

He said, 'This'll do you, mate. If I was you I'd get off the
road. About a mile farther on there's a wog village. You might
find somewhere to kip but I wouldn't trust the bastards. They'd
stick a knife in you soon as look at you.'

John jumped down from the cab and went to the back of the
truck to retrieve his rifle and equipment. Frank joined him and
let down the tailboard.

'Just a minute,' he said and climbed into the back of the truck.

John opened his small pack and found his balmoral and put it
on. He threw the steel helmet into the scrub at the side of the road.

Frank came down from the truck with three tins of corned
beef and a packet of hard-tack.

'You'd better take these. Better than fuck-all. Let me put them in your pack. Save you unbuckling . . . I'll fill your water-bottle too . . . Hang on, I'll get the jerry-can.'

John uncorked his water-bottle and Frank filled it.

'That'll keep you going for a day or two. If you last that long.'

John strapped the bottle on to his webbing and picked up his rifle.

He said, 'Well, thanks. I'm sorry I wasn't better company. I felt knackered. Feel a lot better now though. So all the best and thanks again.'

'Think nothing of it.' Frank climbed up into the driver's seat, leaving the cab door open. Then he reached down and held out the tin of cigarettes. 'You'd better take these, mate . . . Yeah, come on. Take 'em. Plenty more where they come from . . . go on.'

John hesitated.

'Go on, take the fucking things. I can get more when I get back. You got matches?'

John said, 'Yes . . . but. . . Christ, it's bloody nice of you.'

'Forget it. And good luck, mate. You'll fucking need it.'

The door slammed and the truck snarled and wheezed as it began to move away throwing up sand and dust. John saw Frank's arm waving from the cab. He waved back once then turned away and left the road for the inhospitable terrain beyond. Then, for the first time since he had walked away from the scene at Wadi Akarit, he felt lonely. It was a sudden and poignant sensation of desolation and a kind of fear that was quite unlike the fear he had experienced in battle, an ache of separation, of loss, of hopelessness as if he were the sole survivor of some atrocious calamity that had devastated the world.

He stood quite still for what was probably no more than a few seconds though he was not conscious of time at all. For those moments it seemed that he had been drained of humanity, that he was no more a sentient being than the rocks or dry vegetation of the land about him. Then he began to walk, quite quickly, as if movement was a way of affirming his humanity.

After he had walked for about half an hour he realised that Frank's notion of what constituted the outskirts of a city was that of a man accustomed to mechanical transport, for the barren and uninhabited country showed no sign of changing. John left the road and walked through the sandy scrubland out of sight of the vehicles that could intermittently be heard passing to and from Tripoli. He tramped on and as darkness began to thicken in the cooling air the sense of loneliness returned. But it was now manageable. It could be held off by a kind of blank resolution, a refusal to be overwhelmed.

Gradually he began to sense that the landscape was changing. At first there was no identifiable difference in the terrain which still felt the same beneath his feet, but he thought that the air now carried a hint of something other than the dry, faintly ordurous breath of the desert; a rumour of soil, of verdancy. And so, in darkness, he stumbled into what seemed to be some kind of plantation where the ground was soft and where his groping hands encountered the slender trunks and branches of small trees. By this time he was again very tired and when he took off his equipment and lay down with his head pillowed on his pack he fell asleep at once.

Waking was sudden and immediately alarming. He opened his eyes to the brightness of sunlight and before full consciousness had returned he was stabbed by a feeling of imminent danger. He was being watched. Slowly he raised his head and looked first to his right and then to his left. Then he saw the lean yellowish dog with its pale red-flecked eyes fixed intently upon him. It was about the size of a small Alsatian with a short-haired coarse coat and wolfish head. It looked very threatening. John remained quite still. Then, very slowly, he began to move his right hand towards his rifle which lay on the ground well within reach. Stories of rabid dogs prowling the boundaries of Arab villages were plentiful and alarming among British servicemen.

His fingers touched and closed round the butt of his Lee Enfield. He inched the rifle towards his side. The magazine was loaded. If the dog attacked him he would have a couple of seconds to get himself upright, slam a round up the spout, release the safety-catch, take aim and fire. Knowing his own uncertain marksmanship he might do better, he thought, to use the weapon as a club. So he stayed quite still, his muscles taut, ready for speedy action. The man and the animal stared at each other. Neither moved.

This motionless exchange of gazes went on for what seemed to John a long time but was perhaps no more than a further half minute or so. Then the dog turned away and loped off through the small trees and out of sight.

John waited for a couple of minutes to see if it would return but, when it did not reappear, he climbed to his feet, put on his equipment and for the first time since waking inspected his surroundings. He was in a grove of lime trees. He reached up and felt the fruits, but they were small and green and hard. They would not be ripe for another two or three months. The thought of tasting fresh lime-juice was tantalising and he was acutely aware of his dry mouth and the soreness of his tongue where he had bitten it. He unstrapped his water-bottle and took a small drink but it did not do much to freshen his palate. Before moving on he worked the bolt of his rifle to force a round into the breech in case the dog was waiting among the trees. Then, carrying the weapon at the ready, he made his way cautiously through the lime trees and emerged into a clearing in which a small, square house had been built of a kind of white stone that, like so many Arab dwellings, looked as impermanent as the casing of a meringue yet at the same time gave an impression of timelessness. The entrance to the house was veiled by a curtain of beads and, as John appeared, a woman in a black burnouse rose quickly from where she was seated with a man in white and disappeared into the house. The man remained seated on the ground with his back to the wall, a large earthenware bowl in front of him in which he had been stirring some kind of mixture which John could not see.

John said, 'Sai-eeda,' hoping his barrack-room Arabic greeting would be recognised and accepted in a spirit of friendliness.

The Arab did not reply. He sat quite still and stared at John, his dark eyes showing no expression at all. The long face was set, grim and immobile, as if carved in stained wood or cast in bronze. There was no welcome in that regard.

John did not blame him for his lack of geniality. If the man had encountered British soldiers before, and he almost certainly had, no doubt he would have been treated at best with derisive jocularity or quite possibly with brutal contempt. John looked around for the dog but could not see it. He shrugged and turned away and walked back through the lime trees towards the road. He thought that, sooner or later, he would be picked up. Attempts to delay the event were a waste of effort. It did not matter to him whether they got him now or the next day or in a week's time. The consequences would be the same, though the exact nature of the consequences was something that his mind was unable to contemplate, partly because he had only a vague idea of the procedures that would follow his arrest but also because the future had become unthinkable. It seemed almost as if he had been left with the dead soldiers on the stony hillside at Wadi Akarit and that he was now his own ghost walking back over the ground that his living self had traversed in fear, privation and pain during the advance from Wadi Zessar towards the Mareth Line.

He reached the road and trudged on towards Tripoli. The sun was gathering strength; it throbbed in the sky like an infected wound. It occurred to him that he ought to have attempted to shave but he knew that he would have dismissed the idea had it earlier suggested itself. He had shaved on the previous day as much to please Frank as from any hope of making himself look respectable enough to escape the curiosity of the military police. When he had walked away from the battle area he had turned his back on military conformity. He had asserted the human individual's right to choose and to act according to that choice. He had ceased to be a minute component in the gigantic machinery of military organisation. And yet, he thought ruefully, he had hung on to his rifle. The Lee Enfield 303. The 'Soldier's Best Friend'. He had thrown away his steel helmet but he could not discard his rifle. At least part of him remained a soldier. The months and years of conditioning had done their work. Perhaps from now onwards he would always be a kind of hybrid, part soldier, part civilian, like one of those clownish figures that used to appear on the stage of provincial music-halls in baggy civvy trousers and a service tunic and cap.

He tramped on and soon the empty landscape on each side of the road began to show signs of the approaching city, at first a few scattered white buildings, similar to the one near the lime grove, and then the more solid-looking houses of the suburbs. There was plenty of traffic on the road, convoys of troop-carriers, some tanks and Bren-carriers and trucks similar to the one in which he had been given his lift. But, if anyone noticed him, he was not aware of it. He plodded along, his rifle slung on one shoulder, his eyes lowered to the ground in front of him. He was now walking on properly paved roads with buildings on either side and palm trees planted at intervals along the pavements. There was something in the air that was strange and pleasant. Above or below the dominant smells of the town, of petrol fumes, spices and sewage, was the faint and elusive counterpoint of another scent. John slowed his pace, sniffed and felt it move from nostrils to somewhere in his head where it wavered and teased like a half-recollected melody. And then recognition chimed. It was the sea.

For the first time since his desertion he felt a stirring of excitement. The sea meant ships and ships were more than mere symbols of escape and freedom: they were practical agents of these things. If he could get to the docks where no doubt troops were employed unloading the ships it might be possible to sneak aboard a merchant vessel and hide. Fantasy began to project its unlikely, sanguine images on the walls of his mind: he saw himself hiding in a cargo hold and being discovered by a sympathetic sailor who would keep his presence a secret and bring him food and drink and civvy clothes.

His reverie was abruptly smashed by the squeal of tyres as a fifteen hundredweight truck skidded to a halt in the gutter at his side. A corporal of the military police came quickly out of the driving seat simultaneously shouting, 'Hey! You! Jock! Just a minute! Hold on there!'

John had stopped walking as soon as the truck had arrived. He felt no impulse to run. After the first ugly jolt of being shocked back to reality he was quite calm. Perhaps it was the calmness of the stunned, numbness rather than conscious indifference, but whatever it was he was mildly surprised to find how little apprehension he felt. Two aircraftsmen on the other side of the road stopped to watch the encounter between John and the redcap who said, 'What you doing here? Where you from? Stand to attention.'

John said, 'I'm at the Transit Camp, waiting to join the battalion.'

'Corporal! You're talking to an NCO. What do you think these are, laundry-marks?' He tapped the two blancoed stripes on the sleeve of his KD shirt.

'Corporal,' John said equably.

Something in his tone of voice or general manner seemed to enrage the redcap. His big, lightly freckled face beneath the peaked cap fattened and darkened with anger. 'Look at you!' he shouted. 'Look at the fucking state of you! You're manky. You're filthy. Look at them boots. You haven't had a shave. You've been sleeping rough. You're on the bloody run, aren't you? You're not at no transit camp. Don't give me that bollocks.'

'No,' John said.

'No? What you mean, no? And I told you, use my rank when you talk to me.'

'I mean no I'm not at the Transit Camp. You're right, I'm on the run. Corporal.'

'Where from? Where d'you fuck off from? Where you stationed?'

'Wadi Akarit. Up past Gabès.'

'Never heard of it.'

'You're lucky.'

'Here. You give me that rifle. Take your webbing off. Give it here.' The redcap slung the rifle and equipment into the back of the small truck. 'Right. Get in. I'm taking you to my HQ. We'll soon find out what you been up to. And you won't get funny with Sergeant Hammond or he'll kick your teeth in. Don't think I'm kidding. I've seen him do it. Often.'

John climbed into the truck and the redcap drove off. Soon they were in the centre of the city. There were civilians among the uniformed people on the pavements, women, some in European clothes. The colour, the delicacy of their dresses, the lightness and grace of their movements pierced with a sweet violence and left an ache of cancelled promises and loss. The truck pulled up in front of the military police barracks.

'Okay,' said the redcap. 'Let's go and have a chat with Sergeant Hammond.'

★　　★　　★　　★　　★

The sergeant did not seem to be as ferocious as his subordinate had promised. Not that he was in the least sympathetic. He sat behind a scrubbed trestle table which was covered with official-looking papers and the customary utensils of military bureaucracy. Both the sergeant and the corporal looked very clean and well-nourished. Their khaki-drill was recently laundered and meticulously pressed. Their webbing was blancoed to the whiteness of sugar-icing, their boots shone like black enamel and both closely shaven faces looked fresh with recent soap and water and with good health. Each exuded a kind of solid complacency, a self-congratulatory sense of untarnishable virtue. John felt grubby, smelly and corrupt.

Sergeant Hammond said, 'All right. Let's have your name, number and unit.'

John gave him the information he wanted and watched him write it carefully down.

'And when did you leave your battalion?'

'Two days – three days ago. I think.'

'What d'you mean, you think? You must know when you fucked off.'

But John was uncertain. The events at Wadi Akarit seemed to
have occurred a long time ago and his journey to this impersonal,
white room with the slowly turning electric fan above the
scrubbed table and the walls bearing typed orders and schedules
had already become peculiarly dream-like. He tried to remember
how many nights had passed since his desertion. There had been
the Gurkha camp, the tea and chapatis. He had slept that night
in a wadi off the road. He had fallen and bitten his tongue. He
could feel the soreness now. Then there had been the lift with
the airman, Frank. That was only yesterday. It was difficult to
believe but he had been away from the front for only a couple of
nights.

He said, 'It was only two days ago.'

'At this place Wadi what's-it?'

'Akarit. Yes.'

'You said that's up near Gabès.'

'Past Gabès. We rested near Gabès just before the attack.'

'But that must be a hundred miles or more. How d'you get
here in two days?'

'I walked.'

Sergeant Hammond's eyes widened and seemed to protrude a
little. His voice rose almost to a shout: 'Don't you come the
funny man with me sonny or I'll make you wish you'd never
been born. Understand? Now let's start again and no pissing
around this time. I asked you how you got to Tripoli from up
near Gabès in a couple of days.'

'I got a lift.'

'Who from?'

'I don't know. Just a bloke driving an army three-tonner.'

'What was he in? What unit?'

'I don't know. RASC I suppose.'

'You mean you sat four or five hours in a truck and the driver
never mentioned what mob he was in.'

'I don't suppose he thought I'd be interested. And he was
right.'

'That so? Well, I'll tell you something you might be interested
in, Private Bain. We'll get a signal off to your CO. He's probably

worried about his wandering boy. As soon as they get the word they'll send an escort to take you up to your unit for Court Martial. You know what you're likely to get? No, I thought not. Well, I'll tell you. Between five and ten years penal servitude, that's what you can expect. Penal servitude. That surprise you? Did you think you'd get a few months detention? Remission for good behaviour? It's not like that, sonny. A year's the maximum detention. Any punishment longer than that's got to be a civvy sentence. That's what you'll get. In peace-time or in Blighty you'd be discharged and sent to a civvy nick. But they don't waste good shipping space on you lot. So you do your time down in Egypt. Cairo or Alex. In a military prison, God help you. And I'll tell you something, sonny. You'll wish to Christ you'd never fucked off. You'll wish you was anywhere but in one of them places. They make hell seem like a rest-camp. I'm not kidding. You'll wish you'd never been born.' Hammond smiled at John with a curious mixture of self-satisfaction and excitement. Then he said, 'Take him away, Corporal. See he gets cleaned up a bit before you put him in the cells. We don't want him stinking the place out.'

'Come on, Bain,' the corporal said. 'Leave all your stuff here except your small pack. We'll see if we can find you a nice cosy cell.' When the door of the office had closed behind them he added with a relish that mocked the meaning of his words, 'You know something? I feel quite sorry for you, you poor miserable bastard. I really do.'

Part II

DOING TIME

THE TRUCK JOLTED to a halt outside the great iron-studded door that looked almost jet-black against the high white walls of the Military Prison and Detention Barracks. The sergeant in charge of the escort-party jumped down from the cab, walked round to the back of the truck and lowered the tail board.

'Okay,' he said, 'escorts first and then the prisoners. Hurry it up. Down you get!'

The three private soldiers acting as escorts clambered down and stood waiting for their prisoners to join them on the ground. They had been detailed for this job by the CO of the Transit Camp in Tripoli. They were infantry-men, not policemen, and they did not relish this task. Each man carried a rifle and wore belt and bayonet. They scowled in the brilliant Egyptian sunlight and avoided meeting the eyes of the prisoners who, handcuffed together in pairs, awkwardly scrambled over the lowered tail board to the ground. The six prisoners all wore full marching-order, large valise, small valise at the side, ground-sheet, rolled blanket, water-bottle, belt and empty ammunition pouches. They did not, of course, carry arms.

'Get fell in,' the sergeant ordered. 'One escort on each side, one at the rear.' He looked nervous, unsure of what attitude to adopt. During the short voyage down the Mediterranean he had been more relaxed and, with the rest of the escort, he had shown some sympathy for his charges, but now that he was confronted by the huge frozen face of the prison he seemed uneasy as if he might, too, be incarcerated behind those high blind walls.

'Prisoners and escort, stand-at . . . ease! Atten . . . shun!'

He turned away from his small squad and approached the door and pressed the bell-button on the wall at its side. In a few moments the sound of footsteps could be heard from behind the door. They halted. There was a grating noise and a small panel was opened to show a barred aperture through which someone peered. Then a voice issued from the indistinct face, 'Yes, Sergeant? What can I do for you?'

The sergeant was now holding some papers in one hand and these he held up as if they were necessary guarantees of his authenticity and authority. He said, 'I've got six prisoners. Sent down from Tripoli. I've got their documents here.'

'Very good. We're expecting you. I'll open up.'

The aperture was closed, then more and louder metallic sounds were heard before the great door swung inwards and its custodian revealed himself in full to the sergeant and the little assembly of prisoners and their escorts. He was dressed in immaculate khaki drill and he wore a service cap with the peak low over his eyes, almost touching the bridge of his nose. The shining metal badge above the peak was a plain GR without wreath or other embellishment.

He said, 'Bring them in, Sergeant. I'll take their documents. Your escort can stay outside. You can take the cuffs off first.'

The sergeant returned to his waiting squad and went to each pair of prisoners unlocking and removing the hand-cuffs. Then, after handing a pair to each of the escorts to look after, he ordered the prisoners to march through the open door.

The moment the six men had crossed the threshold the guardian of the gate took command.

He ordered them to halt outside the office just inside the gate. Then he said, 'From now on you are S.U.S.'s – Soldiers Under Sentence. You will do everything at the double. You understand? Everything. You do not move unless it's at the double. I'm Staff Hardy. I'm going to hand you over to Staff Henderson. He'll look after you. Right. Double . . . march! *Left*-right, *left*-right, *left*-right, *left* . . . Mark time! Get them knees up! *Left*-right *left*-right *left*-right *left* . . .'

The prisoners had trotted forward on to the large stone parade-ground and were now marking time at the double in the flogging heat of the afternoon sun. The square of the parade-ground was overlooked on all sides by rows of cell doors, on both ground level and above where there was a quadrangular second tier of cells. These could be reached by stone steps set at each corner of the parade-ground leading to a balcony and the upper tier of cells. Another staff-sergeant was standing in the limited shade of the balcony and, as the prisoners appeared, he began to walk towards them.

Hardy yelped, 'SUS's . . . halt! Stand-at . . . ease!' Then he called to his approaching colleague, 'Six on, Staff Henderson!'

'Very good, Staff.'

As Henderson drew close Hardy handed him the papers he had taken from the sergeant in charge of the escort and returned to the reception office. The six prisoners stood sweating under the weight of their equipment and the stinging heat.

Henderson was dressed in the same fresh and well-pressed khaki-drill as Hardy and he, too, seemed almost to be balancing his cap by its peak on the bridge of his nose. He stood in front of the prisoners and examined the sheaf of papers. Then he looked up at them and grimaced, a contortion of the mouth and a screwing up of the facial muscles that looked like a mixture of snarl and smile. Then he ordered them to attention. His voice, like that of Hardy, was not the loud bark of the drill-sergeant on the barrack-square. It was, rather, high-pitched, the commands not abrupt but drawn-out, a kind of angry whine.

'SUS's . . . shun!' The six prisoners came to attention. 'Answer your names!' He consulted one of the sheets of paper. '2991658 Private Morris P!' His accent was Glaswegian.

'Sarnt!' answered one of the prisoners.

Henderson's teeth showed again in a grin of rage. He yelped, 'Not Sarnt, you dozy man! Staff! You call us Staff . . . Understand? Staff's what you call us. All except the RSM and the commandant. You call them Sir. So let's try again and get it right this time. 2991658 Private Morris P!'

'Staff!'

Henderson called two more numbers and names before he reached John Bain's. He paused, called them out, waited for the response and, after it had come, he paused again. Then he said, 'I see you're in the Gordon Highlanders. What's your regimental motto?'

'Bydand,' John said.

'Staff!'

'Bydand, Staff.'

'Bydand. Aye. And what does that mean, Private Bain?'

'Stand fast, Staff.'

Henderson nodded slowly a few times without speaking. Then he said, 'Stand fast. That's the motto of the Gordon Highlanders and they've always lived up to it. Till now. They never retreated. Not in the whole history of the regiment. But you didn't stand fast, Private Bain, did you! You horrible man. You took a powder. You got off your mark. You're a disgrace to a great regiment. My father fought with the Gordons in the Great War. He stood fast, Private Bain. He didna take a powder. So I'm going to keep a special eye on you, Private Bain.' He nodded again, then resumed his calling of numbers and names.

John felt the sun's heat punishing the exposed skin of arms, face and neck. The whiteness of the walls dazzled.

Henderson said, 'You'll find a list of orders pinned up in your cell. Read it. Take note. You'll also find a diagram for kit lay-out. Reveille's at O-six hundred hours. You lay out your kit for inspection as soon as you get up. You get your tasks handed out after dinner and you're banged up at seventeen hundred hours. You will work on your tasks till lights-out at twenty-one thirty hours. And there's no communication at any time except on communication parade. I hope that is quite clear to everyone of you. If you're caught talking at any time you'll be on a charge and you'll get punished. Three days solitary on PD One. That's Punishment Diet Number One. Bread and water.' His lips curved back exposing his teeth in that mad, ferocious grin. 'Known as jockey's diet or bread and desert soup. Right. SUS's stand-at . . . ease! Stand easy. Take off your equipment. At the double. Get it down there on the ground . . . Right. Spread out your groundsheets and blankets. Spread them out and put your equipment on them . . . Now, I'll give you just one minute to get your clothes off. Everything. All your clothes down there on your blankets. Move! Come on, you. Don't be shy. There's no young ladies in here! So get them clothes off, everything. Boots, socks, the lot.'

In a few moments the prisoners stood naked before the piles of equipment and clothing on the blankets at their feet.

'Right,' Henderson said. 'Open your packs, both of them, and empty them out. I want to see everything you own in this world, you horrible men. I'll have no contraband smuggled here. No tobacco. No tinder. We know the tricks. All of them. And you can't fool us.'

Henderson, quite slowly and with many gestures and express-ions of fastidious distaste, examined each item of clothing and equipment while the six prisoners stood naked in the sun. Then they were ordered to put on only their socks and boots and wrap up the rest of their possessions in the groundsheets and blankets, which had to be secured from each corner so that each man made a bulky parcel. Then, ludicrous in their nakedness, the prisoners were ordered to lift the unwieldy packages above their heads and given the command to double-march.

There was a tiny moment of hesitation before the order was obeyed when it seemed possible that rebellion might explode before such gross humiliation. Henderson's snarling grin widened and his eyes seemed to gleam in the shade of his cap's peak. His freshly-creased, cool khaki-drill, the surgical whiteness of his webbing and stripes of rank made him seem powerfully unnaked, invulnerable. The impotence of the prison-ers was absolute. They raised the great bundles high above their heads and began to trot across the parade-ground; at first they were shamefully aware of their grotesque appearance but, as they were ordered to wheel and turn and straighten their sagging arms, pain and fatigue soon neutralised the humiliation and all they longed for was relief from the physical torment.

John felt sweat running from drenched hair down forehead and neck and down his flanks. His vision was blurred from its salty stinging and from the cruel whiteness of the prison walls. The aching in the muscles of his arms as he held his burden above his head was becoming intolerable. His mouth and throat were parched and there seemed too little oxygen in the burning air to satisfy his tortured lungs.

Henderson was yelping out orders as the six naked men ran round the square: 'Get them knees up! Straighten them arms! Left-right, left-right, left . . . Right . . . wheel! left-right, left-right, left . . . Mark time! For . . . ward! Left-right, left-right, left . . . Right . . . wheel! Keep them arms straight! Get them knees up! Left-right, left-right, left . . .'

At last, when it seemed that to keep going was no longer possible, Henderson brought them to a halt and opened one of the ground-level cell doors.

'Lead on inside. Drop your kits and get your clothes on, you disgusting men. Get moving!'

The cell was long – about fifty feet – but quite narrow, no more than eight feet in width, and there were three small barred windows set high in the wall facing the cell door. The ceiling was high, some ten feet or so, and there were no windows overlooking the parade-ground. A swathe of brightness from the open door cut through the gloom but the rest of the cell was dark and cold in contrast to the heat and brilliance outside. It stank of piss and ordure. There were three men already inside at the end furthest from the door and they were squatting on the stone floor at the side of their blankets and kits. Each of them was rubbing with mechanical vigour at a large, rusty bucket or dixie. None looked up or appeared to take any interest in the six newcomers.

Henderson stood just inside the cell and watched John and his five companions put on their clothes.

He said, 'There's twelve blankets, there, in that corner. You will take two each. That means each man's got three blankets. You'll see from the diagram on the wall how to fold them for inspection. You will also see there's a chocolate-pot for each man. That's what you filthy men will use from when you're banged up at seventeen hundred hours until reveille. In the day-time you use the latrines – at the double and only under Staff's supervision. We don't want any of you drowning yourselves in the bogs, do we? We're now going to get you your tasks . . .

Outside! Line up . . . SUS's . . . stand-at-ease! SUS's . . . shun!'

Again the prisoners were out in the stabbing heat. Henderson slammed and bolted the cell door. Then he gave the command to double-march across the parade-ground, ordering them, when they drew away from him, to mark time until he caught up and sent them forward again. The cookhouse was next to the arch which led to the reception office and gate. There each prisoner was given a large rusty and dirty metal platter or dixie and the little squad was double-marched back to the cell.

Inside it Henderson said, 'You can get your beds down now on that interior-sprung concrete. From now to lights-out you work on your tasks. You will see over there a little pile of sand and some rags. That's what you use to clean your tasks with. I want those tasks shining bright tomorrow. I want to be able to see my face in them. And remember. No communicating. I shall be watching you. Like God. And I shall be listening. If any of you whisper a single word I'll have your dinner for the next three days.'

The spasmodic mirthless grin twisted his features for a couple of seconds before they assumed their more usual grim impassivity as he turned away, left the cell and slammed the door, ramming the outside bolts into place. The six new prisoners laid out their groundsheets and blankets on the stone floor with their packs serving as pillows and, after an exchange of rueful grimaces, they squatted down and began to rub at their tasks. John looked down the length of the cell. In the chill, malodorous twilight the seated figures bent over their tasks reminded him of some gloomy and frightening picture from his childhood, a print or an illustration in one of his grandparents' Victorian books of moral exhortation, showing wretches in poorhouse or gaol, or even the damned themselves in an infernal cave of eternal desolation. John's bed-space was almost opposite the cell door and he realised that either by ill-luck or the cunning of his fellow-prisoners he had been given the worst position to occupy, for the door had a small hole in the centre, about eighteen inches below the lintel, through which he could be observed from outside.

The man next to him was a machine-gunner in the Middlesex

Regiment who in the journey down from Tripoli had introduced himself as Chalky White. Beyond him was an infantry-man from the Durham Light Infantry called Bill Farrell. It was Bill who was the first to risk speaking. When he did so it was in a hoarse whisper issuing from the side of motionless lips like someone parodying an incompetent ventriloquist.

He said, 'What would I give for a fucking smoke.'

Neither Chalky nor John replied. There were a few whispered exchanges from farther down the long cell but nothing comprehensible at that distance and the main sound was the gritty rubbing of the sandy cloths on metal and, very faintly, drifting through the small barred windows, the faint, attenuated noises of the city of Alexandria. The artificial twilight deepened slowly into the gloom of evening's dusk. Once John looked up from his senseless and largely ineffective work and felt a small sting of shock which caused a quick intake of breath and a following chill at the spine. The hole in the cell door was alive; it gleamed with a watchful eye. The door had an eye in the middle of its forehead. He bent again to his work and when he glanced up again a minute or so later the socket was empty, dead. The door was blind again.

Involuntarily whispering, John said to Chalky, 'Somebody looked in a minute ago. Through that peephole.'

'Yeah, I saw him.'

'I didn't hear a thing.'

''Course you didn't,' Chalky whispered. 'The bastards wear gym-shoes at night. He's like as not out there right now, listening.'

Bill Farrell, in his old lag's mutter from the corner of frozen mouth, said, 'They're worse than screws in civvy nick. I'm telling you. Give 'em half a chance and they'll kick shit out of you.'

'You been in civvy nick then?' Chalky said.

'Aye. Armley in Leeds. Six months.'

'What was that for?'

'Minding my own business.'

Chalky took a couple of moments to digest the reproof. Then

he said with petulance, 'I only asked.'

'Aye. I heard you. But it's the first lesson you learn in nick. Never ask what nobody's in for. But I don't mind telling you. We – me and my mate – was done for pinching lead off a church roof.'

'And they give you six months for that?'

'Aye.'

They rubbed away at their dixies for a few minutes. Then Chalky said, 'I done fifty-six days in the glasshouse, Aldershot. That was fucking murder.'

Bill grunted. Then he said, 'I was in Northallerton. But they reckon these places out here is worse. Looks as if they're right 'n all, the way that bastard Henderson went on. The first week's going to be sheer fucking hell. That's the way they work. Make your life sheer fucking misery for the first week or two, then maybe ease off a bit.'

There was no more conversation for a long time and the cell was almost in darkness. John clenched his mind tight against the past and future, against regret and fear and hope. He rubbed mechanically at the dixie and waited for the next senseless happening. When it came he was again startled for he had become drowsy. The bolts were pulled back and the door swung open.

A voice that belonged to neither of two members of staff they had previously encountered yet which carried the same note of taunting, affected prissiness whined, 'SUS's . . . stand by your beds!'

John could see, framed in the open door, a shape taller than either Hardy or Henderson but thinner, less compact and less erect. All the prisoners stood to attention.

The staff said, 'In three minutes it will be lights-out. For the benefit of you new SUS's I'm Staff Pickering and I'm a proper bastard. You'll hear the whistle blow and that means you get into your kip. I shall be round listening for any sound of communication. If I hear as much as a whisper I'll put the whole lot of you on the peg. That understood?' A few seconds' pause and he said again, in a muted squeal of fury, 'Is that understood?'

'Yes, Staff,' muttered the prisoners.

'All right.' He waited in the doorway for a little longer then turned away, stepped outside and slammed the door. The bolt grated into place. The prisoners began to undress.

John crawled beneath the two upper blankets as a whistle shrilled outside. He could hear someone at the other end of the cell using his pot. It sounded as if the man had diarrhoea and the already oppressive stench noticeably thickened. John put his head beneath the blanket and waited for the brief mercy of sleep.

★   ★   ★   ★   ★

John awoke to the squeal of whistles from the parade-ground outside and in that vulnerable moment of unprepared semi-consciousness he experienced a drench of pure horror as the full knowledge of his circumstances drove like a bayonet to the gut. Then as the other men began to rise, with whispered curses and muffled groans, he too threw off the blankets and climbed to his feet and, automatically, his defences were resumed, the vision adjusted so that no more than a few feet in front of him could be seen, mind and body clenched against the threats of pain and humiliation as the refusal to think of more than a minute ahead, to foresee a more distant future, swiftly gathered strength and grew adamantine. He dressed and began to fold his blankets and lay out all of his kit in the order shown by the diagram that had been stuck on the wall near the door. The air was grizzled and chill; it stank of unclean bodies and bodies' waste, the reek of disgrace and captivity.

The bolts securing the door snarled back and the early morning light cleaved the gloom of the cell as Staff Pickering appeared in the open doorway.

'Stand by your beds!'

The prisoners stood by the side of their folded blankets and kit lay-outs.

'SUS's . . . stand-at . . . ease! SUS's . . . shun! Each SUS will pick up his pot for slopping out. You will fall in outside with your filthy stinking chocolate-pots. When I blow my whistle you will proceed at the double to the latrines where you will slop out. Then you will fall in again outside the latrines and wait for the order to return to your cell. You will then get your washing-kit and fall in again outside the cell, faces to the wall. You will wait there till I bring the razors. Each SUS will be issued with a razor. You will then be double-marched to the ablutions, next to the latrines where you will wash and shave. In five minutes. Anyone not finished by then will be put on a charge . . . Right . . . SUS's . . . pick up your pots and fall in outside.'

Pickering moved back from the doorway on to the parade-ground and waited for the SUS's to line up clutching their unsavoury burdens. He was, as John had seen on the previous night, taller than Hardy and Henderson but he was slightly stooped, hollow chested and his forearms and knees were thin and bony. His cap seemed ill-fitting, perhaps a size too big, and his ears, which were unusually large, grew well away from his skull. John guessed from the pale, gingery eyebrows that he was red-haired. His nose was long and pointed and his upper teeth protruded slightly. Although he wore, of course, the same garb as his colleagues – the khaki-drill, short-sleeved shirt and shorts – the uniform did not suit him as it did them. With Hardy and Henderson the clothes seemed to be a natural, unalterable part of the men; you could not imagine them dressed in any other way. Pickering's KD shorts were too long, not perfectly pressed, baggy. He seemed almost to slouch. His eyes were pale blue, bloodshot and secretively resentful.

When the slopping-out had been completed, the razors were distributed. These were kept on a kind of tray covered with small holes into which the razor-handles fitted, and as soon as each prisoner had shaved, or done his best to do so with the blunt blade he had been given, his razor was returned to its place on the tray. John's face felt raw and he knew that he had cut himself on the chin. The man who stood next to him at the kind of trough in which they washed was a muscular blond heavyweight, one of the three SUS's who had been already installed in the cell when John's group had arrived. In the centre of his broad chest was tattooed the perpendicular image of a dagger from which dripped little pear-shaped tears of blood and, horizontally, beneath the point of the blade was an elaborate representation of a scroll bearing the words *Death before Dishonour*. Later, and without surprise, John learnt that this man was serving a ten-year sentence for 'Desertion in the Face of the Enemy'.

Back in the cell John had scarcely had time to restore his washing gear to its place in his kit lay-out before he and the other SUS's were ordered outside again.

Pickering brought them to attention. Then he said, 'Staff Brown will be taking over now. I'm going off duty. You're on fatigues till breakfast parade . . . ah, here comes Staff Brown . . . Nine on, Staff!'

The NCO advancing towards them across the square was short, not a great deal over five and a half feet, but he looked powerful, his shoulders wide and the exposed forearms thick and muscular. He had a neat dark moustache and his eyes were small and very bright, like berries.

'Very good, Staff,' he said as he drew level with Pickering who, looking more slovenly than ever compared with his smoothly turned-out colleague, set off towards the gate.

Prisoners from other cells were double-marching across the parade-ground in the charge of other, as yet nameless, staff. Whistles were blown and orders were shouted in those curious whining tones which seemed to sneer as well as threaten.

Brown gave the order to stand at ease then immediately brought them to attention again.

He said, 'You're going to be on fatigues till breakfast. That means we have one hour. In one minute from now I'm going to send you over to the stores. For the benefit of you new SUS's that's the green door over there next to the cookhouse. Each SUS will collect a bucket and scrubbing-brush. You will fill the buckets at the ablutions and you will join those other SUS's over there near reception and you will get down on your knees and scrub the barrack-square.' His bright little eyes looked at the faces of the prisoners, seeking perhaps evidence of incredulity, but already the new SUS's had become virtually impervious to surprise. 'All right . . . SUS's . . . Shun! Right . . . turn! Double . . . march!'

For the next hour John, in a line of twenty or so other SUS's, made his slow way across the square on all fours with his bucket of water at his side scrubbing the unsurprised stone. While they did this Brown and another staff-sergeant, bored and malignant, strolled round the line of prisoners making occasional insulting and provocative comments all of which, John suspected, were taken from a stock of traditional usages. The heat of the sun was growing steadily stronger and by the time the SUS's had finished their senseless work John was sweating.

On breakfast parade each SUS carried the two parts of his mess-tin to the cookhouse where one half was filled with thin porridge or gruel served by a prisoner wielding a ladle and the other with tea, measured and poured from a chipped and grimy enamel mug. On top of the gruel was placed a lump of bread with a pat of margarine on it. Since the SUS's had to double-march back to their cells once they had been served with their rations it was inevitable that a good deal of the tea would be spilled. Back in the cell they spread the margarine with the handles of their spoons for they were not permitted to use either knives or forks since these could serve as weapons. When they had eaten, Brown inspected their tasks and kit lay-outs. John's dixie was still blackened from years of use though he had managed to remove most of the rust.

Brown said, 'You want to use more elbow-grease. If that's not shining so's I can see my face in it tomorrow morning I'll have you on jockey's diet. You've got ten minutes before PT. So get on with it now.'

Physical Training – or, as it was far more accurately called by the SUS's, Physical Torture – was conducted by Staff Henderson. John and his cell-mates joined the prisoners from all the other cells on the square. They did not wear PT kit but their usual khaki-drill and heavy boots. There was no need for Henderson to demonstrate any of the exercises which were familiar to all of the SUS's from their earliest days in the army.

Having brought them to attention Henderson shouted, 'Astride-jumping, hands clapping above your heads, be . . .

gin! . . . hup-two . . . hup-two . . . hup-two . . . hup! Come on . . . slap those hands! – hup-two . . . hup-two . . . hup!'

The SUS's began the exercise with a fair degree of synchronism but as it proceeded their efforts became more and more ragged, with the stronger and fitter still managing to keep up something like the pace at which they had begun while those with less stamina grew slower and feebler, the weakest of them scarcely leaving the ground with their jumps.

Henderson did not appear to notice their distress but continued to yelp out his directions, 'Hup-two! . . . hup- two . . . hup-two . . . hup! . . . Slap those hands!'

Through the noise of the irregular crashing of boots on the parade-ground and clapping of hands could be heard the gasps and sobs of exhaustion as the weaker SUS's struggled to continue the exercise. John was able to keep up with the fitter men but when at last the order to halt was given he was soaked in sweat and was gulping greedily at the warm air. There was to be little respite. Some bending and stretching exercises followed and then came the command, 'On the hands . . . down! . . . As you were!' Henderson's grin of rage appeared. 'You dozy man!' he yelped. 'You never done PT before? Listen and get it right. On the command "Down!" you crouch, knees full bent with hands on the ground in front of you. You then shoot out your legs behind you into the press-up position. And you do it together, like this – *crouch* two-three! legs *out* two-three! Right, let's try it again . . . SUS's . . . on the hands . . . down! Arms. . . bend! Stretch! . . . Bend! Get those greasy bellies off my nice clean parade-ground! Stretch . . . too much rich food. We'll have to do something about that . . . bend! . . . too much blanket-drill . . . stretch . . . too much wanking . . . bend! . . .'

Henderson patrolled the ranks of groaning, perspiring SUS's as they desperately tried to press themselves up from the ground. When one of them collapsed face down Henderson kicked him in the ribs – not heavily but hard enough to make him grunt each time the brightly polished toe-cap connected – until the prisoner, with agonised groans and grunts, managed to press his torso clear of the ground again. By the time the exercise was brought to an end a dozen or more SUS's were struggling on the square, gasping for air like stranded fish and trying desperately and in-effectually to press their bodies clear of the ground. More exercises followed – running on the spot, further stretching and bending, but the worst was over. Henderson it seemed had, at least temporarily, satisfied his need to see his charges suffer and had become bored by the whole business.

After the PT session all of the SUS's except for those in the punishment cells on the upper landing were mustered on the square. Staff-sergeant Brown again took charge of the occupants of John's cell.

He said, 'You SUS's that came yesterday are for Comman-dant's Orders. The RSM, that's Mr Grant, he'll be on parade in a couple of minutes to inspect all of you. When he gives the command to fall out you'll be told to stand fast. Then he'll march each one of you in front of the commandant, Captain Babbage.'

By now the sun had risen high enough to flood the square with its brilliance and heat. The white walls ached in the glare. There must have been about two hundred SUS's on parade and they were lined up in drill formation while staff-sergeants moved around and along the ranks carrying out a preliminary inspection before the arrival of the regimental sergeant-major. John stood to attention and felt the heat on his neck and bare arms. The parade was facing the gate and from a door next to the reception office came the RSM. Instantly the staff-sergeants fell in at the side of the men they had been inspecting and, with a great crashing of boots and general show of military smartness, they came to attention.

The RSM was dressed much like his subordinates but his KD was of even better quality than theirs and it looked to be tailor-made. His peaked cap, too, was of the superior kind worn by officers. He also wore what looked like an officer's highly polished leather Sam Browne belt and on one wrist was a thick leather band upon which had been fixed the shining brass insignia of his rank. As he came close to John saw that his face bore the bitter, clenched and potentially vicious expression that seemed to be part of the uniform of the corps. He was very pale and his jaw and upper lip were dark though smoothly shaven. He did not look physically strong but despite and even, perhaps, because of this his presence carried with it a powerful sense of menace.

He stood in front of the SUS's for a few moments without speaking. Then he shouted, 'SUS's . . . stand-at . . . ease!' A pause of three seconds. Then: 'SUS's . . . shun!' His voice was perhaps louder, less of a whine, than the standard word of command adopted by the staff-sergeants but it still contained something of the same note of outraged contempt that they affected. 'Open order . . . march!'

The ranks of SUS's opened smartly to facilitate the RSM's journey of inspection during which he was joined by the staff-sergeant in charge of the men at that time under his critical regard. A few men were put on charges and the attendant staff-sergeant dutifully noted down names and numbers of the unlucky SUS's. When the RSM reached John his eyes rested on his face for a moment, flickered down to his feet and back again. Those eyes looked impersonal yet hostile, as if they were contemplating something inanimate but offensive. Then he moved on and John felt a sense of momentary reprieve.

When the parade had been inspected the RSM returned to the place on the square from which he issued his orders.

'SUS's . . . close-order . . . march! . . . On the command dismiss all SUS's will turn smartly to the right, pause, then double back to your cells in formation. The SUS's that came in yesterday will stand fast.'

The orders were given and John and his five cell-mates were left in a line facing the RSM.

He ordered them to stand at ease, then said, 'You SUS's are going to be taken in front of the commandant, Captain Babbage. To save time, you won't see him individually. I'm going to march all six of you into the commandant's office together. You will march in at the double. I give the commands mark time, then halt and then right-turn. You will then be facing Captain Babbage. He'll have your documents in front of him. He'll read out your sentences, which you already know. Then he'll read out the official rules and regulations of Number Fifty-Five Military Prison and Detention Barracks. He'll ask you if you've got anything to say. My advice is to keep your mouths shut . . . Right . . . SUS's . . . shun!'

The six SUS's were double-marched across the square towards the door from which the RSM had earlier emerged and there they marked time until he reached them. He ordered them to halt and stand at ease. Then he went through the door into what was evidently the commandant's office to reappear after only a few seconds. He stood close to the door with his hand on the shining knob.

'SUS's . . . caps off! . . . In the right hand you dozy man! . . . SUS's . . . shun! Right . . . turn! Double . . . march! Left . . . wheel! . . . Mark . . . time!' He opened the door but remained outside as he ordered them forward into the office where they marked time until he followed them in and closed the door. 'SUS's . . . halt! Right . . . turn! . . . The new SUS's . . . sah!' He saluted.

The commandant sat behind his desk and, after a pause, looked up at the six SUS's. John felt some foreboding and a sense almost of incredulity that the man could be quite as repulsive as he was. There was about him nothing of the military smartness that the RSM and most of the staff-sergeants so obviously valued. He was very fat and the sparseness of the colourless hair that was spread in ineffectual thin strands across the pale and lumpy baldness of his head made it difficult to guess his age. The open collar of his KD shirt showed his almost imperceptible chin disappearing into folds of flesh and his mouth was half open and sagged slightly to one side. The rest of his features were smudged and blurred; his eyes were ill-tempered and bilious-looking and the pudgy hands on the desk were noticeably tremulous.

'Thank you, Mr Grant,' he said. His voice was fat, too, squeezed out with wheezing effort. Although it was quite cool in his office a film of sweat gleamed on his forehead, jowls and upper lip. He looked along the line of SUS's, peering for a moment at each face. 'Answer your names when I call them,' he said.

After each SUS had acknowledged the calling of his number and name the commandant read out his crime and his sentence. When he reached John, who was last in the line, he said, 'Three years penal servitude. Desertion in a forward area.' He threw down the army forms from which he had been reading and picked up a single sheet of printed paper mounted on a board. He looked at it for a few seconds then put it back on the desk. 'Before I read through the rules and regulations I'll just say a few words so that you won't have any funny ideas about what you're doing here. You're here to be punished. You're here because you've committed crimes. In your case – all of you – it's the crime of desertion. You're all cowards. You're all yellow. You think you're tough guys but you're not. You're soft and you're yellow. If you weren't you wouldn't be here. You'd be with your comrades, soldiering, fighting. Well, you listen to me. You thought you'd leave the dirty work to your comrades. You'd have it nice and easy here. In fact I wouldn't be surprised if you don't wish to God you were back with your units. Wherever they are. We're going to punish you. Make no mistake about it. And if you think you can play the Bolshie in here you'll find you're very much mistaken. You get funny with us and we'll smash you.' He allowed a pause for his rhetoric to be absorbed. Then he picked up the printed paper on the desk and began to read quickly and mechanically: 'No SUS is allowed to keep personal effects such as photographs. Smoking or the possession of tobacco will be severely punished. No communication is allowed. If communication takes place *both* SUS's will be regarded as equally guilty. There is a daily communication parade of ten minutes when SUS's may converse. Each SUS is allowed to write one letter per fortnight. The letters will be written each second Sunday afternoon and handed in unsealed for censorship by the commandant. Sick parade is after muster parade and Commandant's Orders at 0930 hours. Any SUS reporting sick must notify the staff-sergeant on night-duty on the previous night before lights-out. Malingerers will be punished. Any complaints will be made to the commandant. SUS's making frivolous complaints will be punished. Punishments consist of

Punishment Diet Number One: eight ounces of dry bread at 0730 hours and a further eight ounces at 1600 hours. A bucket of drinking water will be placed in the cell. The SUS on PD One will undergo solitary confinement. Punishment Diet Number Two is the same as Number One except that a pint of gruel is given with the first eight ounces of bread. SUS's who are, or threaten to be, violent may be subject to mechanical means of restraint. That means body-belts or strait-jackets. So, as I said, you get funny with us and you'll soon find out who's boss. Any questions?'

Captain Babbage belched slightly. 'Very good, Sarnt-major. Take 'em away.'

The RSM yelped out his orders and the six SUS's double-marched out of the office into the heat and glare of the parade-ground. Staff-sergeant Brown was standing in the shade of the upper tier balcony on the other side of the square.

'Caps on,' Grant commanded. 'Remember what the comman-dant said and don't try and come the old soldier in here. We've seen your kind before. Thousands of you. And you're all the same. Shit. Now, SUS's! stand-at . . . ease! SUS's . . . shun! Right . . . turn! Double . . . march! Over to Staff Brown . . . Six on, Staff!'

Brown called back, 'Very good, Sir!' and moved from beneath the balcony's shade into the brilliant sunlight. His shadow was almost black on the pale stone square.

John and his cell-mates were directed to their cell where they put on full Service Marching Order, large and small packs, ammunition pouches, water-bottle, rolled gas-cape and ground-sheet and they were then drilled on the square for an hour, double-marching, wheeling, turning, marking time, half-blinded by the thrashing heat and the sweat and gasping from the pain of tormented lungs and limbs. When at last this ordeal was brought to an end they were returned to the cell to work on their tasks until tiffin parade at noon. Tiffin was the same as breakfast except that, instead of gruel, each man was given a small serving of tinned jam with his bread and margarine. After tiffin there was more pack-drill, this time under the supervision of Staff

Henderson. The entire parade-ground was filled with SUS's responding at the double to the barks and yelps of staff-sergeants. At first John found the pain of muscles already stiffened from the morning's PT and pack-drill almost unendurable but he doggedly forced himself to obey each command until a dark numbness settled over both mind and body, neutralising much of the discomfort and defusing both anger and impatience.

After the session of pack-drill came communication parade. For this all of the SUS's – again excepting those in the punishment cells – were mustered on the square in double ranks. The RSM who was in charge of the parade gave the command for each second rank to about turn so that the double rows of SUS's were facing each other with only a yard or so between them.

'Communication . . .' yelped the RSM, 'be . . . gin!'

The prowling staff-sergeants at once started to patrol the lines, exhorting those SUS's who were silent to start talking. John found that he was facing a small, swarthy man wearing a forage-cap without a badge who said, 'You just come in, mate?'

'Yesterday,' John answered.

'You'll get used to it.'

A pause.

John said, 'What mob are you in?'

'Artillery. Twenty-five pounders.'

'How long you been here?'

'Too fucking long . . . seven month.'

There did not seem much else to say. Staff Brown who was moving along the double line came close enough to observe that neither John nor the man opposite him was speaking and immediately barked, 'You two dozy men! What's wrong with you? Get talking. That's what this parade is for. You're quick enough at the whispering if you think nobody's got their eye on you. So talk! Go on, talk!'

'What you do in civvy-street?' the swarthy man said.

'I worked in an office. Insurance company.'

'Yeah. Thought you sounded posh.'

'What did you do?'

'Watney's. Brewery.'

Brown, satisfied that they were indeed conversing, moved on and no more words were exchanged. From the ranks of SUS's rose an uneven low muttering noise punctuated by the occasional shouts of the staff-sergeants encouraging speech. The RSM, who had disappeared into the commandant's office after he had given the order to communicate, came out, looking at his wrist-watch.

He shouted, 'Two more minutes! Make the most of it!'

Staff Brown was again moving towards John and his supposed interlocuter who said quickly, 'Better start talking.'

For a few seconds John could think of nothing at all to say. He was aware of Brown coming dangerously close. Then he said, 'Read any good books lately?'

Surprisingly this seemed to tickle the artillery-man who grinned and gave a little grunt of amusement as he began to reply but Brown interrupted whatever he was going to say: 'Here! You two SUS's! What the hell you think you're laughing at? This is communication parade not funny time. I catch you grinning again I'll have your dinners.'

Then the RSM brought the parade to an end, ordered each alternate rank to about turn and the SUS's were double-marched back to their cells to collect their mess-tins and parade for dinner which consisted of a scoop of sweet-potato-and-mutton stew and a scoop of rice. After dinner the cells were locked and the SUS's were told to get on with polishing their tasks until lights-out. John had completed a full day, one which, with perhaps minor changes, would be the model for every other week-day he would spend as a prisoner in this place.

After lights-out he crawled between the blankets and drew the top one over his head in an attempt to minimise the stink and the intermittent hoarse whispering from the far end of the cell. In the few minutes before sleep he found that he was reviewing the day's events with a feeling that was close to disbelief. Like every soldier in the British Army he had heard enough stories of military prisons, some recounted by men who had actually served time in them, to have a fair idea of what awaited him in this one but he had not been prepared for what seemed to him the sheer lunacy of the regimen. The physical hardship and cruelty were to be expected. What had taken him by surprise was the incessant mockery, the sneers, the provocation, the quite systematic processes of humiliation and the insulting madness of everything the SUS's were compelled to do which had been epitomised by the crazy ceremony of communication parade. He had not been fully prepared either for the sheer awfulness of the staff.

He had encountered bullies and manic disciplinarians during his army training at the depot and elsewhere but never such dedicated sadists as these seemed to be. And that fat sweating lard-bag of a commandant: had he been chosen by some fiendish process of selection to ensure that his physical presence alone was a sustained insult to his victims before he had performed an action or said a word? And what of the few words he commanded, John thought, seeing again the gross, baleful face glaring across the desk, mouth through spittle: 'You're all cowards! You're all yellow!'

It was strange that not only was this the first time that the accusation of cowardice had been levelled at John but it was the first time that he himself had considered the matter. At the Court Martial his defending officer, a lieutenant from another company, who had no previous knowledge of John, had seemed embarrassed and almost apologetic when he had conducted a brief interview a couple of days before the trial took place. He had murmured something about the possibility of John having 'things on his mind', 'troubles at home perhaps' and when his unco-operative client had said that he had no troubles at home and that he had walked away because he was sick of the whole hideous business of war, the lieutenant sighed and said, 'I'll plead it was a sudden impulse that you now regret. How would that be?' John remembered saying, 'It just happened. It seemed inevitable. I didn't seem to have any choice.'

And now, trying to recall that morning at Wadi Akarit, the motionless, broken bodies scattered among the rocks and sand gilded by the morning sun, his walking away down the slope, the jeep giving him a lift to B Echelon, it all seemed dream-like and certainly those events possessed the sense of inevitability that he had spoken of to his defending officer. But cowardice did not seem to have anything to do with what had occurred. He had been afraid often enough to know that what he felt at Wadi Akarit was not fear, or not the kind of fear he could recognise. What he had felt was a kind of hopeless disgust, disgust with his comrades who were looting the corpses, with the lunacy of war, with his own impotence. His defending officer had made the point to the court that when John had deserted the fighting had ended and the enemy was in flight. But the truth was perhaps more complex than John himself had believed. Perhaps the vague dream-like quality of his recollections was a kind of screen erected by his own guilt to protect him from seeing his actions for what they were, the behaviour of a coward. Perhaps in those dead Seaforths he had seen his own mortality, the likelihood of his being killed in some future battle, and he was in flight from his own premature and violent death. Yet, even if this were true he felt nothing of the guilt that he assumed the coward should, and usually did, experience. He did not *feel* that he was a coward, though this might be because of a deficiency in moral sense. Perhaps, when he got out of this place, he would have himself tattooed like the man he had seen in ablutions that morning, except that his own inscription would read *Dishonour before Death*. There was a small, grim smile on his face when he turned on his side to solicit sleep.

The days went by and, in retrospect, seemed to merge into one long painful and exhausting sequence of parades, whistles, double-marching feet drumming on the square, the whining exhortations and objurgations of the staff, stench, heat and sweat, and the continuous thin ache of hunger. On alternate Sundays air-mail letter-cards were distributed among the SUS's with two pencils to each cell. Every man had to write a letter, whether he wished to or not. John wrote to an imaginary father and addressed his letters to an equally fictional Radcliffe Hall,

Long Willerton, Hampshire. He expressed contrition for the
shame he had brought upon the family and begged father not to
let Uncle Henry know of his disgraceful conduct. He made
references to his young brother, Quentin, who was at Eton, and
to his sister, Isobel, who must be sorely missing her hunting. He
also used as many long and difficult words as he could think of in
the almost certain knowledge that Captain Babbage would be
forced to make frequent recourse to a dictionary or remain in a
cloud of incomprehension. John derived sour amusement from
this fortnightly exercise and did not greatly fear the hoax being
discovered. Each time he handed his letter to whichever staff-
sergeant was on duty he thought, with grim relish, 'I am taking
the piss out of that fat bastard of a commandant.'

When he had served six weeks a slight change to the days'
pattern occurred. One afternoon the gate was opened and an
uncovered lorry carrying a load of sand was driven on to the
square. Two SUS's from another cell were issued with shovels
and the other prisoners, pounding out their session of pack-drill,
could see the unloading of the sand on to one corner of the
parade-ground. The lorry drove off to reappear half an hour later
with another load for disposal. This happened three times, after
which there was a substantial hillock of sand on the square, the
purpose of which the SUS's discovered the next morning when,
instead of pack-drill, each man was given two buckets and
ordered to double-march with them over to the sand-pile. There
he filled his buckets under the supervision of a staff-sergeant
who made sure that the buckets were as full as possible, and
carrying these very heavy burdens, the SUS doubled diagonally
across the square to the opposite corner where he unloaded the
sand. There was a constant double stream of SUS's moving
from one corner to the other and in half an hour or so the
pyramidal sand-pile had disappeared from one corner and
reappeared in the other. When this had been achieved the order
was given to reverse the process and the sand-pile was moved
back to its original corner. This exercise became a regular feature
of each day's activities.

Chalky White and Bill Farrell were the first of the new SUS's to be put on a charge. It happened in the early evening when tasks were being worked on and the usual whispered comments were being interchanged. Chalky, in the past few days had become rashly confident of his ability to fool the 'screws' and he would quite often keep up a lengthily sustained diatribe against particular members of the staff, the entire British Army, officers in general and Captain Babbage in particular. Whether he was addressing John on his right or Bill on his left he did not turn his head in either direction but kept it lowered and the words dribbled from the side of his stiffly motionless mouth. On the evening of his being charged he was in a nostalgic mood, recalling the delights and freedom of his peace-time life, when the bolts of the door were noisily pushed back and Staff Hardy appeared in the open doorway.

'Stand by your beds!'

Everyone stood to attention.

'I've been watching you,' he said to Chalky. 'And I've been listening too. You've been communicating, haven't you?'

'No, Staff!' Chalky said.

Hardy reacted to Chalky's denial with a small scream of rage: 'No Staff! What d'you mean, No Staff? I saw you! I heard you! You were communicating, you horrible little man, weren't you?'

'Yes, Staff,' said Chalky.

'Yes, Staff. That's more like it. And what were you talking about?'

Hardy looked first at John and then at Bill. To John's relief he addressed himself to Bill: 'He was talking to you, wasn't he?' Bill did not answer. 'Wasn't he, you dozy man?' Hardy yelped.

Bill said, 'Dunno, Staff.'

Again the high-pitched yell of anger 'You don't know! Of course you bloody well know! What was he talking about?'

'I don't know. I wasn't listening, Staff.'

'Don't give me that shit. Takes two to communicate. You're both on a fizzer.' He brought from one of his breast pockets a pencil and a small pad. 'You,' he said to Chalky. 'Your name and number.'

When he had written down the details he required from both

men he again looked at John, who felt a quick stab of uneasiness.

'You,' he said. 'What's your name?'

'Bain, Staff.'

'All right, Bain. I'm going to give you the benefit of the doubt. But watch out. I'll be keeping an eye on you. Unless you're very careful you'll find yourself on bread and desert soup.' He looked along the line of SUS's, examining each face. Then he said, 'Stand-at . . . ease! Stand . . . easy! Carry on with your tasks,' and he went out silently on his plimsolled feet and slammed and bolted the cell door.

'You stupid cunt,' Bill said distinctly to Chalky. 'You've got us both on PD One.'

The next morning the two communicators were brought before the commandant and sentenced to three days' solitary confinement on Punishment Diet Number One. When they returned to the cell after they had served their sentence they were noticeably subdued for a few days but after a week had passed Chalky again began his slurred and muttered monologues and when Bill told him to shut up he re-aimed his discourse at John who lacked the self-protective toughness of Farrell though he despised himself for his softness. But when John did receive his own dose of PD One Chalky was not involved and the punishment was not for the crime of communicating.

On this day the first parade after tiffin was pack-drill and the SUS's were released from their twilit cells into the shrill brilliance of the afternoon sun to be lined up for inspection before the drilling began. The harshness of the light reflected from the white walls cut at John's eyes like a thin lash and involuntarily he half-closed them, screwing up his features against the dazzle.

Staff Pickering, who was in charge of John's cell for that parade said, 'You there! What do you think you're grinning at?'

John did not at first realise he was the one being addressed.

Pickering came close and pushed his face near to John's and his voice rose to the familiar squeal: 'You horrible man! Answer when I ask you a question. What do you find so funny? Why were you grinning?'

'I wasn't grinning, Staff.'

'Are you calling me a liar? I saw you grinning. What's the joke? What were you grinning at?'

'I was frowning. The sun was in my eyes. I've got fuck-all to laugh at.'

'You're right! You've got fuck-all to laugh at. And you'll have a bit less tomorrow when you're on jockey's diet. Name and number . . .'

The next morning John was brought before the commandant and charged with 'Smiling on Parade'.

The RSM read out the charge.

Captain Babbage was toying with a fly-switch. John could see the dark sweat-stains spreading from the armpits on to the KD shirt.

'Have you anything to say?' the commandant asked, looking at John with suspicious and angry little eyes.

'I wasn't smiling, Sir. The sun was in my eyes. I was frowning.'

Captain Babbage seemed to wince with irritation. 'If the staff-sergeant says that you were smiling that's what you were doing, smiling. So I'll give you something to smile a bit more at. Three days PD One. Take him away, Sarnt-Major.'

'Sah! . . . Right . . . turn! Double . . . march . . . left-ri' . . . left-ri' . . . left . . . Mark . . . time . . . Halt!'

Out on the square the squads of SUS's were just beginning to shift the sand-pile. Bill Farrell passed quite close with his two buckets but he did not look in John's direction.

The RSM said, 'All right, Smiler. You heard the commandant. Three days PD One. I'm going to hand you over to Staff Hardy on the upstairs cells. There he is, look, waiting to tuck you up nice and cosy.' Then he shouted, 'Staff Hardy! One on, Staff. Three days PD One for this SUS.'

From the upper tier Hardy called back, 'Very good, Sir!'

The RSM said, 'Off you go, at the double . . . March!'

John trotted across the square and ran up the stairs to where Staff Hardy was waiting for him.

'Mark time,' Hardy said. Then: 'Halt!'

He unbolted the door outside which they were standing.

'In you go,' he said.

The cell was small, about six feet by eight, and there was one aperture, of no more than nine inches by five, high on the wall opposite the door. On the stone floor beneath this window were three folded blankets and next to these a piss-pot and a bucket of water. Hardy followed John into the cell.

He said, 'Pick them blankets up and put them outside next to the door. You don't get them till lights-out. You'll get a cob of bread at sixteen hundred hours and that's your lot till breakfast tomorrow when you get another. You can drink as much water as you like. I heard somewhere you can get pissed on it if you drink enough.'

When John had put the blankets on the ground outside and returned to the cell the door slammed shut and the bolt was rammed into place. He stood for a while in a kind of paralysis of misery. Except for the bucket and pot the cell was entirely bare and it was cool, almost cold. He thought, 'I've got to stay here for three days, seventy-two hours, with nothing to do, nothing to read, nothing to look at. I shall go mad.' He could hear the shouting of the staff and rhythmic tramp of double-marching feet from beyond the cell door and he almost envied the men who were working on the sand fatigue. Lack of reading-matter was the worst deprivation to endure. In Tripoli one of the military policemen had thrown some paperback thrillers and a batch of old *Lilliput* magazines into the cell and John had read every word of every page. Since he had been here, in Alexandria, he had read nothing and he craved for the printed word as some of his fellow prisoners craved for tobacco. Absence of cigarettes, after the first few days of imprisonment, had not troubled him. It seemed that the artificial craving for nicotine had been displaced not by the natural pangs of continuous hunger for food but by the starved imagination which ached for sustenance.

John had been able to read from an unusually early age and had displayed a precocity of literary taste which would have surprised his parents had they been at all interested, which they were not. He had been brought up in a home environment that was working-class but with aspirations of an entirely materialistic kind towards a stifling gentility. His father was not simply indifferent to all of the arts, he was positively hostile to and contemptuous of them as 'women's stuff' that any healthy-minded lad should steer clear of. John's mother, who was more intelligent and was herself a product of that genteel, 'superior' working-class that pressed close to the frontiers of the bourgeoisie, read library novels in which she sought a nice story, nothing depressing or sordid, and showed no interest in her children's literary diet. Consequently John did not encounter in his childhood any of the traditional literature for the young that forms part of the early cultural development of more privileged people. He simply read whatever was available and this proved to be a weird mixture which included some novels by Edgar Wallace, the property of his maternal grandfather who also provided *Ivanhoe* and *The Pilgrim's Progress*; a couple of his grandmother's Sunday School prizes, earnest Victorian moral tales, a steady supply of Sexton Blake novelettes supplied by an uncle, and his mother's library books. As he had grown into adolescence he had become aware of something called 'literary taste' and for a time an ill-informed snobbishness directed his choice of reading but this had little to do with his discovery within himself, at the age of fifteen, of an unfeigned and delighted response to poetry.

He stood quite still in the cell, staring at, but not seeing the door. Then, suddenly aware that self-pity was nibbling at the borders of his resistance, he rebuked himself sharply and began to pace the floor. He remembered buying his first book of poetry. He had been looking through a shelf of cheap second-hand books outside a junk shop in Aylesbury where his family was then living and he picked up an anthology of modern verse chosen by A. Methuen with an introduction by Robert Lynd. He opened it somewhere in the middle and read the poem by Thomas Hardy called *Afterwards*. He read the other poems by Hardy then he flicked back the pages and stopped at Walter de la Mare's *Farewell*. He could remember the first stanza now:

When I lie where shades of darkness
Shall no more assail mine eyes,
Nor the rain make lamentation
*   When the wind sighs*
How will fare the world whose wonder
Was the very proof of me?
Memory fades, must the remembered
*   Perishing be?*

He spoke the lines aloud but quietly, and he grinned faintly as he wondered if you could be charged with communicating when you were in solitary. Then he set himself to discover how much poetry he could recall by heart. He began with the first poem he had read with pleasure, at the age of nine, *He Fell Among Thieves* by Sir Henry Newbolt, and in the act of remembering – not all of it but quite a lot – he re-experienced a spectral reflection of the frisson which had mysteriously and pleasurably disturbed him all those years ago, and with this recollection came other memories of childhood. Occasionally he stopped his pacing of the cell and closed his eyes with the effort of summoning up words from the past. He was surprised by how much he could remember and interested by the way in which fragments of verse now appeared as milestones on the journey to maturity: lines from the *Ode to a Nightingale* had brightened the gloom of the shabby office where he worked among dusty files and the smell of old documents and dry rot; Housman's *Tell me not here . . .* brought the first fragrance of lilac on a summer evening and a clear image of the sweet, stupid face of Kathleen, his first girl; Lawrence's *Giorno Dei Morti* and Eliot's *The Love Song of J Alfred Prufrock* both conjured up, oddly, the smell of embrocation and memories of the piercing excitement and apprehension of dressing-room tension before going into the ring. That, he thought, would have surprised those two poets, as it surprised himself. He must have first become acquainted with the work of these writers in the winter of 1938 when he was boxing in the Junior ABA Championships at the Holborn Stadium Club. In the following autumn, just after the declaration of war, he had met Barbara.

Again he stood still and felt himself grow suddenly watchful
and taut as, involuntarily, his defences against the seductive and
emasculating temptations of romantic nostalgia asserted themselves. Barbara, he told himself, was probably bringing comfort
and joy to some well-hung GI. And good luck to her. He had
always known that she would not remain faithful to him and,
while the thought of her being enjoyed by someone else was
painful, he knew that, given the chance, he would have betrayed
her without compunction. Still, that long and golden summer of
1940 had been a lyrical interlude of sheer pagan bliss, its warmth
and shimmer and sweetness intensified by the encroaching
darkness, and whether or not his protestations of love had been
untrue he still felt much grateful affection when he thought of
her and the reflex resentment was there only to combat the sense
of loss.

He had grown tired of pacing the cell so he sat down on the
floor with his back to the wall, his knees up and head cradled in
his crossed arms. He closed his eyes but the hoped-for
drowsiness did not come. The noises from the square had
stopped so he knew that it was past noon but not yet two o'clock
when the drill or fatigues would start again. The SUS's would
now be having tiffin. He thought of the bread and margarine and
tinned apricot jam with longing, and the four hours that lay
between this moment and his piece of dry bread stretched before
him like a long and arid desert-track. The hardness and
coldness of the stone floor became uncomfortable and he was
conscious of the beginnings of an enfeebling self-pity gathering
inside him. He jumped to his feet and began to move around the
cell, shadow-boxing, throwing jabs and hooks and slipping
imaginary punches. Then he began to let the hatred of the
commandant and his staff focus itself and grow strong. He had
often heard Chalky muttering to himself a kind of litany of
loathing: 'I hate that fucker . . . I hate the fucking lot . . . I'll kill
the bastards . . . I'll get them, I swear to God, I'll get the
bastards . . . I'll murder them . . . you wait and see . . . I'll
murder the fuckers' and he had deliberately distanced himself
from Chalky's rage, feeling instinctively that this reaction was

the one that was expected by the staff and to give way to it was to play the enemy's game. But now he surrendered to the same passion of detestation, the same rage to avenge. He thought of abbage's fleshy, petulant face, the loose, lop-sided mouth and hostile glare, and he imagined smashing his fist into it then slamming one into that great sheriff's belly, watching the fat bastard fold up, slobber and beg for mercy. 'I'd show him who's yellow,' John said to himself. 'And that slimy bastard, Pickering, too.'

He imagined a scene in a bar set in an indefinite future, the war over, and John seeing a tall, untidy figure drinking alone. John approached this man and said, 'I think we've met. Do you recognise me?' The man, Pickering, looked at him uneasily and said, 'No, I don't think so. I'm sure we haven't.' 'Does Mustapha, Alexandria mean anything to you?' The panic was evident in the shifty eyes. 'No. No, I've never heard of it. Don't know what you're talking about.' 'I'm talking about 55 Military Prison and Detention Barracks where you were one of the screws. Where you got me three days PD One for smiling on parade. I wasn't smiling, Staff. Or do I call you Mr Pickering? I wasn't smiling, and I'm not smiling now.' Pickering started for the exit but John gripped him by one arm . . .

Outside, from the barrack square, a whistle shrilled and a voice shouted, 'One on, Staff,' and John's vengeful little fantasy ended abruptly.

He found that he was curiously embarrassed, even a little ashamed, as if his fantasising had been observed, and after a moment's thought he realised that this kind of deliberate daydreaming was not much different from erotic fantasy-weaving and that its after-effects were similarly joyless and debilitating. Anger was sustaining, he thought, but it should be kept pure.

After a while he sat down again and tried to hasten the passing of time by setting himself childish tests of memory and knowledge: he tried to supply the name of a novelist beginning with each letter of the alphabet, then a composer, a boxer, a poet, a cricketer, a politician and so on, but quite soon his thoughts began to stray back to his childhood and early youth in natural flight from the intolerable present and finally he became drowsy so that the grinding of the bolt and creaking of the cell door startled him. He scrambled to his feet and became aware that he was painfully stiff and cold.

Staff Hardy was looking at him with a faint smile in which there was no trace of sympathy. He held out a lump of bread. 'Here's your dinner,' he said. 'Try not to make a pig of yourself.'

John took the piece of bread.

Hardy paused before slamming the door shut. Then he said, 'I expect we'll be having steak again in the mess. Fried potatoes. Real spuds not them wog things. Nice salad. I'm not much of a man for duff. I'll just make do with a bit of fruit and cheese. Then a few drinks in the bar. How's that sound?'

This attempt to torment was too crude to be effective.

John said politely, 'It sounds very nice, Staff.'

Hardy must have heard the note of patient indulgence that John had aimed for, the tone adopted by parents when provoked by naughty children, and the artificial smile disappeared.

'You fancy yourself, don't you?' he said. 'You think you're a fly man. Well, you're not. You're nothing. You're nobody. And let me tell you this. There's a few of us got our eyes on you. I'm not the only one that thinks you fancy yourself as a wide-o. We talk among ourselves. We take note. So watch your step, my lad, or you're going to get a lot worse than PD One.'

John stood, holding his piece of bread, and said nothing.

Hardy nodded to himself and the mirthless smile returned to his mouth. He said, 'You're a horrible, dirty, stupid little man. What are you?'

John remained silent.

Hardy's voice rose to an angry yelp. 'I said what are you!'

A slight pause then John said, without expression, 'I'm a horrible, dirty, stupid little man. Staff.'

Another nod of the head and Hardy left the cell and bolted the door. John sat on the floor and ate his bread, chewing each mouthful slowly, making it last as long as he could. All the SUS's were locked up in their cells. Whichever of the staff were on duty would now be wearing plimsolls so the absence of sound was almost total. Just occasionally, through the small window, drifted the very faint sounds of the city. John finished his bread, drank a little water from cupped hands and paced about the cell for a time before he returned to his sitting position against the wall and settled down to the long wait until lights-out.

Again his thoughts went back to the past and to his elder brother, Kenneth, who was serving, as far as he knew, in Blighty with the Royal Engineers. John would have used his fortnightly letter-card to write to Kenneth had he known where he was stationed or the branch of the REs to which he was attached but, without any of this information, he had to remain ignorant of his brother's circumstances. This was troubling because they had always been very close friends and had joined the army at the same time and served together for a year before Kenneth had been transferred from the infantry to the Royal Engineers. There was a difference of only two years in age between them and in early childhood Kenneth had been protective and later they had been firmly united against the unpredictable violence and cruelty of their father and in their shared enjoyment of the literature and music which the old man detested. Even their pleasure in boxing was spoilt by their father's manic insistence on the absolute importance of victory and the intolerable disgrace of defeat. But it was *his* triumph he demanded and *his* shame that he feared, for this vain, vicious and essentially cowardly man was interested in his sons' performance in the ring only insofar as he believed that he could claim credit for their success and enjoy the euphoria of conquest.

Still, John thought, by no means all their enjoyment in boxing had been destroyed. He remembered winter nights returning in the coach with the rest of the team after boxing in a club tournament at the Kentish Town Baths or Letchworth or Barnet. The ordeal of the contest was passed and you had the warm feeling of achievement even if the verdict had gone against you, because you knew you'd fought well and done your best and everybody in the coach knew it, too. They sang the popular songs of the day, often through split lips, and they were happy.

At least the old man couldn't spoil those moments nor, for that matter, those times when you were actually in the ring and the fight was going just the way you wanted it to go, you were on target with the jab, you felt it connecting cleanly, with the knuckles, and you saw his head jerk back as if on an invisible puppet-wire and you slipped or blocked the counter and jabbed again until the opening offered itself and you threw the big right hand or whipped in the left-hook and he faded away and he was on the floor and the crowd in the darkness beyond the white brilliance of the arc-lamps was just a great tidal-wave of noise sweeping over you, warm and exalting.

Gradually the grey half-light began to thicken into darkness and after a while John stood up and performed a few exercises and again did a round or so of shadow-boxing to get his circulation going; then, some time later, he heard the bolts being tugged back and the door was opened. Staff Brown was now on duty.

He said, 'Get your blankets inside. You can kip down now, you lucky man.'

John carried the blankets into his cell and dropped them on the floor.

'I'd use one of them for a pillow if I was you,' Brown said, 'and keep your clothes on. Gets cold in the night.'

The door was shut and the bolt pushed into place. It was impossible to tell whether Brown had moved away because of the silent plimsolls he was wearing.

John did as had been suggested, folding one of the blankets for a pillow and wrapping the other two around him before he lay down. He was surprised at Brown's recommending this. It was the first flicker, however faint, of anything approaching humanity that any of the staff had displayed. He found it strangely troubling, difficult to come to terms with, and he decided he would prefer it not to have occurred. Until now every one of the staff had behaved with total heartlessness and apparent indifference to, or positive pleasure in, the SUS's pain and discomfort. This meant that he and the other prisoners could respond with complete hatred which seemed in time to produce a kind of protective carapace that blunted to some extent the weapons of the enemy. A show of consideration, however slight, was disconcerting and potentially enfeebling. John curled into a foetal position and closed his eyes. 'Fuck 'em all,' he said to himself, 'including Brown. I detest the lot of 'em.'

★   ★   ★   ★   ★

He awoke as the cell door opened and the metallic light of early morning clanged in the gloom.

Brown said, 'Out of that wanking-pit and on your feet! Get them blankets outside!'

John threw aside the blankets and scrambled to his feet.

'And get your boots on!'

He folded the blankets and put them on the ground outside the cell and then he laced up his boots.

'Right. Pick up the pot and bucket. You're going to slop out and get fresh water. Come on, pick 'em up and get outside.'

And so the second day of his punishment began.

At seven-thirty he was given his eight-ounce piece of bread. He remembered the previous day's painfully long wait for the second piece at four in the afternoon so he decided, hungry as he was, to break the bread into two portions, eat one now and save the other until he heard the SUS's collecting their tiffin. Then, at least, he would have something to eat at mid-day. When he had split the bread in half he put one piece into the pocket of his KD shorts and ate the other as slowly as he could. After he had swallowed the last mouthful he was powerfully tempted to eat the second piece and he knew that he must distract himself through physical action if he were not to succumb. So again he began to put himself through a sequence of exercises and ended with a round of shadow-boxing. After this he tried to settle down to endure the sluggish movement of the passing of the minutes.

He sat on the floor, his back to the wall, closed his eyes and let his thoughts drift against the sounds of whistles blowing, the crunching spondees of the double-marching feet, the shrill commands of the staff. Images of very early childhood floated in the misted depths of the mind; incidents and objects, the factual existence of which he was uncertain, teased his memory, the veiled recollection of a wood, bluebells, the sun shafting through the leaves and his emerging into a glade where, sunk deep into the earth, the roof alone showing above the grass, was a sunken house. Could he really have seen this? And if he had not, how account for its presence in his mind? He could feel, too, a small but identifiable echo of the feeling which the sight of the roof had evoked, a tremor of fear, of troubled awe. He could not remember if Kenneth had been with him on that day. One day he must remember to ask him.

More precise memories surfaced and he burrowed into the past, finding there a precarious sanctuary against the vileness of the present. This seemed to work for quite a long time and when he was forced back into the present by stiffness and cold the noise from the barrack square had, unnoticed, come to a temporary end so he knew that the SUS's must be locked up for tiffin. At once he felt the importunacy of hunger but for a few moments he moved round the cell, working his shoulders and punching at the air to restore circulation and warmth. Then he brought the piece of bread out of his pocket, broke a small piece off and put it in his mouth. He began to chew, slowly, forcing himself, with difficulty, not to gobble it down. Still masticating with hard-won deliberation, he sat down on the floor opposite the door when some instinct prompted him to look up at the judas-hole. Shock needled his heart, caused a quick gasp of breath. The hole was alive. He was being watched.

Then the bolt was shot back and the door was swung open. Staff Henderson stood there. He took a pace inside the cell and gave his puppy-bark: 'Get on your feet! To attention!'

John stood up straight, his hands at his sides, one of them holding the piece of bread.

'What's your name again?' Henderson said.

'Bain, Staff.'

'Bain. Aye. I remember you. The cocky wee Gordon, the pride o' the Fifty-First. Is that no' right?'

'Yes, Staff.'

'And what are you holding in that hand? . . . Yes, that hand there? Show me!'

John held up the piece of bread.

'Give it here.'

'It's my ration.'

'I said give it here! Move!'

John handed it over and Henderson looked at it carefully as if checking to ensure that it was truly a piece of bread and not something less innocuous disguised as one.

'And what are you doing with a cob at this time of day?'

'It's half my morning ration. I kept it, Staff.'

'You kept it! You've been hoarding food. You expecting a siege or something?' Henderson's familiar, mad, mirthless grin showed his tobacco-stained teeth. 'You are not allowed to hoard food. You eat your ration at the proper time or not at all. You understand?'

John said nothing.

'Do you understand?'

'It's my ration. I'm entitled to it.'

'You're entitled to fuck-all you horrible greedy man. And if you've got any complaints you know what to do. You see the commandant, and you'll find out where that gets you. I'll tell you if you like. I'll tell you where it'll get you. Right back in here sonny, where you belong. Right back in a single flowery for another wee dose of desert soup. Now do you understand?'

John felt anger filling his chest, rising, thick in his throat. Henderson's toothy, snarling grin blurred. John's hands had bunched involuntarily into fists.

Henderson said, 'Don't you look at me like that, lad!' but he moved quickly away to the open door as he spoke.

One leap and John could still be on him. But he hesitated and the moment passed as the door slammed shut and was locked.

John stayed where he was standing to attention; he stared at the door as if he could will it to open and show Henderson there, attainable, smashable, killable, but he knew that his chance had gone and, when it had been there, he had lacked the courage to seize it. He felt sick with frustration, rage and self-disgust. He began to tremble and he turned away and sat on the floor slumped against the wall. There was a bitter taste in this throat and mouth. After a while he got up and drank some water but the taste remained. He began to pace the cell again and very slowly the sickness faded, leaving an inner emptiness and a great weariness. All right, he thought, they were right, the commandant and the rest of them. He was a coward. If he hadn't been a coward he would have knocked Henderson's dirty teeth down his throat. He hadn't done it because he was afraid. He was afraid of the consequences: the body-belt, that wide leather waist-band with a steel cuff on either side to pin the prisoner's hands down so that he was a man without arms, defenceless against the time when they crept, silent at night on plimsolled feet, to burst into the cell and use him as a punch-bag and a football; he was afraid of longer periods of solitary confinement and PD One, of losing the wish to go on living, of going mad, of dying the death. He was afraid. He had surrendered to his fear. He was a coward.

The following half hour was perhaps the worst he had experienced since arriving at the prison. Until now he had been able to retain a small, secret self-regard in spite of all the calculated strategies of humiliation that the staff had practised; he had convinced himself that, if he had been put to a test of courage against any one of them, on equal terms, he would have proved the better man. He had not feared any of them as individuals; what had prompted caution in his dealings with them had been the knowledge of the almost illimitable power that supported them, the whole vast punitive machinery of the British Army. But the collision with Henderson had surely been a situation where prevarication was no longer possible: he should have attacked whatever the cost to himself. But, very gradually, John began to assemble self-protective arguments against the despair that threatened to overwhelm him. Henderson had been scared. You could see it in his eyes. He had got out of the cell pretty fast when he'd spotted the danger-signals. If he'd stayed another five seconds John would have had him and he knew it. If he tried anything like that again John wouldn't hesitate, not for one second. He'd smash the bastard.

So with at least a little self-esteem restored, John's engulfing and debilitating misery was eased and he was able to apply himself simply to the business of coaxing the seconds to flow more swiftly past. Again he rummaged in memory for words: *Tomorrow and tomorrow and tomorrow, creeps in this petty pace from day to day . . . The bailey beareth the bell away, the lily, the lily, the rose I lay... O rose, thou art sick! The invisible worm that flies in the night, in the howling storm has found out thy bed of crimson joy, and his dark secret love does thy life destroy . . .* And against the remembered words the noise of the yapping commands and the tramping of feet on the square composed their grim counterpoint.

The afternoon went by; the drills and fatigues ended, and the SUS's were locked up at the end of another day. John's cell door was again flung open and again Henderson stood there. Significantly perhaps there was no yelping command of 'On your feet!' and John rose quite slowly from where he was sitting and stood in a relaxed position. He felt a flicker of curious excitement. Perhaps Henderson would provoke him again. If he did John was ready.

Henderson did not enter the cell. He stood in the open doorway and held out the lump of bread. 'Here you are, Bain,' he said. 'Your second ration.'

John stepped forward and took the piece of bread.

Henderson seemed at first to avoid looking directly into John's face but he did so as he turned away and there seemed to be the smallest hint of amusement in his eyes. He said, 'Eat all of it this time,' and swung the door shut and rammed the bolt into place.

John remained for a moment looking thoughtfully at the door and the sightless judas-hole; he nodded once to himself, in recognition of a very small but unequivocal feeling of victory. He thought he would not be fooling himself if he believed that Staff Henderson would be a little less provocative in the future. Then he sat down and began to eat his bread.

The third day and night of John's solitary confinement passed without any remarkable event and, after he had eaten his breakfast of dry bread, he was released from the cell just before muster parade and returned to the company of his fellow prisoners. Very quickly he adapted himself to the rhythm of each exhausting and senseless day and he found that, while he would not have welcomed another period of PD One, he was not intimidated by its possibility. He had survived it once and he knew that he could face it again if he had to. The confrontation with Henderson over the piece of bread troubled him still and he swore that, if he found himself again in a similar situation, he would not back down, whatever consequences might ensue. And so the days grew into weeks, each one beginning with the rhythmic swishing of scrubbing brushes on the barrack square, followed by the agonising choreography of physical training; then muster parade and pack-drill before the respite of tiffin; out again into the lacerating heat of the afternoon for the mind-and-muscle-aching sand fatigue, all accompanied by the blasts of whistles and the barks and whines and yelps of the staffs' insults and commands. Then came the banging-up of the cell and the long stretch of whispering and pan and dixie-scrubbing until lights-out and, despite the interdict on communication, the irrepressible appearance and spread of rumours.

Some of the rumours originated in letters from home, others from some mysterious and unidentifiable source, perhaps the bored, self-deceiving or even malicious imaginings of SUS's driven by the need to assert their possession of a power that the authorities could not interfere with. A very small number of SUS's, who were serving maximum sentences and had already spent three or four years in the prison, worked in privileged jobs such as cookhouse assistants, office cleaners and mess orderlies waiting on the staff, and these were able sometimes to smuggle information overheard in the course of their duties to the ordinary prisoners. Some of the rumours were of a military nature, perhaps reports of allied successes or disasters in various parts of the world and, most persistently, tales of a Second Front having been, or about to be, established in Europe. Then one day, after dinner, when the cell had been locked until reveille, a quite fresh and not entirely implausible piece of news was produced by Chalky White.

'Hey,' he muttered, his head lowered over the tea-pail he was rubbing away at, 'pssst! You listening, mate?'

John grunted.

'Listen. I was on communication parade opposite a bloke what's been on office cleaning.' He paused to glance up at the judas-hole, and then continued: 'He reckons he heard one of the screws going on about suspended sentences. With the Second Front coming up they need all the cannon-fodder they can get. He reckons they're going round the nicks letting out the blokes they think'll soldier on.' There was another wordless interval; then he continued: 'These interview boards are going round the nicks. They ask you if you'd fight if you went into action like. You tell 'em and they let you out on a suspended. Me, I'd volunteer to be a human torpedo to get out this fucking place.'

Again John grunted agreement.

They both worked at their tasks for a few moments before Chalky spoke again: 'You'd stand a good chance, mate. You was done for scarpering in a forward area, wasn't you? That's not as bad as in the face of the enemy. That's right ennit? You wasn't done for the face of the enemy job was you?'

John looked up at the judas-hole; then he said, 'No. I fucked off in the arse of the enemy.'

Chalky was quiet. Then he said, 'What you mean?'

'Jerry was on the run. Got his back to us when I took a powder.'

Chalky tried to smother his laugh, choked and began to cough.

Bill Farrell hissed, 'Shut up you two silly cunts! You'll have us all on PD One!'

Chalky had to make a show of bravado. He said, 'I'm not scared of a bit of jockey's diet. Fuck the screws. I'll talk if I want to.' But he did not speak again until lights-out when, from his coarse cocoon of blankets, he muttered, ''Night, mate. Sleep tight . . . Christ, what couldn't I do to a pint of Bass right now!'

During the days and weeks that followed, the rumour that

prisoners were to be released on suspended sentence did not, in the manner of previous canards, disappear completely and it was quite often discussed on communication parade, though it did occur to John that sheer lack of conversational subject-matter might be one cause for its survival. The summer was moving towards its end though the only evidence of this was the slight decrease in the intensity of the heat of the day and the marked increase in the chill of the night. Bill Farrell became ill with dysentery but would not report sick because he knew that the only treatment ever prescribed by the Medical Officer was 'light diet' which simply meant a reduction to half of the normal rations. Bill could not eat his meals but he would far rather distribute them among the other SUS's in his cell than accept the punitive 'light diet'. He grew thinner and weaker and John could hear him groaning during the night, much of which he was forced to spend on his pot. When he collapsed on sand-fatigue Staff Pickering, who was in charge of the party on that afternoon, ordered him to get to his feet, giving him a couple of nudges in the ribs with the bright toe-cap of his boot, but when it became quite evident that Bill was unconscious two SUS's were ordered to carry him into reception and, after that, he was not seen again. A few days later his kit was taken out of the cell and the only too believable rumour was floated that he had died.

'Bill's kicked the bucket,' Chalky hissed as he plied his rag on a metal meat platter, 'the bastards killed him. I'll get one of them fuckers for this, I swear to God. If it's the last thing I do I'll get one of 'em. I'm going to come back here and I'll spend every minute I get off duty watching the fucking gates. Sooner or later one of them's bound to come out and I'll get him. I'll kill the fucker.'

Ron Lewis, who had taken Bill's place, said, 'You never see the bastards. When did you ever see one of them GR badges outside the nick? You never have. They never leave the fucking place. That's why it's all laid on for them inside. They've got everything they want. Bloody great bar, all the booze you can drink. Smashing grub. Brothel bints come in regular. It's a known fact. They never leave the fucking place.'

Ron did not make a serious attempt to conceal the fact that he was speaking. It was true that his voice was lowered a little and he affected the twisted corner-of-the-mouth delivery of the old lag, but he did not bother to ensure that the judas-hole was empty before he spoke, nor did he look down at the floor or in the opposite direction from the person he was addressing, so he was an unnerving person to have as a neighbour. He was lean, dark, gipsy-like, with a slight squint and mad, wolfish grin. There was some difference of opinion among the SUS's as to whether he was truly insane or pretending to be in the hope of working his ticket as a nut-case. Sometimes he would abandon his task, throw down his rag and, in a squatting position he would raise both outstretched arms in front of him until they were just above the level of his eyebrows. Then he would very slowly gyrate to the left or right, pause, and still keeping his arms rigid he would jerk them backwards in a spasm of recoil and utter a booming noise. He was, he explained to anyone who might be interested, a pair of six-inch naval guns. He had served more spells of PD One than anyone else in the cell but he claimed that he was completely undismayed by the prospect of facing further punishment.

More days passed, each an ugly replica of the one that had gone before. The temperature became cooler during the hours of parades and fatigues and the cell was colder than ever at night. Bill Farrell was no longer mentioned though John suspected that he had not been wholly forgotten. The rumours of the possibility of being released on suspended sentence were revived at intervals and they flared from the embers of cooling credibility to a blaze of optimistic conjecture when three strange officers were seen coming out of the commandant's office accompanied by Babbage, but when a week had passed without any sign of an interview board being established and no further sight of the officers, hope died away. And still John managed to avoid a second spell of PD One though Ron Lewis was given yet another three days for alleged insolence.

Monotony, strategies of humiliation and insult, exhaustion and a growing sense of injustice steadily undermined John's determination to protect his identity, his private conviction of his own wholeness and humanity, and with increasing frequency and importunacy he experienced moments when a great voiceless howl of protest swelled inside him and clamoured for release. It was outrageous that the mean, stupid and sadistic staff, not one of whom had ever been within range of any missile more dangerous than a flying cork, should be able to abase, mock and abuse men who were, in many cases, their physical, moral and intellectual superiors or at least had been tested in circumstances of pain and terror beyond the imaginings of their present captors and whose failures surely merited something other than this kind of punishment. Self-pity and despair were the most insidious of threats and John found that the only way to cauterise these cankers was through the cultivation of anger and hatred. Although he did not voice his longing he, too, like Chalky, dreamed of maiming, smashing, mauling, killing the fuckers, and if he heard a faint inner whisper of warning that he was allowing the enemy to fulfil their purpose and fundamentally change him into something more like themselves he dismissed it, believing, perhaps correctly, that rage alone could prevent his submission and collapse. So hatred grew in the darkness of his spirit and mind like a malignant flower, its perfume poisonous and heady, and he knew that before long it would have to find means of expression.

Another day of whistles, shouts, and double-marching feet drew to its close and the SUS's were lined up for communication parade. The man opposite John was someone he had not noticed before, rather older than most of the prisoners, perhaps a little over thirty, tall and bony with a lugubrious comedian's face.

'Haven't seen you before,' John said. 'How long you doing?'

'For ever.'

'No remission for good behaviour?'

The man grinned. 'That's life,' he said.

A pause.

'Where do you come from?' John asked, not really interested but because Staff Henderson was approaching.

'The Midlands. Near Coventry. What's left of it.'

'What was your job in civvy street?'

'Printing trade. What about you?'

'Insurance office. Tea-boy really.'

Another pause.

Then the Coventry man said, 'I was reading the other day that the Yanks in Blighty get more pay than our officers. I mean their other-ranks, enlisted men as they call them, GIs. An ordinary private gets more than one of our lieutenants. No wonder they're fucking all our women.'

John nodded, 'Lucky sods.' Then the significance of what had just been said suddenly flared, like a match struck in the darkness: 'What was that? What do you mean you read it the other day? How? Where? How d'you get anything to read? Who gave it to you?'

'Steady on, chum. Don't get excited. It was only an old number of *Reveille* or something.'

'But who gave it to you? I've never seen a single word of print since I've been here.'

'You're entitled. It's in the Regulations. In the bit Babbage never reads out. When you've served more than fifty-six days you can ask for a book or magazine. I've seen it written down. You ask one of the screws. He can't say no.'

'You can get books?' John said.

'Yeah. You ask one of the screws, tactful like. Try and get one that's in a good mood.'

At that point communication parade came to an end and the SUS's were returned to their cells.

John thought very carefully about which of the staff to approach and decided finally that Brown was probably the least overtly hostile and sadistic though he reflected that his looking for a sympathetic screw was rather like trying to find an iceberg in the desert. Having made his decision he waited for what seemed a propititious time to present his request. It came two days after the Coventry man's revelation, as Brown was about to lock up the cell for the day.

The little staff-sergeant came just inside the cell and looked around it. Then he said, 'Right. Get on with your tasks. I want to see them dazzling bright tomorrow.'

As he turned to step outside John said, 'Excuse me, Staff.'

Brown paused and faced this bold SUS who had dared to speak before spoken to and his bright, curranty eyes widened a fraction: 'Well? And what do you have to say for yourself?'

'I wondered if I could get something to read.'

Brown continued to stare. The cell had become completely silent. Then somebody at the end farthest from the door was heard to stifle a grunt of laughter.

'Shaddap!' Brown snapped. 'All of you! On your feet! Stand to attention. Don't let me hear another sound or the whole lot of you will be on a fizzer.' The SUS's scrambled to their feet and stood to attention. Brown's eyes came back to John. 'What did you say?'

'I said I wondered if I could get something to read, Staff.'

'And what put that into your head? Why do you suddenly come up with this?'

'It's in the Regulations. Any SUS who's done fifty-six days or more is entitled to a book or magazine.'

Brown's eyes seemed to gleam even brighter. He allowed a few seconds to pass before he spoke again. 'And when did you get to see Regulations?'

'I haven't seen them, Staff. I was told about it.'

'And who told you about it?'

What small expectation of success John might have entertained now faded away. He simply wanted to bring the dialogue to an end. 'Someone on communication parade, Staff.'

'Who? What's his name? Unit?'

'I didn't ask him, Staff.'

There was another longish pause. 'So you want something to read, do you?'

'If I'm entitled to it, Staff.'

Each looked steadily at the other. John tried to eliminate all expression from his face. Then Brown nodded to himself a couple of times, before he said, 'Yes. You're entitled to it, Bain. What about the rest of you? Anybody else want to claim his rights?'

None of the other SUS's spoke.

'So it's just you, Bain. You're the great reader, are you? And you know it says in Regulations you're entitled to reading matter. You're quite right. It says SUS's that have completed fifty-six days of their sentence is entitled to printed reading matter such as newspapers, magazines and books as and when obtainable. All right. You can fall out, all of you. Get on with your tasks. And I'll be back shortly with your reading matter, Bain.' He swung round, left the cell and slammed and bolted the door.

For a few seconds the only sound in the cell was the susurrus of sandy cloths applied rhythmically to rusty metal; then Ron Lewis said, 'I bet he don't come back.'

'You never know,' Chalky said. 'He said he would di'n't he?'

'Yeah. Well, we'll see.'

The SUS's went on working. Then they heard the brisk click of boots on the square, coming closer, then stopping outside the cell. The bolt growled back and the door swung open. Brown stood there holding what looked like a magazine or paperback book in his hand. He raised it and flicked it through the air so that it fell close to where John was sitting on his folded blankets. Brown remained in the doorway looking into the cell. John picked up the book. The light in the cell was poor although the sun had not yet set, but it was just bright enough for John to see that the cheaply produced magazine was printed in Arabic. Brown stayed in the doorway; the little dark eyes were very bright and there was a suggestion of a smile or smirk at the corners of his mouth.

'There's your book,' he said. 'Satisfied?'

The accumulated anger of months rose in John's throat and roared in his ears as it was focused on the neat, simpering little man in front of him. He gave a muffled, wordless shout of rage and hurled himself forward in a dive towards his target in the doorway. But Chalky was quick to grab one leg and send John sprawling on his face as Brown skipped back and swung the door shut and bolted it.

'You little shit!' John yelled. 'I'll kill you!'

Ron Lewis had by now joined Chalky and the two of them held him down and tried to gag his shouts.

'Fuck's sake Johnny,' Ron gasped, 'they'll get you in a fucking body-belt and kick the shit out of you. They won't let you get away with it. For our sakes Johnny. They'll take it out the whole fucking lot of us. So for Christ's sake shut up!'

Chalky was lying across John's face, pressing close with his body. John was smothered and sickened by the stink of Chalky's sweaty flesh and his muffled attempts to ask for release were inaudible.

'Get off his head,' Ron said, 'the poor fucker can't breathe.'

Chalky moved away and John was released by both of his restrainers. He breathed deeply and sat down on his blankets.

Ron picked up the magazine. 'The bastard,' he said. 'It's in fucking wog writing.'

'Let's have a shufti.' Chalky took the magazine and turned a few pages. 'How you supposed to read that fucking stuff? No wonder the wogs is all ignorant.' He dropped it and picked up his cloth and resumed work on his task.

Ron said, 'You should've kept quiet, Johnny. That little bastard'll get you. Him and his mates. You see. You did just what he wanted. You'll be on a fizzer tomorrow. Then on PD One in a single flowery. They'll wait till you're asleep and come creeping up in them fucking gym-shoes and they'll be into the cell and have you strapped up in a body-belt before your fucking eyes are open. Then they'll kick shit out of you. That's what they do. They did it to a mate of mine in the Black Watch. He put the head on one of the screws – made a right mess of the bastard an' all – but they got him all right. They half killed the poor fucker.'

John was scarcely aware of what Ron was saying. The explosion of fury had left him trembling and sick. He knew that he had reacted to Brown's little joke in a way that must have given his tormentor great satisfaction. Controlled anger and contempt were healthy, sustaining forces, but his abandonment of all restraint and reason, his moment of homicidal lunacy, for that is what it had been, was a gift to the enemy. The hard centre of resistance that he had nurtured had been smashed. He felt

weak and vulnerable and ashamed. Tomorrow he would be
brought before the commandant for punishment. The solitary
cell was waiting for him, the unfriendly cold stone floor, the
twilit freezing of time; then darkness and trying to fight off sleep
because once he had surrendered to it he was defenceless and
they would come creeping through the night on silent feet, the
eye of the door would come to life and peer down at his sleeping
form and then the door would burst open and boots and fists
would split the wincing skin and thump and thud on unpro-
tected bone. Somehow he must try to reassemble his broken
defences, his centre of resistance, his sense of wholeness of
being. But he doubted his ability to accomplish this.

The next morning he moved through the early routine of
slopping out, washing and shaving and scrubbing the square in a
state of partially numbed apprehension. At breakfast he could
not finish his piece of bread. Chalky pounced on what he left and
devoured it with heartless relish. Then came muster parade and
Commandant's Orders. This was the time when John would be
called out to join the malefactors who had been placed on
charges. His name and number were not called by the RSM. At
first he felt a brief uplift of spirit, a feeling of reprieve, but almost
at once it was vanquished by the gloomy reflection that Brown
had obviously forgotten to submit the charge-sheet to the
commandant's office and this lapse would be corrected today so
that John would be brought before Captain Babbage the
following morning.

That evening in the cell Chalky was optimistic. 'You scared
the shit out of the little bugger,' he said. 'He's not put you on a
fizzer 'cos he's bloody scared.'

It seemed to John that Chalky was presenting providence with
unbearable provocation. 'I'll be on a charge tomorrow. I expect
he forgot.'

'No,' Chalky was quite confident. 'You're going to get away
with it, mate. You see if I'm not right.'

Ron was less sanguine. 'I hope you're right Chalky boy. But I
doubt it. I can't see him letting Johnny off. He might be scared if
it was just the two of 'em, man to man like. But Brown's got the

whole fucking army behind him. He's got nothing to be scared about. Johnny'll be on the peg tomorrow.'

But the next morning's muster parade again passed without John's being called up before the commandant and astonishingly it seemed that Chalky was right. Brown had not charged him. When yet another day passed with no summons from the RSM John at last accepted that, for whatever reason, he had been let off the very serious charge of using threatening and obscene language against an NCO and probably attempting to strike him.

One evening it was Staff Brown's turn to slam and bolt the cell door on John and his cell-mates after dinner. About twenty minutes later the SUS's heard the smart click of footsteps coming closer, then stopping outside the cell. Everyone began industriously rubbing at dixies and platters. No-one looked up at the door until it swung open and Brown stood there. They began to climb to their feet but he yelped,' As you were! Carry on with your tasks!'

John who, with the others, had begun to rise, sank back on to his blankets. He thought, 'Whatever the little sod says or does I'll keep my temper.' He did not look up but began to work at his rusty tea-pail.

'Here you are, Bain,' Staff Brown said and threw something down which landed close to John's feet.

As John looked up Brown was already pulling the door shut. The bolts grated home and they heard his brisk footsteps crossing the square towards the gate. Then John saw that he had thrown a book on to the ground. He reached out slowly and picked it up, wondering what trick was being played on him this time. But there was no trick. The book, a stained and tattered but – as a rapid inspection confirmed – quite complete Penguin, was in English. It was *Esther Waters* by George Moore.

Chalky whispered, 'What's he give you, Johnny? What is it?'

'A book,' John said.

'Is it in English?'

'What kind of book?' Ron asked.

'It's a novel. A story.'

John held the book close to his face so that he could see the print in the dim light. He thought: 'I have a book. I shall read it, a little each day, and it will make me human again.'

Chalky hissed: 'I told you, Johnny. You've scared the little bastard. He's arse-creeping. That's why he give you the book. He's scared you'll belt him one.'

'Bollocks!' John was suddenly very angry. 'What's he got to be scared of? I'm the one that was scared.'

'Well what you think he give you that fucking book for?'

'I don't know.'

'I tell you. He's shit-scared.'

John did not bother to argue. He found himself curiously moved by Brown's giving him the book. It was the first gesture from any member of the staff that could be regarded as human or humane and he was conscious of a disproportionately strong sense of gratitude that, for a few seconds, seemed like a kind of love. Whatever Chalky might say or think, Brown was not afraid and he must have chosen to give John the book in order to make amends for the cruelty of his 'joke'. He was capable of remorse and of compassion. The knowledge brought with it strength and warmth.

John thought, 'I'll read about ten pages a day. At that rate it'll last me well over a month. And if I don't get another book I'll just turn back to the beginning and read it again.'

But as events transpired, he did not reach the end of *Esther Waters* for, three weeks later, he was summoned before the commandant after morning muster parade and told that at 14.30 hours he was to report for an interview with the Sentence Review Board.

Babbage said to the RSM, 'He can rejoin his squad now – what are they on?'

'Pack-drill, Sah!'

'Right. He can get back on the square. But after tiffin he's to get smartened up for the interview. Who's in charge of his squad?'

'Staff Hardy, Sah!'

'Very well, Mr Grant. Tell Hardy that this SUS is to be brought here, to my office, at 14.30 hours on the dot. The

Review Board will be sitting here. So he won't be on parade after tiffin. He can wait in his cell till Hardy fetches him. That clear?'

'Sah!'

'Carry on, Sarnt-major.'

'Sah!'

So, at half-past two in the afternoon John was marched into the commandant's office again, though this time Babbage was not present. Behind his table sat three officers, a lieutenant-colonel in the centre flanked by two majors. They were not wearing their caps so John could not tell what unit or units they belonged to.

Staff Hardy, who had escorted John into the office, barked '2991874 Private Bain J, Sah!'

'Wait outside Sarnt, will you,' the colonel said with that slightly irritable langour that senior officers usually adopted when speaking to NCOs.

'Sah!'

Hardy turned smartly and marched out of the office.

John remained at attention.

The colonel said, 'I'll briefly explain why you're here – ah – ah, oh yes, Bain. And why we're here, too. We're here to ask you a few questions and we want – we absolutely demand – straightforward, honest answers. Don't try to pull the wool over our eyes because it won't work. Straightforward, honest answers to all questions. That understood?'

'Yessir.'

'Very well. First thing, let me tell you what this board is about. You may or may not know that in the near future the allied forces will be launching a big offensive against the Germans somewhere in Europe. The Second Front. A considerable number of the troops involved in this campaign will be inexperienced. They won't have seen any action. I'm sure they will acquit themselves well. But it's only common sense to make sure that they'll be, as it were, stiffened by a fair number of battle-hardened troops. Now part of the Eighth Army has already been repatriated, including your own division, the Fifty-first Highland. They've been sent home to prepare for the

Second Front. Obviously they're well under strength and the numbers will be made up by reinforcements from the training centres. But the point is this. We need every battle-experienced man we can find and so we've been taking a look around the various punishment establishments to see if we can find chaps who've learnt their lesson and are prepared to soldier on. I don't mean in some cushy billet in Blighty, or out here for that matter. I mean by soldiering, fighting, going into action, facing the enemy. We've had a look at the details of your case and it seems like one of the less disgraceful kind.' He looked from one to the other of his companions each of whom nodded and looked thoughtful. Then he went on: 'Don't misunderstand me. You deserved the sentence you were given. You deserted in a forward area. It was a damned bad show. You let your comrades down. Or you might have done.' He paused again. 'Yes, a damned bad show. Now, the question is – would you do the same thing again? Would you turn tail and run? Would you, to put it very simply, let the side down. Or would you give us your word that you would soldier on and make up for blotting your copy-book at Wadi Akarit? That's what we want to know. Are you ready to go back to your battalion and, when the time comes, fight.'

'Yessir,' John said, trying hard to sound sincere and manly.

Again the colonel looked at his colleagues.

Then he said, 'Can you promise us that you would not do the same thing again, the thing you were sent here for?'

'Yessir.' John managed to capture a nice note of vibrant earnestness.

'Ah, yes, mm . . .' The colonel looked at the papers on the table in front of him. Then he said, 'Have you any questions you'd like to ask, gentlemen? What about you, Major Taylor?'

The officer on the colonel's left said, 'Looking at the details of your Court Martial you didn't seem to have any kind of defence. I mean what made you do it? Jerry was on the run, you weren't in a hot spot. Couldn't have been sudden panic. I don't understand why you did it.'

John did not know whether he was supposed to answer.

The colonel said, 'Well? Why did you do it?'

'I don't really know, sir,' John said. 'I think it was exhaustion and worry about things at home.'

'Ah, things at home,' the major who had not yet spoken said, and it seemed clear to John that here was something comprehensible, if not excusable. 'What kind of things exactly?'

'I'd had a letter saying my girlfriend was pregnant.'

'Well, there's not much –' the major began; then he paused and frowned. 'But . . . I mean how could she . . . you'd been out here for what? The Fifty-first left the UK in June forty-two, didn't they? So you'd been away for at least nine months by the time you got up to Gabès. You must have . . . oh, I think I see your problem.'

'Yessir.'

The colonel said, 'You mean you're not the father?'

'Yessir. I mean no, sir, I'm not the father.'

'I see.' The colonel tapped with his finger-tips on the table and pondered for a few moments. Then he said, 'Well, hard luck and all that, but these things happen in wartime. I still don't see how running away from your unit is going to help matters.'

'No sir. I think I was confused, Sir.'

'Why didn't you mention this at your Court Martial?' Major Taylor asked.

'I didn't think it was any excuse, Sir.'

'Then why mention it now?'

'I've had a lot of time to think about it, Sir. I came to feel that it had upset me more than I realised at the time. I think I felt that we were supposed to be fighting to protect our loved ones at home and that was the kind of thanks we were getting. I know it's no excuse but I think that's what I felt subconsciously.'

'Never mind about subconsciously,' the colonel said briskly. 'The fact is you deserted. What we want to be sure of is that you wouldn't do it again.'

'No Sir.'

'You mean you wouldn't? You're quite sure of that?'

'Yessir.'

'All right.' He shuffled some papers before he spoke again. 'You realise that if we send you back to your battalion it'll be on a suspended sentence. Do you understand what that means?'

'I think so, Sir.'

'It means this. If you commit any other serious crime – I don't mean dirty brasses or an idle boot-lace – I mean something serious like desertion or refusing to obey an order, that kind of thing. If you commit another crime you'll have to serve the rest of your present sentence – what have you got left? Two and a half years, isn't it? – you'll have to serve all that on top of the sentence you're given for the new crime. You understand?'

'Yessir.'

From outside could be heard the double-marching tramp of boots on the barrack square and the staccato barkings of the staff.

The colonel looked at John steadily and John gazed at a point above the officer's head and tried to exude resolution and reliability.

'Very well,' the colonel said. 'If we decide to release you you'll be out of here in twenty-four hours. You'll go to the infantry base and wait there for the next troopship home. When I tell you to dismiss I want you to go outside and send that staff-sergeant in here. You'd better wait for him to come out again. Understood?'

'Yessir.'

'No more questions for this man, gentlemen?'

The majors shook their heads and made vague negative noises.

'All right. Dismiss!'

John left the office and went out into the bright afternoon. Hardy was waiting in the shade of the upper tier balcony.

'They want to see you, Staff. They told me to wait till you came out again.'

'Right. Stand easy.'

Hardy unnecessarily straightened his cap, advanced to the office door, knocked on it and went inside.

The SUS's were jogging across the parade-ground with buckets or sweating under the weight of their equipment as they double-marched, wheeled and marked time to the yapping of the staff. The white stone of the cell walls ached in the acerbic light. A feeling of unreality, not dream-like but distanced, remote, seemed to settle over John's senses. He was a spectator not a participant. In the past few minutes he had ceased to be an SUS. The shouts and the metronomic tramping were filtered, made fainter by his non-involvement. He did not feel anxious about the decision of the interview-board. Somehow he knew that he was going to be released.

The door of the office opened and closed. Hardy approached. He stood looking at John for a few seconds with an expression of cynical wonder. Then he said, 'You're going out tomorrow.'

John did not speak.

'Did you hear me? You're going out tomorrow.'

'Yes, Staff.'

'You've persuaded them you're going to be a good boy. That right?'

'Yes, Staff,'

'All right. You'll be discharged after muster parade. Until then you won't do any more parades. In a couple of minutes you'll go and get all your kit out of your cell. I'll take you up to one of the punishment cells. That's only because we don't want you talking to the SUS's in your cell. You'll spend your last night on your tod. After muster parade you'll see the commandant. He'll give you your documents and travel-warrant and instructions. Then you'll be out in the big free world. All right?'

'Yes, Staff.'

'And in a month or two from now you'll be back in Blighty.'

'Yes, Staff.'

'And I'll still be here, chasing horrible little men like you up and down the square. Do you think I envy you?'

John did not answer.

'Well, do you?'

'I don't know, Staff.'

'I do not. I do not envy you at all. Not one little bit. And do you know why I do not envy you?'

'No, Staff.'

'I'll tell you why. The only reason you're being let out of here is because they want all the poor buggers they can get hold of to start the Second Front. They're letting you out tomorrow and they're going to send you home. And then they're going to get you killed. That's what you're being let out for. To be killed. You understand that?'

'Yes, Staff,' John said, 'I understand.'

Hardy frowned. He looked worried, a little anxious.

'Don't you believe what I'm saying?' he said. 'Don't you believe that's what they're letting you out for? To get you killed?'

'I believe they'll try,' John said.

Part III

GUNSHOT WOUNDS

THE TRAIN SNORTED and rattled to a halt. John rubbed at the vapour on the window and peered at smooth blackness and the spectral reflection of his own face. The civilian sitting opposite him, a middle-aged man in a navy-blue overcoat and bowler hat, said, 'This is Chalfont, son. That's the station you said you wanted, isn't it?'

'Yes. Thanks.'

John heaved his kit-bag and webbing down from the rack and put on his balmoral and greatcoat. He opened the carriage door and dumped the equipment and kit-bag on to the platform. He picked up his rifle from where it had been resting in one corner of the compartment and stepped down into the darkness.

'Goodnight,' the civilian said. 'I'll close the door.'

Rain fell steadily from the hidden sky. John turned up the collar of his greatcoat then felt for his webbing, found it and buckled it on. He closed his eyes for a few seconds then opened them and thought that he could make out a low fence on the side of the platform opposite to the track and the outline of what must be the booking-office. He slung his rifle over one shoulder and picked up the kit-bag, carrying it by the neck, and moved cautiously towards what he hoped was the exit. Then above the sound of hissing rain he heard a metallic click and the squeak of unoiled hinges, as a door opened to spill a little feeble light like watery egg-yolk on to the black glossy stone of the platform. A moment later he was out of the rain and into the dimly lit hall of the booking-office where a short, elderly man wearing a big raincoat and official railway company cap was asking to see his travel-warrant.

'How do I get to Vache Camp?' John said.

As he spoke he heard the sound of a motor-engine and a gear-change from beyond the station exit and the ticket collector said,

'This'll be one of your lot. There's always a truck comes up to meet the last train from town.'

Outside, the engine was switched off and very soon after a Gordon Highlander private came into the hall straightening up from the crouching run that had brought him from his vehicle.

'Jesus Christ,' he said, 'that fucking rain hasn't stopped since yesterday dinner-time. You for Vache Camp, china?'

John said that he was.

'Okay. Let's have your kit-bag. Chuck the rest of your stuff in the back and you can sit in with me.'

John followed the driver out to where his fifteen hundred-weight truck was parked; his rifle, kit-bag and webbing were slung into the back and the two soldiers scrambled into the front. In the restricted light of the masked headlamps the rain flickered like needles. The driver peered into the darkness, restarted the engine and drove away. John could smell the doggy pungency of wet khaki.

'You're lucky there wasn't an officer on that fucking train,' the driver said, 'or you'd be in the back.'

'Is the camp far?'

'No. A couple o' mile.'

'What's it like?'

'Fucking terrible.'

'How? What way terrible?'

'Vache Camp they call it. You know what that means, Vache? It's French for "cow". The four-legged kind with horns. Christ knows why they've got to give it a French name. I'll tell you one thing though. You'll be up to your bollocks in mud. Pig Camp'd be a better name for it. You know what they say, happy as a pig in shit. Well, only a pig'd be happy in that fucking dump.'

At the entrance to the camp he slowed down to be recognised by and exchange jovial insults with the sentry and then he pulled up outside a Nissen hut the shape of which was just discernible in the rain-filled dark.

'In there, china. You can get your own stuff out the back. I don't want to get fucking soaked again.'

John climbed out of the truck, retrieved his belongings and

felt his way to the door of the guard-room and went in. He
blinked in the white glare from the naked bulb which hung
above the scrubbed trestle-table behind which a corporal sat with
an enamel mug of tea at his elbow. In the centre of the hut a
stove was burning and on top of it stood a tea-pail. Two privates
sat on a bench in front of the stove smoking cigarettes and a third
lay, wrapped in his blankets, asleep on the floor.

John let his webbing and kit-bag fall to the floor. He said,
'2991874 Private Bain J.' He unbuttoned his battle-dress tunic
pocket and brought out a piece of paper and handed it across the
table. 'My leave-pass.'

The corporal took it, looked at it, consulted his watch and
dropped the pass on to the table.

'You're in B Company,' he said, 'but you'll kip down in the
reception hut tonight. One of the guards'll show you where it is.
Tomorrow you'll see your company commander and get detailed
to a platoon.' He turned to the two men seated near the stove.
'Beattie, show this man to reception. You can give him a hand
with his kit.'

'Right corp.'

'Take the torch and you'd better put your gas-cape on unless
you want to get drowned.'

They went out into the smothering darkness and rain and
John stumbled and squelched after his guide who led him to
another Nissen hut which contained wooden beds with thin
palliasses. Some were made up for sleeping; others had three
folded blankets at the head. There were five soldiers sitting
round the stove.

'Here you are then,' John's guide said, dropping the kit-bag.
'Grab yourself a bed. HQ Company's orderly-sergeant'll be
round at reveille. He'll tell you about ablutions and breakfast
parade and what to do an' all that. Okay?'

John thanked him and got rid of his webbing and rifle, took
off his damp greatcoat and began to spread the blankets on one
of the beds. The men sitting round the stove seemed to be dumb
and almost paralysed with boredom or misery. John got
undressed and took a paperback book from his small pack and

lay under the blankets, his head propped on a pillow of equipment and folded battle-dress. The book, Eric Linklater's *Poet's Pub*, could not hold his attention and he was not displeased when the orderly-sergeant looked into the hut and shouted, 'Get to kip you men! Lights-out in five minutes!'

John lay awake in the darkness listening to the rain rustling on the roof and he tried to hold away the weight of dejection that pressed upon his spirits. He remembered an earlier and similar feeling of misery and desolation when, almost exactly three years ago, he had sat in the NAAFI canteen at Fort George, that dark grey promontory that lay in the Moray Firth like a fossilised leviathan, and he had known, suddenly and with utter certainty, that the war would not end during his lifetime, that he was condemned to remain in this drab khaki world, becoming steadily more and more dehumanised, until all memory of a previous existence was extinguished by death or indifference. He had sat there with his mug of tepid stewed tea as from the loudspeaker on the wall issued the lachrymose, nasal wailing of Vera Lynn making mendacious promises of peace and laughter and happy-ever-after, and he had not possessed even the price of a pint or two of anodyne beer. 'Well,' he thought, 'at least it looks as if the war might come to an end now, though an awful lot of us won't be around to celebrate.'

★   ★   ★   ★   ★

The rain had stopped by the time breakfast was over and John was being interviewed by Captain Forbes, commanding B Company.

Forbes wore an unfashionably heavy black moustache and spoke with a plummy, public-school accent. He said, 'You'll be joining Number Two Platoon. Lieutenant Mitchell is your platoon commander and Sergeant Thom, platoon sergeant. You were in B Company before . . . ah . . . I mean when you . . . er . . . left the battalion at Wadi Akarit, weren't you?'

John was chagrined to find that his forehead and cheeks were tingling with a wholly unexpected embarrassment. He muttered, 'Yessir.'

'You'll find a few changes. Major Walker – Captain as you'll remember him – is at Battalion HQ as Intelligence Officer. Lieutenant Fergusson was killed in Sicily. Unfortunately. I believe your platoon is out firing the Piat this morning so you can get your kit over to B Company lines. Sergeant-Major Maclean will direct you to your hut. So you can just sort of settle in, make yourself at home an' all that till dinner-time. Then Lieutenant Mitchell will tell you what section you're in and so on. Oh yes, and Bain . . .'

'Yessir?'

'I want you to know that nothing is going to be held against you. You know what I mean, what? It's a completely fresh start. So carry on and good luck to you.'

John saluted and left the company office.

Company Sergeant-Major Maclean was waiting outside. He said, 'Pick up your kit from reception and take it over there, number five hut. See it? The one in the middle of that lot there. I know there's a couple of free beds. Take either one. And report to Lieutenant Mitchell when he gets back from the range.'

In daylight the camp was quite as depressing as the driver on the previous night had promised. A single rough road ran from the entrance with a few even rougher paths leading from it to the six-deep rows of Nissen huts on either side. Among the sixty or so huts were a few larger but no less ugly structures which served as dining-hall, cookhouse and the sergeants' and officers' messes. A spacious area next to the guardroom had been concreted over and, on part of it, Bren-carriers and variously sized trucks were parked, the rest of the space presumably being reserved for guard-mounting and other parades. John splashed his way through the muddy pools on the track to collect his kit and then carried it to the hut to which the CSM had directed him.

He backheeled the door shut and stood looking down the hut. On each side was a row of wooden beds, with rolled-up palliasses and neatly folded blankets at their heads and above every one was a dark green, metal locker, nearly all the doors of which were decorated with pictures of some kind, photographs of wives or girl-friends or, in the cases of those who possessed neither, or none whose lineaments they wished to exhibit, pictures of film actresses or models in more or less extreme states of undress. The wooden boards of the floor were well-scrubbed and the stove, which had not yet been lit, was black-leaded and polished, so the place was clean with that specious cleanliness on which inspecting NCOs and officers insisted; but the air, though chill, was heavy with the migled odours of unwashed feet and clothes, stale tobacco-smoke, rifle-oil, leather and the sickly, persistent smell of old blankets and the various bodily emissions they had absorbed. John moved to one of the beds which had no kit-bag or other signs of occupancy on or around it and dumped his rifle and equipment on to the floor at the side of it. He opened the locker to ensure that it was empty and began to transfer some of the more personal contents of his valises to its shelves. Then he found his paperback book, sat on the bed and forced himself to concentrate on the novel's uncompelling pages, but after about half an hour he began to feel drowsy so he lay down on his back, his knees bent and his head propped against the folded blankets and fell asleep.

He was awakened by the Number Two Platoon's return from the firing-range. The door flew open as if it had been assaulted by a battering-ram and boots clattered on the wooden floor as the men, already pulling off their webbing, made for their lockers exchanging amiable insults or simply voicing profane opinions of the weather, the camp, the ineptitude of officers in general and Lieutenant Mitchell in particular. John swung his feet down to the floor and sat up, looking for familiar faces. For a moment he thought there was no one there he knew and then, with an unexpectedly sharp sense of pleasure, he recognised Hughie Black's short, stocky figure and round, battered face, which looked like a very tough baby's, and he jumped up and crossed to where Hughie was hanging up his equipment.

'How you doing, Hughie? Remember me?'

Hughie turned and looked at John as if he suspected him of being an impostor and then a slow, very wide grin brightened his usually pugnacious and suspicious features and he said, 'Fucky Nell, look what the tide's brought in.' Then he called to someone on the other side of the hut: 'Hey, Alec! Come here a minute. Somebody I want you to meet.'

The man who joined them was of medium height, and he had clear blue eyes, intelligent and amused, and the well-seasoned complexion of a country man who enjoys his drink.

Hughie said, 'This is Johnny Bain. I've told you about the bastard. Meet Alec Stevenson, my mate. He's no' bad considering he's a neep.'

'Neep' was the word used by the city fly-men of Glasgow and Edinburgh to designate the slow-witted yokel from rural Aberdeenshire or Banffshire.

John and Alec shook hands.

'Listen,' Hughie said. 'You'd better go and see Mitchell. We're in Number One Section. Tell him you'd like to get in with us, you've got old mates in the section. Mitchell's no'a bad bloke. He'll likely fix it for you . . . ah, here comes Gordon. Better still. Get Gordon to talk to Mitchell. That'll be a cert. Gordon's our section leader now.'

Gordon Rennie, whom Johnny had known and liked, had risen from private to full corporal and he came up with his right hand outstretched, a big toothy smile on his broad, slightly mongolian face. 'Johnny Bain! How are you man? It's great to see you.'

They shook hands.

Hughie said, 'I was just saying, Gordon. You could have a word with Mitchell and get Johnny into our section, couldn't you?'

'Shouldn't be difficult. But look. We'll have to have a wee celebration. None of you's on guard tonight, is that right. We'll go and have a few pints then, the three of us. How's that sound?'

John said, 'It sounds fine. But I'm broke. Just back from leave.'

'Never mind. We'll manage all right,' Gordon promised. 'See you later.'

Hughie said, 'You didna get home for Christmas or Hogmanay, then?'

'No. We were hanging about at the base in Egypt for a couple

of months before we got on the boat. We landed a couple of
weeks ago and I was sent on leave from a kind of transit camp near
Southampton.'

'Where d'you go.'

'A couple of days at home. Not far from here. Aylesbury.
Then I went to London and stayed in the Union Jack Club at
Waterloo.'

'What the fuck d'you do that for? What's wrong with home?'

John grinned. 'You don't know my home, Hughie. My
mother was frightened I'd eat her butter-ration and the old man
tried to avoid being on his own with me in case I tried to tap him
for a couple of quid.'

'What d'you do in London? You know people there?'

'No. I boozed, as much as I could afford to. Went to the
pictures. Watched the Yanks getting off with all the women.
The last couple of days I couldn't afford anything more than a
cup of tea and a wad in the Union Jack canteen.'

Hughie brought out a packet of Woodbines. 'Here. Have a
fag.'

John took one and they both lit up. 'First smoke since
yesterday morning,' he said.

'Yeah?'

'Smoked my last one in bed at the Union Jack, Wednesday
morning.'

'You as broke as that then?'

'Flat.'

'Take a couple of these fags.'

'No, it's all right.'

'Take 'em. Here.'

Hughie pushed four cigarettes into John's hand.

'Better get ready for dinner,' he said. 'Get your eating-irons.
They'll be shouting us out on parade in a minute.'

★   ★   ★   ★   ★

The public bar of the village inn was small with a low ceiling and
dingy, smoke-stained wall-paper, and it was inadequately lit as if

it had been the landlord's aim to make the place as unappealing as possible. The landlord was as unwelcoming as his bar, a heavily built, bald man of middle age and ill-tempered aspect. It was quite plain that he was not pleased to see the four soldiers.

Gordon Rennie paid for the drinks and they raised their glasses and toasted each other before taking the first swallow.

'Fucking terrible beer,' Hughie said and Gordon, who was, unless strongly provoked, the most pacific and easy-going of people, glanced anxiously around to see if the landlord was within earshot, but he had moved into the saloon-bar out of range of insult.

Alec Stevenson said, 'There's no bad beer. Some's better than others, that's all.'

Hughie scowled. 'This isna beer. It's fucking gnat's piss.'

John said, 'It needs livening up. A bottle of Guinness'd do the trick.'

'Next round,' Alec promised, 'I'll get black-an-tans.'

After the second round had been drunk and they were starting on their third pint John felt more cheerful but Hughie seemed morose and taciturn.

Alec said, 'You used to box, didn't you, Johnny? I saw you on the troopship. You beat a sergeant from the Camerons.'

'Why? You interested?'

'No. Well, just to watch. Football's my game.'

John tried to dispel Hughie's gloom by involving him in the talk. 'You're a football man, Hughie. You played in civvy street, didn't you?'

But Hughie just grunted and scowled into his beer.

When the time came to refill their glasses Gordon said, 'This'll have to be the last one lads or I'll be skint.'

Hughie and Alec counted their money but between them they could not afford another round so a quarter of an hour later they all trudged back to the camp and were back in the hut well before lights-out.

John went over and sat with Hughie on his bed.

'You seemed browned off tonight.'

'Aye.'

'Any particular reason?'

Hughie shrugged and relit a half- smoked Woodbine. At first
he avoided a direct answer.

'Och, I'm just fed up.'

'You'll feel better tomorrow.'

'Aye. Maybe.'

John waited for a few seconds then said, 'Well, goodnight,
Hughie. I'll see you tomorrow.'

'Aye . . . wait a minute, Johnny. There's something I want to
ask you.'

'What's that?'

Instead of asking his question Hughie said, 'You've changed,
Johnny. You know that?'

'I'm older. . . All right. How? How have I changed?'

'I dunno. You're just different. Harder.'

John nodded. 'Yeah. Well, I'm not surprised.'

'Was it tough in there. In the nick?'

'Pretty tough.'

'Listen. What you do it for? I mean what made you fuck off
like that, Johnny? At Wadi Akarit. I thought we were pals. I
couldna believe it when I looked round and you wasna there.'

John felt guilt spurt, spread and almost immediately it was
converted into aggression against his friend. 'I don't know why
the fuck I did it. We can't all be bloody heroes.'

Hughie's gingery eyebrows rose. 'Hey! I never said nothing
about heroes. You know me better'n that Johnny. There's no
heroes. We both know that. I just couldna understand why you
never told me what you was going to do. I'd've been with you
like a flash. But . . . well, you know what happened. I looked
round and there you was. Gone. I thought "The bastard! He's
fucked off without a fucking word and I'm supposed to be his
china." I couldna believe it!'

John began to grin and the grin grew into a chuckle.

Hughie said, 'What's so funny? What the fuck you laughing
at?'

'I don't know. I thought . . . .'

'You thought what?'

'I thought you were getting a bit regimental – you know, I shouldn't have let the side down an' all that, old boy. I thought you were going to give me a white feather or something.'

Hughie looked incredulous. 'Jesus Christ, no! I was just mad you'd gone without me! And listen, I'll tell you something, pal. If you'd a had me with you you'd've been away a lot longer than you was. We might still be there, kipped up with a couple of bints in Tripoli or somewhere instead of in this fucking hole. I knew fine you wouldna get far on your tod.'

John was relieved to know what had been the cause of Hughie's ill-humour. He said, 'I wish to God you had been with me. But Hughie, I didn't think. It wasn't something I'd planned. I just turned round and walked like a machine or a ghost or something. It was unreal. I can't understand it myself. I can hardly remember anything for sure. I just remember all those dead Seaforths lying out there and our blokes going round, settling on them like fucking flies, taking their watches and wallets and Christ-knows-what and I just got up and walked. It was like a dream. Why didn't anybody stop me? I just floated down that fucking hill like a ghost or the invisible man. Christ, Hughie. If I'd planned it, if I'd been thinking about it I'd've sure as hell told you what I was up to. I didn't have any idea I was going to do it. It was like a kind of trance, like being hypnotised or something. You understand?'

'Aye . . . sure. Yeah, I understand now. I understand . . . and what about this fucking lot?'

'What d'you mean?'

'What the fuck d'you think I mean? I mean the Second fucking Front. We're gonna be in the first fucking wave. It'll be like going over the top in the last bloody war. We're going to be cannon-fodder, pal.'

'I don't know.'

'You take my word for it. Cannon-fodder.'

'I mean I don't know what I'm going to do.'

'Well, think about it, Johnny. And if you make up your mind to take a walk let me know this time and I'll take a walk with you. Okay?'

'Don't worry. I'd let you know.'

'We could fuck off up to Glasgow. I've got mates up there. They'd see us all right. We could get into civvies, get a job. You don't have to have cards nor nothing if you know your way around. There's blokes been on the run two three years up there. Sitting pretty.'

'I'll think about it.'

'Aye. You do that. I'll think about it myself.'

'I couldn't face the nick again.'

'Better than being dead. Or having your balls shot off.'

'Maybe.'

'Not maybe. Stay alive and in one piece. Doesn't matter what the bastards do to you, they've got to let you out sooner or later. I've seen too many killed already. Or worse. You remember Jimmy Rae? Wee dark-headed bloke?'

'I think so. On two-inch mortars wasn't he?'

'Aye. Well, he got blinded in Sicily. And Peter MacFarlane – you remember him? – Aye, I thought you would – he went up on a mine and got both legs blown off. There's worse things than the nick.'

'You've not been inside. You don't know what it's like.'

'It doesn't matter what it's like. You're alive and in one piece. That's all that counts.'

Outside, in the night, a bugle played the Last Post, the throat of brass hoarse with an ancient grief. Then the pipes began their own slow lamentation, keening in the darkness and the cold.

'Lights out!' Gordon shouted. 'Into your kip everybody!'

John said to Hughie, 'See you tomorrow,' and hurried to his own bed before the lights in the hut were extinguished.

Under the blankets he lay and listened to the sounds of the other men grunting and coughing as they settled for sleep. A few were continuing earlier or initiating fresh conversations. A match scratched and flared as a cigarette was lit. John began to feel drowsy.

Gordon's voice again: 'No more talking now! Let's get to sleep! Goodnight.'

The talk was reduced to an occasional mutter and then it faded

away completely. Someone began to snore. John pulled the
blankets over his head and went to sleep.

★   ★   ★   ★   ★

During the next few weeks John settled into the familiar,
repetitive routine of life with the battalion. Gordon was able
without difficulty to arrange for John to join his section of the
platoon and Alec, who had been Hughie's number two on the
Bren-gun, readily relinquished this office in John's favour and
became a plain rifleman. He seemed to accept quite cheerfully
his own demotion, a reduction not in the military sense but in
the order of intimacy, and he amiably took his place as the
auxiliary member of the trio. Gordon Rennie, as a full corporal
and their section-leader, was obliged to limit his friendship in
order to avoid charges of favouritism, but there could be no
denying the warmth of feeling which existed among the four of
them. This feeling of friendship, reciprocal trust and confidence
of support was the one thing that made life tolerable. The rest
was boredom, cold, exhaustion, squalor, lack of privacy,
monotony, ugliness and a constant, teasing anxiety about the
future. Fresh rumours were floated almost daily: the battalion
was going to be converted to airborne; it was going to move up
to Scotland; there had been a rape in the village; General
Eisenhower was coming to inspect them; the Highland Division
was going to be used as a diversionary assault force on D-Day
and it had been written off as totally expendable; the Germans
had a secret weapon that would destroy the entire invasion force;
Hitler had been assassinated; Vera Lynn was coming to sing at
Vache Camp; Churchill was coming to inspect the battalion; the
Germans were about to surrender; the battalion was moving to
Kent. This last one proved to be true.

At the beginning of March 1944 they moved to Halstead, a
few miles from Sevenoaks, where they were stationed in a camp
which was little improvement on the one they had so willingly
left. The boredom and irritability of the troops were exacerbated
by the local pubs being frequently shut because of shortages of

beer and by the presence of a large unit of American soldiers who effortlessly captured the attention of all the local girls.

In May the battalion made another move, this time to a vast tented camp near Grays on the Tilbury to Southend road. Here the men slept in large bell tents and the dining-quarters and NAAFI canteen were housed in roomy marquees. The camp was a large city of canvas and it accommodated not only the Highland Division but an airborne division too. Active training was abandoned and the time was spent on a few lectures, fatigues, football matches and other games. There was no doubt in anyone's mind that D-Day was very close. Every day and night great fleets of heavy bombers passed over on their way to smash the defence positions and lines of communication in France and the Low Countries. In daylight the sky would darken with their presence and at night the noise of their engines seemed to throb in the ground beneath the feet. The tension among all ranks expressed itself in different ways: the officers were serious, thoughtful and, in many cases, uncharacteristically solicitous of the welfare of the men under their command, less peremptory and even, at times, indulgent of minor breaches of discipline. Among the NCOs and men there was a wider variety of reaction: those who had already been under fire in North Africa or Sicily were, in the main, quieter and more reflective than the eighteen-year-old reinforcements who had joined the battalion straight from the depot, though there were times when a kind of wild hilarity would explode in the ranks of the veterans, horseplay and laughter so irrational as to verge on madness.

One of the reinforcements in John's section was a Londoner who, apparently, had volunteered to serve in a Highland regiment, impressed by what he regarded as the more glamorous image presented by the Scottish units compared with the English county regiments. He was of a type that John and, in varying degrees, most of the other old hands found it very difficult to respond to with any sympathy. His name was Victor Denham; he was eighteen years old and he had the firm, regular features and steady, utterly humourless gaze of a Head Boy or a Rover Scout patrol-leader. It was the kind of face that would have pleased the Chief Scout or served as a model for illustrations to *Boy's Own Paper* yarns of youthful adventure. If a voice of a schoolboy was going to rally the ranks, John thought, it would be the voice of Victor Denham.

Denham was an extraordinarily smart young soldier. Conscientiously he pressed his battle-dress trousers every night by carefully disposing them beneath his bottom blanket so that the weight of his sleeping body supplied sharp creases that were noticeably lacking in the garments of most of his comrades. His webbing was always kept freshly blancoed and his cap-badge sparkled from daily applications of metal-polish. And it was not simply the uniform that afforded him such pleasure and satisfaction; he was continually oiling and cleaning his rifle and to Hughie's grim amusement he would frequently ask if he could dismantle and clean the Bren. He spoke quite often of his desire to kill a few Jerries and on one of these occasions Hughie spoke out.

'Shut your fucking stupid mouth,' he said. 'You know fuck-all about action. It's not a game. You won't be playing cowboys and Indians over there, son. So don't let me hear you talking about killing anybody. Jerry's the same as us. We're all Jock Thompson's bairns. You ever heard that saying? You'd better remember it.'

'They're the enemy,' Denham protested. 'It's our job to kill them. It's what we're trained to do.'

'They're not the fucking enemy. Not the German soldiers. It's the generals and the fucking politicians, ours as well as theirs, they're the ones, they're the fucking enemy. They're the ones that want to get us killed. Our job's to try and stay alive. You'll find out soon enough son.'

Denham started to speak again but Hugh interrupted: 'I've told you to shut your fucking mouth. I won't tell you again. I'll shut it for you.'

Hughie, at five feet six inches in height, must have been conceding about six inches to the young firebrand but there was something in his aspect which told Denham that it would be prudent to hold his peace.

In the early evening of that day John and Hughie went to the NAAFI wet canteen and settled down with a pint of beer each. Alec, who would normally have been with them, was playing in an inter-company football match. John produced a packet of cigarettes and they lit up.

'I canna stand that young fucker, Denham,' Hughie said. 'I know I shouldna get annoyed but I canna help it. There's something about him.'

'I know what you mean. He always seems to be looking at himself in a shop window. I suppose we ought to feel sorry for him. He's just a big kid playing at soldiers.'

'Aye. Maybe. But I wish he'd go and play somewhere else.'

John took a drink and then said, 'Christ, they make me feel old those kids. But when you come to think, I'm only three or four years older than they are.'

'Right enough, but it's three or four years of being shot at and generally fucked around. It's experience, Johnny, that's what makes the difference. I know what you mean. I'm a wee bit older'n you, but no' that much. And I feel like a fucking grandpa.' Hughie drew on his cigarette and drank some beer. Then he said, 'It's going to be any day now. They could have us away on to the boats inside two or three hours. I bet we don't get much warning. In case we fuck off.'

John did not say anything. He was listening to the faint but steadily increasing droning of bomber engines drumming steadily in the early summer sky.

Hughie said, 'What we going to do, Johnny? You made up your mind yet?'

'I don't know.'

'They're handing out twenty-four hour passes. We could get a couple tomorrow and that would give us a great start. We could be in Glasgow before they missed us. What about it, Johnny?'

'I don't know.'

'Oh fucky Nell, if you don't know, who the fuck does? Come on now, Johnny. It's not like you. What's it going to be?'

John stubbed out his cigarette and drained his glass. 'Drink up, Hughie – I'll get another couple o' pints.'

When he came back to their table with the fresh drinks he sat down again and said, 'I'm not taking a powder, Hughie. I don't want to go into all the reasons for and against, but the main thing is I'd rather face anything than go inside again. Simple as that really.'

'Maybe you've forgotten what action's like.'

'Maybe. This one's going to be a lot different from the desert though. Whatever it's like I'll take it sooner than the nick.'

'But that's no way to look at it, Johnny. It's no' a straight choice between the two. We don't have to get caught. I know some that's been on the run for bloody years. If we use our heads we could stay away for good.'

The planes were directly overhead now, the roar of their engines a sustained and hugely magnified growl, a dark heavy noise, pressing down on the senses.

John waited until the sound had begun to fade and then said, 'If I was going to go on the run there's nobody I'd rather go with than you. But I'm not. I can't. It's more complicated than I said. It's not just the nick. It's true I'd rather be dead than go back inside but that's not the only reason.'

'What else? What other reason?'

'I don't know. I don't think I can explain without sounding stupid or crazy. It's not easy. I don't really understand it myself. It's to do with – Christ, I sound like a fucking padre or something – but it's to do with my own feelings about myself. Self respect I suppose you've got to call it. When I fucked off at Akarit it wasn't planned. I told you, didn't I? It was like being hypnotised, as if I'd got no choice.'

John stopped to take a drink.

Hughie said, 'Go on.'

'What I'm trying to say is I never thought about being a coward. Not till I was in the nick. Then that's about all I heard. I'd been yellow. I'd run away and left my mates to face it. That's what they told me. I was a gutless bastard. A coward.'

'Who told you? What you mean? You talking about the screws?'

'The screws and the commandant, a fat bastard who'd have

shit himself if he'd heard a thunderflash go off.'

'But Christ, Johnny, you can't pay no attention to cunts like that. You said yourself, they'd shit themselves if they was anywhere near the big bangs.'

'I know. But that doesn't mean to say they're wrong. Maybe it takes one to spot one. All I know is I began to think about it and the more I thought about it the less sure I was whether they were wrong or not.'

'For crying out loud, Johnny, you're no' a fucking coward! Cowards don't go in the fucking ring do they?'

'That's different.'

'What's different about it? Och, come off it china. You're no' a coward. And what the fuck's it matter if you was. Better a live coward than a dead hero. That's the old saying and it's true.'

John grinned. 'Here, have a fag.' They lit their cigarettes. 'That's it, Hughie. I'm not going to take a powder. I've got to have another go. And I don't mind telling you, I'm shit-scared. But if I fucked off now, I'd never know, would I? And I don't know why, but somehow I've got to know. I've got to find out if those bastards in the nick were right or wrong.'

'You're a bloody head-case, Johnny. Why get yourself killed for they fuckers? We've had more'n our share of it. Let somebody else have a go. Let fucking Denham do it. He's rarin' to go. He's dead keen. Let Denham do it.'

John drank some beer. 'Listen, Hughie. I've made up my mind. I think it was made up all the time really. But listen. You don't have to go along with me. You know that. I've got to go on this bloody Second Front thing for my own reasons. But you don't. You don't have to go. Don't think I'd blame you for one second if you fucked off. In fact I think you'd be daft not to.'

Hughie sounded shocked: 'I wouldna go without you Johnny. You know that fine. Hey, drink up, it might be our last.'

★　　★　　★　　★　　★

Three days later, on 25th May 1944, the camp at Grays was 'sealed'. This meant that the barbed-wire fencing which already encircled it was patrolled on the outside by armed military police and every exit was heavily guarded for twenty-four hours of each day. Unlike conventional security measures these were aimed not at frustrating penetration from outside but at preventing the escape of those within the camp. Excitement among the troops simmered steadily and every now and then it boiled over in wild exhibitions of buffoonery or anger and violence. John felt moments of sudden apprehension that were close to pure dread but he was surprised by the infrequency of these attacks and by his more usual equanimity. He recognised that this relative calmness was, at least in part, due to the fact that his subconscious instinct for self-protection had woven a kind of veil which blurred and softened his perceptions of reality. The days that followed the sealing of the camp were oddly lacking in substance; they were not so much dream-like as chronologically dislocated; it was as if he were remembering these events and sensations rather than experiencing them for the first time.

Each morning after breakfast, there was an inspection of weapons and equipment and then the day was taken up with more games of football, more lectures and fatigues. On one early evening the pipes and drums of the division played the Retreat and again John was surprised, this time by the poignancy of the sound and sight of the ceremony, and that night, when the lone company piper played Lights Out, he recalled the massed pipes and drums, the colours and the skirl and beat of the march which held at the heart of martial arrogance a melancholy acceptance that war meant separation, suffering and the loss of young lives. He was angered and humiliated by the power this sound and spectacle possessed to move him, despite his rational rejection of them as part of the mendacity of the army's glorification of the essentially inglorious.

For a time Hughie became withdrawn and taciturn but, after the camp had been sealed for four days, he cheered up as if he had finally accepted whatever the future held for him. Alec was as equable as ever and Gordon Rennie, too, showed his customary good-natured stoicism and was noticeably helpful and encouraging to those young reinforcements who were showing clear signs of trepidation. Victor Denham was not one of these. The prospect of landing in occupied France clearly held no terrors for him. When Lieutenant Mitchell gave an open-air lecture to the platoon one morning about the kind of country they would probably be fighting in and the kind of armour the Germans would be employing the only man to respond to the perfunctory invitation to ask questions at the end of the talk was Denham.

'Could you use a sticky-bomb on a Panther or Tiger Tank, Sir?'

Mitchell, who had not expected any questions, hesitated. Then he said, 'I could. But I wouldn't like to try.'

'Sir!' Denham's hand was up again.

'Yes? What is it?'

'You said the Panther and Tiger tanks had a big eighty-eight gun. Well, Sir, if a man could get close up surely he'd be out of range. He'd be able to plant a sticky-bomb on the side and get away before it exploded.'

Mitchell began to look annoyed. 'The German Mark Five and Six tanks do indeed carry eighty-eight millimetre guns. But they also carry at least one machine-gun. And as for sticky-bombs, if you want my opinion – my unofficial opinion, that is – you'd be just as well off with a sticky bun as a sticky-bomb.'

The platoon guffawed.

'Still, I'm glad to see you taking an interest, Denham. I think that'll be all for now. You can dismiss the men, Sarnt Thom.'

Mitchell acknowledged the platoon-sergeant's salute and strode away in the direction of the officers' mess tent.

As the group disbanded Hughie said, 'Your hear that stupid bastard, Denham? Him and his fucking sticky-bombs. I'd like to stick one up his arse.'

Alec who, with John, was accompanying Hughie back to their tent, said, 'Pay no attention to the lad, Hughie. He'll learn soon enough.'

'I'd like to get the bastard before Jerry does.'

'Och, away with you, man. You know you don't mean that.'

Hughie grunted, unconvinced.

Denham was at that moment walking only a few yards in front

of them. John watched the slightly strutting gait, the tilt of the balmoral into which a wire had been inserted to give its shape a smartness that his own conspicuously lacked, and he felt a spasm of something more disturbing than mere irritation, an impulse to hurt, a sharp need to see him humiliated, and he was shocked to recognise it as sadistic. This feeling was followed almost immediately by guilt and by a superstitious uneasiness, a primitive conviction that, by wishing harm to another he was inviting retribution from the god of equity.

That night the three friends sat with pints of beer in the NAAFI tent. The radio behind the bar was playing dance-music. There was to be a boxing tournament between the Highlanders and the airborne troops the next afternoon and John had been entered at middleweight.

Alec said, 'You feeling nervous, Johnny? About fighting tomorrow.'

'No. A little bit maybe. I expect it'll get worse an hour or so before the fight.'

Hughie said, 'You're taking a chance. Could be anybody. That's the trouble with service boxing in wartime. You don't know who's going to be in the other corner. Could be a fucking pro.'

'I can always take a dive.'

'You mightna get the chance. He might knock your head off with the first punch.'

'Oh well. That'd be all my worries over, wouldn't it?'

Alec said, 'You ever been knocked out, Johnny?'

'Once. I've had a few hidings though. Been stopped a couple of times.'

'What's it feel like? Being knocked out?'

'You mean a head punch? You don't feel anything much. A kind of bang inside your head, a few stars maybe, and the next thing you open your eyes and you're looking up at lights above the ring.'

'It doesn't really hurt then?'

'No. Not at the time. You might feel a bit bruised later on.'

Hughie said, 'They say it's like that when you get wounded.

Remember Dave Reid, copped a packet at Alamein? When he came back to the battalion at Sfax he reckoned he never felt it.'

Alec grinned. 'Some of 'em make a terrible amount of noise about it if it doesna hurt.'

'Aye.' Hughie thought for a moment, then said, 'Aye, I suppose you're right. It depends what kind of wound. Dave copped a bit of shrapnel up his arse.'

'That sounds painful enough,' John said.

'Aye, but I think it was just the fleshy part. Took a fucking great bite out of his bum. He showed me the scar. Half of one cheek was gone.'

Alec said, 'I think we'll talk about something else.'

From the radio came the rhythmic syrup of the Inkspots proclaiming that they didn't want to set the world on fire but only start a flame in someone's heart.

'Let's have another pint,' Hughie said.

★   ★   ★   ★   ★

The next day was fine and sunny and it seemed that everyone in the huge camp had turned out for the boxing tournament. John had expected the event to be run with a good deal of improvisation and inefficiency but to his surprise a proper ring had been erected, the ropes were taut and padded to prevent rope-burns and in each corner, to act as second to the boxers, was an Army Physical Training Corps sergeant. John's opponent was a lance-corporal, a paratrooper, who looked strong but appreciably shorter in height and, as soon as the bell sounded for the first round, it was obvious that he was not skilled in the finer points of the Noble Art. He disdained any attempt at a guard and simply charged forward with both gloved fists swinging in scything arcs in the general direction of his adversary's head. John moved back and allowed two of the punches to flail the air. Then he stepped inside the third swing and countered with a short right to the chin. The paratrooper's forward progress was abruptly halted. He staggered a couple of paces backwards, seemed about to fall but somehow managed to regain his balance and stood, his hands at about waist height, a wondering expression in his eyes. John threw a crisp left-hook that was just sufficiently hard to topple his already dazed opponent to the canvas and the referee took up the count. The paratrooper was climbing rather unsteadily to his feet as ten was called. John escorted him to his corner where the sergeant-second said, 'All right, son, I'll take care of him,' adding, as he sat his charge on the stool and sloshed cold water over his head and shoulders, 'You've done a bit before, haven't you?'

'A bit.'

'Yeah. Well, I knew this kid couldn't box eggs but he would have a go. Serves him right. He'll know better next time.'

John left the ring. There was a lot of cheering from the Gordons but now that the bout was over he felt deflated and a little guilty. It was not his fault that his opponent had been a complete novice, and to dispatch him as quickly as possible was really the most merciful thing to do, but the cheers and congratulations of the spectators embarrassed him. He knew that he had achieved nothing that should be admired.

That evening in the NAAFI tent he received more congratulations and something more acceptable in the form of free drinks from admirers, some of whom were strangers from other companies. Hughie and Alec, who enjoyed a share of this bounty were delighted and, after their fifth pint, John's uneasiness dissolved and he began to accept the homage as his due. It was about twenty minutes before the bar was to be closed and John and his friends were beginning to show ribald evidence of the beer they had drunk when the lance-corporal paratrooper appeared in the NAAFI tent and made his way towards their table.

It was Hughie who first became aware of him standing over them. 'Hey! Are you no' the bloke Johnny – here, Johnny, look who's here.'

The lance-corporal was grinning rather uncomfortably. He said, 'I've been looking for you all over the bloody place. I wanted to buy you a pint.'

John, who had at first failed to recognise the paratrooper, got to his feet and shook his former opponent's hand. 'No. I'll get you one. Nice of you to come over to our lines. Good to see you.'

But the lance-corporal insisted on buying the drinks and when he had brought them back to the table he sat down and raised his glass. 'All the best, mate,' he said. 'And the rest of you.'

They all drank.

John said, 'Sorry the fight this afternoon never got going. I was lucky you walked into one before you'd got settled.'

The lance-corporal laughed with real amusement. 'I was the lucky one,' he said. 'If I'd've stayed upright you'd have cut me to ribbons. Best thing you could do for me was put me away like that. And by the way my name's Geoff.'

'Have a fag, Geoff,' Hughie said, extending his Woodbines.

'Don't smoke, thanks.'

Alec said, 'I'll get in another round before they close shop.' He was counting his money. 'I think I've got enough cash.'

Hughie put his hand in his pocket and brought out a fistful of small change and slapped it on the table. 'Take that if it'll help.'

John, too, produced his own small store of coins. 'Take the lot Alec. Get in as much as you can.'

Alec went to the bar and returned to add six more pints to the glasses on the table.

'We can share out the odd two,' he said. 'Cheers!'

'You blokes was in the Middle East, that right?' Geoff said.

Hughie nodded. 'Alamein to Sicily.'

'I've never been in action. Any day now though. It's a bit worrying like – you know – wondering what it's going to be like, whether you've got what it takes. You know what I mean?'

'You've got what it takes all right,' Hughie said. 'You've jumped out of fucking aeroplanes. If you got the guts for that you got the guts for anything.'

'I hope you're right.'

'Sure I'm right. Drink up.'

The big tent was becoming thick with tobacco-smoke and loud with the drab revelry of the drinkers. Just audible above the noise was the sound of a woman singing, faint and sweet like lingering cheap scent.

'You done a lot of boxing?' Geoff said to John.

'Quite a lot.'

'In civvy street?'

'Mainly in civvy street. A bit in the army.'

'I never saw what hit me. Which hand was it?'

'The first one? A short right inside the left swing. Then I clipped you with a left-hook to finish it. I'm sorry. I really wouldn't have gone in if I'd known you'd never – well, I suppose I'm right am I? I mean you'd never been in the ring before had you?'

'Well . . . not really. A couple of times. Once when I was about twelve or thirteen, in the Scouts. And once at the depot. But that was with a bloke even worse than myself. The referee stopped the fight. I expect that's what gave me the idea I could box a bit.' He grinned. 'You taught me different.'

'You'd probably be all right if you were shown a few things.'

'How not to get knocked out for instance?'

'Yeah, well, something like that.'

The orderly-sergeant came into the tent and shouted that the drinkers would have to be out in ten minutes. The bar was closed. Lights-out in half an hour.

Geoff said, 'I'd better get back to our lines. It's been good having a chat with you blokes. Best of luck an' all that.'

They shook hands with him and watched him go.

'He's a good lad that one,' Hughie said.

Alec agreed. 'I wouldna fancy his job though.'

'Christ, no!'

John said, 'Let's drink up and get back to the tent.' The slight euphoria that alcohol and conviviality had induced had begun to fade and he felt unsteady, heavy with the quantity of liquid and the beginnings of depression.

When they got back to their bell-tent most of the section were already in bed but not, it seemed, asleep, for Victor Denham was talking loudly and with his usual confidence to his neighbours, Docherty and Burns, two eighteen-year-old reinforcements who had been posted with him from the depot. John and his friends fumbled their way into the almost total darkness of the tent and began to prepare for sleep.

Denham was in full spate: 'Jerry's a good soldier, make no mistake. Not like the Ities. They're cowards. Everybody knows that. They used to have to chain the machine-gunners to their weapons otherwise they'd run away. That's a fact. Sergeant Devlin told me. He's actually seen them in the desert, chained to their weapons when they've been captured. Jerry's quite a different case. He's disciplined, well-trained. They're like us. They're not cowards. You wouldn't have to chain a German to his gun. They'd fight till the last round of –'

'Shut your fucking trap!' Hughie's voice in the darkness was loud and very angry. 'Another fucking word an' I'll break your fucking neck!'

'I was only –'

'Well don't! Just shut up and get to sleep. And let other people go to sleep as well.'

'They've not played lights-out yet. Any case you've got no right to give me orders. You're just a private like me. You're not an NCO. I'm just as entitled –'

A hoarse and wordless growl of rage came from Hughie and Denham's protest was broken off by a yelp of alarm and possibly pain as he was attacked. A series of sounds that were not precisely identifiable followed: thumps, grunts, gasps, creaks and clatters and then a sharply focused squeal of anguish, recognisably coming from Denham; and John, peering into the darkness at the vague, moving shapes felt an undeniable frisson of excitement.

Then Alec's voice, breathless and clenched, 'For Christ's sake Hughie leave him alone! – Johnny! Help! – For Christ's sake, Johnny, give us a hand!' and John realised that Hughie was being prevented from inflicting further damage on Denham. He hesitated for a moment then dived in the direction of Denham's bed-space, collided heavily with struggling bodies and gasped, 'Who's this? Hughie?'

Alec grunted, 'It's me. Here he is. Grab hold of him. Come on now, Hughie, let's get outside. Give us a hand, Johnny. Drag the bastard outside or he'll kill somebody.'

John, lunging into the darkness, felt his questing fingers touch someone's face and there was an exclamation of anger and pain; then he heard Hughie's voice.

'Get your finger out my fucking eye! You're blinding me! All right, let go. Let go, both of you. I'm coming!'

Behind the voices of the principals was a low counterpoint of muttered protests from other members of the section and a muffled sobbing which John guessed was coming from Denham.

'Let's go out and have a smoke,' John said, and he moved away towards the tent flap and crawled out into the fresh air, followed by Alec and then, to his relief, by Hughie.

John brought out cigarettes and he and Hughie lit up.

Alec said, 'Let's get away from here. Over behind the cookhouse. Nobody'll see us there. The orderly-sergeant'll be round after lights-out. We don't want him to see us.'

They picked their way, stepping carefully over guy-ropes to the secluded place that Alec had commended and there they sat on upturned boxes which had contained tins of McConnochie's meat-and-vegetable stew.

'What did you do to him, Hughie?' John said. 'He sounded a bit unhappy.'

'I got my knee into his bollocks. I tried to put the head on him but I hit the fucking tent-pole.' He touched his forehead carefully. 'It's a wee bit sore. No' as sore as he'd a been if I'd caught the bastard.'

Alec said, 'It's no' worth it Hughie. You shouldna get excited. He's just a wee bairn.'

'Aye. Well, wee bairns need their arses skelpin' now and then, don't they? That's the way to learn them.'

John said, 'That lance-jack, Geoff, was a nice bloke wasn't he?'

'Aye. He was a good 'un,' Hughie agreed. 'It's a pity you didna hit him a wee bit harder and bust his jaw or something. Put him in dock so's he'd miss the fucking invasion.'

It was a mild, clear evening; the stars were very bright, like polished pin-heads.

Alec said, 'Peaceful, isn't it? Out here. Why the fuck do we have to have wars?'

'It's the capitalist system,' Hughie told him, stressing the second syllable of 'capitalist'. 'It's big money. It's they fuckers in their big cars with their fucking top-hats and cigars. An' I'll tell you what. When this lot's finished, I mean when Jerry's licked, it'll be the Russians next. Churchill talks about our Russian allies. Allies be fucked. They'll be the enemy next time. It'll be us and the Yanks against Uncle Joe's lot. An I'll tell you something else. The Russians'll beat the shit out of us like they did the Germans at Stalingrad.'

John said, 'You should have taken a powder, Hughie, before they sealed the camp.'

'I told you. I wasna going without you.'

'That puts a big responsibility on me, doesn't it?'

'What way?'

'Obvious, isn't it? If it wasn't for me you'd be safely out of it. In Glasgow.'

'No, no. It's no' like that Johnny. It's my decision. I'm a big lad. It's what I decided. If anything happens to me it's no' your fault. I could've gone but I decided to stay. Me. I decided. Not you nor anyone else. Okay?'

'Right, if you say so.'

'Any case, nothing's going to happen to me, son. The fuckers tried hard enough when we were up the blue.'

They sat for a time in silence. Then they heard the buglers from the airborne lines and their own pipers playing Lights Out. It was a haunting commingling of sounds and it seemed to linger in the air after the last note had been played.

After a few moments Alec said, 'I hope you've no' done that silly young bastard serious damage.'

'A thump in the goolies won't do him any harm.'

'It didn't sound as if it did him much good, from the noise,' Johnny said, 'though I can't say I feel sorry for him.'

'Maybe he'll shut his mouth when he's told to next time.' Hughie sounded unrepentant.

Alec stood up and belched. 'That NAAFI beer's gassy stuff. Maybe we'd better get to kip.'

Hughie said, 'We'll have one more smoke.'

'Aye . . . Well, I think I'll get the head down. See you the morn'.'

When Alec had left John said, 'I'm not so sure you're right about the war being a wicked plot to make the rich buggers richer. I mean it's not just the poor or the working-class that get killed or crippled, is it? And I don't see what else you could do against Hitler except fight.'

'Aye, sure you get the officer-class, the college boys and aristocrats' kids in the forces. But they've got something to fight for. We havena got nothing. You wait and see. It's going to be like the last fucking lot, nineteen-eighteen. A land fit for heroes, that's what Lloyd George said the lads in the trenches'd come back to. And what did they get? The fucking General Strike and the hunger marches.'

'It'll be different after this one.'

'Don't you believe it, pal. The only way you'll get a change is revolution and the lads that might've had the guts and brains to organise it is killed off in the war or thrown in jail.'

They sat and smoked without speaking. John thought about the thousands of young men sleeping in their tents, in this camp and in other similar camps in other parts of the country. He guessed that most, if not all of them, were convinced that, though inevitably casualties were going to be heavy, they would not be among the unfortunate ones.

He dropped his cigarette-end and put his heel on it. 'I suppose we'd better get some kip, Hughie.'

They both stood up and made their way back to their tent.

On the following day, after breakfast, the whole battalion was mustered on parade; even the clerks and cooks were called from their duties, and it was obvious to everyone that something important was about to be announced. When the companies had been assembled they were ordered by their respective sergeant-majors to stand at ease. At once a low murmur of excitement and speculation started to buzz like an insect swarm. This lasted only a few seconds before the regimental sergeant-major, who was standing with the adjutant in the centre of the improvised grassy square, gave a hoarse scream of fury which modulated into a comprehensible but still agitated command to maintain silence in the ranks. The noise stopped. The battalion waited, but not for long. First the sound of a motor-engine was heard and then a jeep was driven up close to where the RSM and adjutant were standing and the commanding officer climbed out of the passenger seat. The RSM came to attention and saluted, his right hand flashing to the side of his head where it remained quivering for three seconds before it snapped down to his side. The CO's acknowledgement was more like the leisurely doffing of an invisible cap. The RSM turned back to face the ranks. He brought the battalion to attention. Then he roared out his announcement, spacing each phrase as if he were translating from a foreign language: 'Your commanding officah . . . is about to give you . . . some important . . . news! Pay careful . . . attention! . . .' He turned towards the CO and saluted again: 'Sah!'

The commanding officer's manner and speech were in quite dramatic contrast to the style adopted by the RSM. He had a rich, well-fed voice and a slightly pedantic way of speaking.

He said, 'I hope you can all hear me . . . can you hear at the back there, C Company? Captain Sinclair, am I audible to the men at the rear? . . . Good . . . Very well . . . I don't want to beat about the bush. We all know why we're here and what we've been waiting for. Well, now I'm in a position to tell you more. We are embarking tomorrow morning on LCIs which, as I'm sure you all know, means Landing Craft Infantry. We are due to sail at 0800 hours to sectors of enemy-occupied territory somewhere in France. The Second Front is about to be established and we have the honour of being among the first sea-borne troops to land. I wish you all good luck and good hunting.'

He turned away, spoke briefly to the adjutant and then returned to his seat in the jeep which was driven away.

The RSM ordered the battalion to stand at ease. Then he said, 'You will be dismissed . . . in just a minute. When you are dismissed . . . you will go to your company lines . . . and wait till your NCOs . . . give you . . . your . . . orders . . . Right! Bat talion! . . . Battalion . . . shun! Dis . . . miss!'

Walking back to the tent John said, 'Well, that's it, Hughie. Tomorrow's the day.'

'Aye.'

'How do you feel?'

'Shit-scared.'

'Yeah. Me too.'

But this was not quite accurate. John's response to the news was much too complex to be summarised so crudely. The apprehension he felt was not so very different from the feeling he experienced before going into the ring, a draining fear of failure, of being humiliated, rather than the fear of being injured, but added to this was the excitement of the hidden outcome and, though it did not show its features clearly, he knew that the face of death was slyly and malignantly present.

Just before they reached the tent Gordon Rennie caught them up and said, 'What happened last night Hughie? I wasna' in the tent. I was out having a crack with Jimmy McLaren at HQ Company. What you do to young Denham?'

'Nothing much. He was bumming his load, shouting about the Ities being cowards. Playing the fucking old soldier. I just give him a bit of a shaking.'

'Aye. Well, he's put in a complaint. But I think I can squash it. Best thing I can do is get him transferred to another section. If they'll have him. I'll have a word with Mitchell. We've got a good section if we can get rid of that one.'

'That'd be great, Gordon. But I tell you. If he stays with our lot I'm likely to kill the bastard. I'm no' kidding.'

'Okay, Hughie. I expect I'll be able to fix something.'

The rest of the day was taken up by preparations, homilies and inspections. Ammunition was issued and all weapons checked. Emergency ration-packs of an American type were distributed each containing a peculiarly unpleasant chocolate bar, bitter, brick-hard and gritty in texture, a cube of dehydrated porridge, a self-heating tin of soup, biscuits, barley-sugar sweets and cigarettes. After dinner each platoon was ordered to parade for inspection in full battle-order, wearing exactly the same clothing and equipment as that which would be worn when they embarked on the following morning. Each man put on his webbing with ammunition-pouches, water-bottle, entrenching-tool and respirator, and, round the pack on his back, was tied a folded blanket. He wore battle-dress and steel helmet. In a small front pocket of his trousers was kept a field-dressing and he carried a rifle or Bren-gun or a two-inch mortar. The number two mortar-man was laden with mortar-bombs which were packed in sacking and hung about his neck.

When Lieutenant Mitchell had carefully inspected every man in his platoon he said, 'Now you are dressed exactly as you will be in the morning when we embus for Tilbury. Reveille is at 0530 hours. Yes you heard me – 0530 hours. So take my advice and don't overdo things in the wet canteen. You've got to be up bright and early and a hangover's the last thing you need. Breakfast will be at 0600 hours. The whole battalion parades in full battle-order, as you are now, at 0645 hours. Transport will take us to Tilbury where we embark in companies on to the landing-craft. We sail at 0800 hours. Now . . . Private Denham!'

'Sah!'

'You are transferred to Corporal Anderson's section. You can shift your stuff as soon as we are dismissed. Private Webb!'

'Sah!'

'You are to replace Denham in Corporal Rennie's section. Understood?'

'Sah!'

'Very well. Not much more to be said. Tomorrow's the big day, chaps. I'd just like to say I've every confidence in you. We're the best platoon in the best company in the best battalion in the best division in the British Army. Right. Carry on, Sarnt.'

Sergeant Thom saluted smartly and Mitchell responded with his languid officer's version of a salute and turned away.

The platoon was dismissed and the men made their way back to their tents.

Hughie said, 'I'm going to bash the swede for half an hour.

Give us a shout if I'm no' awake for tea.'

John removed his equipment and placed it carefully at the head of his sleeping space ready to be put on again. 'I might take a walk over to the airborne lines, see if I can find Geoff.'

Hughie was spreading his blankets. 'Who?'

'Geoff. The lance-jack we had a drink with last night.'

'Och aye. Give him good luck from me will you? And see if he can come over for a pint tonight.'

Denham came into the tent. He was still wearing battle-order. His steel helmet was tilted at a cheeky angle over the right eye. He would have served well as a model for a propaganda poster or film: the plucky British Tommy, thumbs up, cheery and indomitable. He avoided looking in Hughie's direction as he collected his blankets and kit-bag and, laden with these, went out.

'Fucking good riddance,' Hughie said.

Alec came into the tent. 'They're having a scratch game behind the Company Office. You fancy a kick-about, Hughie?'

'Not on your Nelly.'

'What about you, Johnny?'

'I'm useless at football.'

Hughie said, 'Away and play with your wee friends Alec and let the grown-ups have a rest.'

'It's no' a rest you're wanting. It's a bit of blanket-drill. You're no' fooling anybody. You'd sooner play with yourself than play football.'

John ducked under the tent-flap and left them to their amiable squabbling but, as he was approaching the airborne lines, he realised that he felt no desire for company and he turned aside and wandered aimlessly through the lanes of tents until he came to a small grassy bank close to the wired perimeter and about thirty yards away from the nearest tent. This was as near to seclusion as it was possible to achieve and he sat down and lit a cigarette. He took off his balmoral and battle-dress blouse and felt the sun warm on his face and arms. The thought came to him that this might be the last time he would sit in an English field in the sun, but it failed to generate any feeling except a mild incredulity. He thought, 'Everyone in this camp, the colonels, the cooks, the privates, the sergeants, the eighteen-year-olds and the old-timers, each and every one of them is the centre of his own little world. Like me. I. I will not be killed. I'm different from the others. I'm special. I'm not ready for death. I, I, I. Reason, common sense, makes no difference. All right you know for a fact that a lot – a helluva lot – thousands and thousands of these I's are going to be killed. Or blinded, or smashed up in ways too horrible to imagine. You know it, but it makes no difference. Not you. The others are kidding themselves. You're special. You're different. Just as all the other I's think they're special and different. It's madness. We're all fucking mad.'

He watched the blue wraith of tobacco-smoke rise from the tip of his cigarette and he sniffed its familiar pungency. This was being alive. He did not ask for more than this. It was quite enough to be able to sit on the grass in the early June sunlight and smoke a cigarette. He would like this to go on for ever. Then, faintly at first but growing steadily in volume, he heard the dark drumming in the sky; louder and louder it grew until the enormous, throbbing roar was directly above him and the sun was extinguished and the blue sky concealed by the great wings of the Fortresses, flying quite low and passing over, squadron after squadron, as if there would be no end to this menacing traffic, and he thought each plane was carrying tons of explosive and all those bombs would be sent hurtling down on people, men and women and children, soldiers and civilians, all of them centres of their worlds, all of them I, I, I, all of them special, all immortal, and suddenly he wanted to pray, but he did not know how to because, if he were to be honest, all he could pray for was himself, his own safety, his own life, his own world, for I, I, I.

'God help us,' he thought as he threw away his cigarette butt and started to walk back to his tent under the loud and murderous skies.

★   ★   ★   ★   ★

Rain was falling quite lightly but there was a strong wind blowing the next morning when B Company clambered down from the backs of the lorries which had transported them to Tilbury Docks and clattered aboard the LCI. Each man was given half a dozen bags made of thick tough paper and told to keep one always handy in the likely event of rough weather and consequent sea-sickness. When everyone was on the deck they were led below where they were ordered to settle down as best they could for what would probably be a long wait before sailing. They were permitted to take off their packs but that was all and they sat in the severely limited space smoking and talking in low, lugubrious voices, occasionally laughing but without real merriment. For John, the sense of being distanced from present reality increased. Even the grey misery and discomfort did not seem to penetrate fully the protective carapace that had formed, without any conscious contrivance on his part, over his responses. He sat on the bench that was fixed to the steel side of the LCI and he felt that he was scarcely more animate than his equipment, a heavy bundle of cloth, leather, metal and webbing.

Hughie, who was next to him, said, 'Have a fag, Johnny.'

John took the cigarette and Hughie lit it and then his own. Although the craft was still at anchor it was rolling a little.

Alec, on John's other side, said, 'Christ, I'm going to be sick before we get going. I'm a terrible sailor.'

'Ah well,' Hughie told him, 'it'll take your mind off what's waiting on the other side.'

'Thanks a lot, pal. That's a great comfort.'

It must have been quite late in the afternoon when the LCI, along with a whole fleet of landing craft, sailed out of the harbour, but the voyage to France had not yet started.

B Company commander, Captain Forbes, ordered all ranks to parade on deck and there he told them that bad weather had delayed the invasion and that they would have to put up with the rather cramped conditions as best they could while the craft circled around in the Channel waiting for conditions to improve.

'You'll have to use your emergency rations. We've got replacements for those. But don't open them until your platoon commanders give the order. It's a bit of a nuisance but I know I can depend on you to grin and bear it. I'll give you fresh gen as and when I receive it. So don't get down-hearted. I don't suppose we'll be held up for more than twelve hours or so. Just till this rough weather passes over.'

But Captain Forbes was mistaken. They were in fact held up for over forty-eight hours, two whole days of wretched discomfort and nervous strain, with no easing of the wind and high seas and a large proportion of all ranks repeatedly sick. John was not sick in that he did not actually vomit but he felt ill and feverish and found it impossible to eat. He spent a good deal of time on the open deck, preferring the rain and spray to the fetid air below and his waking hours merged into a timeless grey continuum of sea and sky and falling rain veiling the shapes of the other craft in the invasion fleet. Both Hughie and Alec were sea-sick and only rarely did one or the other feel well enough to join him in the open air and then for only a brief period before the heave and lurch of the craft induced another attack of vomiting.

Then, late on the morning of 6th June, with the seas less boisterous and no rain falling although the skies were still grey, the company was mustered on deck to be addressed by Captain Forbes. They were a miserable assembly, many pale and unshaven, some still sporadically spewing into their vomit-bags. The company commander looked rather less than his usual healthy and confident self. His normally healthy complexion had been drained to a waxy pale yellow and his eyes were dull and seemed to contain something like the reproach that one sees in the eyes of a sick dog. He made what must have been a costly effort to sound brisk and efficient.

'Stand easy. I hope those of you who've been ill – it looks as if some of you are still not too fit – I hope you'll all pull yourselves together and get on your toes. I know it's been hard for you – hard for all of us – but today's the day. We're now approaching the French coast and we should be there by the early afternoon. We go ashore at approximately 0230 hours. We – the fifty-first Gordons – will be the first battalion of the Highland

Division to land on French soil. From signals I've had from BHQ it seems we go in after the Canadians. So, at least the sting will have been taken out of Jerry's punch. The thing is to get ashore and off the beach as quickly as we can. If you hang around you're likely to cop it. Platoon commanders and section leaders will inspect and check all weapons. Stay on deck in the fresh air as much as you can. At least you can look forward to having terra firma under your feet pretty soon. Carry on Sarnt-Major.'

CSM Maclean saluted and gave the order to dismiss and Gordon Rennie gathered together his own section and told them to follow him to a place in the bows of the LCI. He was grinning cheerfully and looked no more concerned than he would on a mere exercise.

He said, 'All right lads. Just check you've got everything. Nothing left below. And a wee word to the lads that havena' been in action before. Docherty, Burns, Webb and Smith. I'm sure you're no more worried than me about this landing. But just in case you've been having a few nasty thoughts about all the shit Jerry's going to be throwing at us let me tell you this. It's amazing when you think of all that stuff being fired – shells, mortars, small-arms, all the rest of it – it's amazing how little of it hits anyone. I'm no' kidding. You ask anybody that's been in action and they'll tell you the same. Okay. That's all I wanted to say, lads. Stay on deck and stay together. It'll no be long now.'

John looked out at the surrounding seas that, close to the LCI, rolled and subsided and swelled like a collapsed silken tent continuously agitated by undercurrents of wind. Farther away the waves seemed smaller except that the other landing-craft could be observed sinking and reappearing in their troughs. The sky and the sea and the ships were all the colour of pewter or of the dull blades of bayonets.

Hughie said, 'How you feeling?'

'Dull. Like the weather.'

'I know what you mean.'

They stayed, in silence, looking out at the bleak undulations of the waves. Around them the rest of the company was also quiet. There were a few muttered exchanges and even an occasional spattering of laughter but it was an unusually silent company that waited and saw, through the thin mist, the darker outline of the French coast rise very slowly from the distant seas.

'That's it,' Hughie said. 'I canna' see any Germans, can you?'

'They've heard you're coming, Hughie.'

Alec, who had been slumped in utter dejection, stirred and spoke for the first time since the company had been dismissed. 'If they've no' all run away from Hughie they'd better keep out of my way or I'll be sick on them.'

The coast-line grew more distinct and soon the shapes of infantry and tank landing-craft could be discerned, still far away but clearly recognisable. John felt no change in his state of glazed apathy and he knew from his experiences in the desert that the only thing that could shatter this shell of apparent indifference was the sudden and violent threat of extreme personal danger which would probably expose the terror beneath. The first sounds of the guns came to him like a memory of a childhood dream. At first it was a low, continuous growl like faraway thunder heard indoors, a mere shadow or whisper of the tumult that it would become. As the sound very gradually increased it still retained its similarity to the noise of distant thunder except that its continuity, while quite steadily sustained, was broken from time to time like a jungle beast whose steady growl erupts into a roar then returns for a while to a low purring snarl of menace.

Then, with shocking suddenness, as if there had been a cinematographic cut from the previous scene, they were close in and John could see that many of the first landing-craft had struck underwater mines and had been holed and tipped over, wallowing on their sides. The artillery-fire seemed to have been reduced to intermittent salvoes though shells or mortar-bombs were still exploding in the sea and, at intervals, came the iron chatter of machine-gun fire.

Captain Forbes was heard, bellowing 'Stand by for landing!' and Lieutenant Mitchell was exhorting his NCOs to get their sections into order for going into the sea. Because of the stranded

LCIs and LCTs their craft could not get any closer to the beach and the waves they were to enter looked dangerously rough and deep. One of the other platoon-commanders, a tall Canadian on attachment to the Gordons from his North American sister regiment, left his equipment behind for someone else to bring ashore and went into the sea with a rope, one end of which was attached to the LCI. As soon as the Canadian entered the water John saw that the waves reached well above his waist and the sea-bottom must be a good four feet below the surface.

'Give me that fucking Bren-gun,' he said to Hughie. 'You'll never manage to carry it in that lot.'

Hughie did not argue and he swapped the light machine-gun for John's rifle.

The Canadian was half-swimming and half-wading ashore playing out the rope as he went. There was one platoon ahead of John's in the order of disembarkation. The Canadian reached the beach and could be seen looping the rope about his shoulders and waist like the anchor-man in a tug-o'-war match. Then he waved to signal for the landing to continue. John watched the first platoon going into the sea, each man clutching at the rope to avoid being swept under the anchored LCI. The platoon commander went first and seemed to stay on his feet without too much difficulty but John noticed that, though he was a man of slightly more than medium height, the waves reached to his armpits. The third section was going in when they lost one of their men. He was a short stocky Glaswegian, very similar to Hughie in build, and as soon as he was into the sea the waves were slapping against his face and little more than the top of his helmet could be seen as he struggled towards the beach. And then he disappeared. The man behind him did not hesitate in his strenuous journey towards land and John knew that he had just observed the company's first casualty in the Battle of Normandy.

He looked over his shoulder and saw at once that Hughie had also witnessed the small man's fate. 'Keep close up when we go in,' John said. 'Alec's behind you. Hang on to my pack if you think you're going. Chuck the fucking rifle away. Just keep your head out of the sea and hang on to me.'

'I canna swim,' Hughie said. 'I hate the fucking water.'

'Don't worry. You'll be all right. Just hang on to me and don't let go.'

The first platoon were continuing to land. John could see them scurrying across the beach, going forward, away from the sea. The mortar-bombs and shells and machine-gun fire were not heavy and although John could see quite a number of still, dark bundles on the ground, which he took to be casualties, he did not see any member of the landing platoon hit.

Gordon Rennie must have been noticing the same thing for he turned his head to look back at his section and said, 'It's going to be a doddle, lads!'

A few minutes later it was their turn to go in. As John feared, the sea was deep, high on his chest, and he knew that Hughie, behind him, must be finding it difficult to keep his head clear of the waves, but with the Bren-gun on his shoulder, one hand grasping the barrel and the other hand clutching the rope, there was little he could do to help his friend. At one point in his struggle to the shore he felt a sudden increase of weight on his pack and he guessed that Hughie was following his instructions to hang on to him. When he reached the shallows he glanced back and saw Hughie and Alec wading not far behind and the three of them reached the beach together.

Sergeant Thom was crouching at the side of the Canadian waving his Sten-gun in the direction his platoon was to go and shouting to them to get off the beach and dig in. John, soaked and squelching in his water-logged boots, felt the pack and blanket on his back dragging at his shoulders with the huge weight of sea-water but he managed to move forward in a stumbling canter across the strand where he now saw that the dead lay quite thickly. From over on his left he heard an explosion followed by hoarse shouts and one high scream and he tried to move faster but the weight he was carrying proved too great and he could only manage to sustain his clumsy lope.

At the top of the sand and shingle of the beach, running parallel to the line of the sea, was a slight declivity of the ground before it rose again forming a shallow natural trench and it was here that the company was beginning to gather. Some of the men were using their entrenching-tools to get more cover while others seemed either too exhausted or too shocked to do anything except lie on their stomachs with their heads down, not even bothering to look out over the low parapet of the long ditch. Lieutenant Mitchell had his field-glasses out and was peering through them with his head well above the small protection of the breastwork. He turned as Gordon Rennie and his section came panting up the beach towards him.

'Get down Corporal! Deploy your section. Check that they're all here. The company's going to assemble along this ditch. Keep your weapons at the ready. No one's to take equipment off. I know it's bloody uncomfortable but that's an order.'

John, Hughie and Alec were by now sprawling, soaked and gasping as they swallowed mouthfuls of air. They could hear the sporadic rattle of machine-gun fire and a few shells were landing on the beach and in the sea but, for the moment, the sense of immediate danger had weakened. To say that they felt safe would be an absurd exaggeration, but at least they did not feel that every missile fired by the enemy was aimed at them and them alone. They had survived. So far.

★   ★   ★   ★   ★

B Company spent the night of the sixth of June close to a village called Banville. Earlier, before dark, Lieutenant Mitchell led his platoon cautiously towards a large farmhouse on the edge of the village and, after circling it a few times and keeping careful watch for signs of occupation, the first section made a nervous entry. It was unoccupied but there was evidence everywhere of the recent presence of German troops. In their hurry to leave they had left behind unimportant articles of clothing, a half-eaten Camembert cheese, a few bottles of wine and Calvados. On the table in one room was an uncompleted and abandoned letter.

'Don't touch anything,' Mitchell ordered. 'Nothing at all. You never know what tricks they're up to. That wine could be poisoned. And whatever you do, don't open cupboards or drawers. And no fires to be lit. Chimney smoke could make us a target. I know you're all soaked. You can wring out your stuff. Get it as dry as you can. But you've got to be quick. We might get the order to move on at any moment.'

The sounds of firing seemed to be coming from a fairly long distance, at least a mile, John thought, but he knew that things could change with shocking suddenness.

He squeezed water out of his shirt. All the contents of his pack were completely sodden so he pressed the water out of his spare socks and shirt, too. He noticed Denham using his pull-through on his rifle. The young soldier still looked keen and alert and his steel helmet had not lost its perky tilt, but his regular, head-boy's features looked a bit pale and strained and his eyes had taken on an almost furtive look as if he were longing to sneak a glance over his shoulder but was prevented by the fear of what he might see.

Mitchell called to the platoon-sergeant, 'I'm off to Battalion HQ for an O-group, Sergeant Thom. Better get the men back into battle-order as soon as possible. And they can eat compo rations. I'll be back in about half an hour. Carry on Sarnt.'

'Right lads,' Sergeant Thom said. 'You heard what Mr Mitchell said. But before you eat anything make sure your weapons is clean and well-oiled.'

Gordon Rennie said to John, 'You going to keep the Bren, Johnny? Maybe better if you did. With your shoulders you could carry a twenty-five pounder. Wee Hughie can be your number two.'

John nodded. 'I don't mind.'

Hughie said, 'Where's that wee fella – Docherty? The one on the mortar. I havena seen him since we got here.'

Gordon looked oddly embarrassed. 'He's no' here. He didna make it.' He spoke quickly, in a low mumble.

'What? What the fuck you on about Gordon? What d'you mean he's no' here?'

'He didn't get to the beach. A wave took him off the rope. He must've went under the LCI.'

Gordon moved away.

'Fucky Nell,' Hughie said. 'The poor wee bastard. What the

fuck they want to hang them bombs round his neck for? He was just a wee bairn!'

Later, soon after sunset, the platoon left the house and were led to a field near the road where they dug in for the night. John and Hughie sat in their slit-trench facing one another, knees bent, helmeted heads just below the parapet. Night was thickening and the sounds of gunfire were broadcast through the dark, but the action seemed to be taking place at a safe distance. The flashes of artillery flickered further inland and its low grumble went on with intermittent pauses. From somewhere on their right they heard the bitter yammering of heavy machine-guns and, when they looked back towards the coast, they could see the tracers from the Bofors anti-aircraft guns flung like luminous oranges by a hidden troupe of jugglers, brilliant, beautiful and murderous against the dark backdrop of the night.

During the next three days John felt himself becoming absorbed and obliterated as an individual by the familiar processes of combat. The differences between the war here in Normandy and the fighting in the Middle East were only superficial. The furnishings, of course, were different. In place of the desert, the sand, the palm-trees and white square buildings in the drumming sun were the fields and lanes, the farmhouses and orchards of a landscape which could have been England. But most of the fields were disfigured by parallel rows of tall wooden stakes which had been driven into the ground and by crashed gliders lying like the broken bodies of great prehistoric birds, for whose destruction the wooden stakes had been planted. An invisible pall of fear and death lay over the countryside and in the pastures the cattle were all dead. Cows and horses lay in the summer grass among the buttercups but they did not look peaceful. They looked grotesque because their bodies were swollen hugely by accumulated gases in their bellies and the mild June air was tinged with the gradually intensifying scent of corruption. The smell of war was the same everywhere, that sweet yet pungent odour of cordite and fear and pu-trescence. And the essential experience was just as it had been before and would always be: the sense of being dehumanised, reduced to little more than an extension of your equipment and weaponry, the constant feeling of being used as an object, manipulated by blind, invisible hands, controlled by a force that was either malignant or stupid, the sense of being quite lost, of staggering about with no conscious direction in a metaphorical and quite often literal darkness, of being exhausted, frightened, sick, sometimes so weary that you slept while on your feet like a horse. And ignorance, stupefying, brutalizing ignorance. You never knew where you were or where the enemy was, what you were supposed to be attempting to achieve. There was no hatred of the Germans, only fear and loathing of the impersonal machines of death and mutilation that they employed, the self-propelled guns, the Nebelwerfers – mobile multi-barrelled mortars that were known among the British troops as Moaning Minnies because of the banshee howling noise of the half dozen and more bombs as they were released on their lethal errands – the jagged white-hot chunks of shrapnel, the insectile whine of sniper's bullets, the trip-wires, the jabbering, murderous Spandau machine-gun.

The battalion had been on French soil for five days of constant movement, taking up positions and digging-in only to be ordered, almost as soon as the men had settled in their slit-trenches, to move on to some other location. Most of the time they were under fire, mainly from self-propelled guns and mortars though snipers concealed in trees were a nerve-teasing menace. Captain Forbes was wounded in the throat by a shell fragment and sent back to the Casualty Clearing Station near the beaches so B Company was led by the second-in-command, Captain Urquhart, in their first large-scale attack on a small village called Touffréville. The company moved in darkness to the starting-line and an artillery barrage opened up behind them. John and Hughie lay side by side in the field while the guns thundered and the shells whined overhead. Machine-guns hammered away, the tracer-bullets slid through the slick dark from the direction of the German positions like little burning embers as the heavy machine-gun battalion on B Company's left flank answered with their own streams of luminous rounds so that the criss-crossing points of brilliance seemed to be stitching the darkness. Then they heard the crazed howling noise of the Nebelwerfer releasing its cargo of mortar-bombs and, seconds later, the earth around was being smashed and torn and hurled into the air as the bombs exploded.

John clenched his teeth, but he could not stop them from chattering.

Hughie said, 'Fuck this for a game. I'd fuck off if there was anywhere to run to.'

John did not say anything but he told himself that this was even worse than he remembered such attacks being in the past. Or perhaps he was becoming less able to endure the terror.

'You all right, Johnny?'

'Yeah. Terrific.'

'All I want's a blighty one. A nice clean cushy one.'

John thought, 'I'd take anything rather than this . . . Even Alexandria? Even the nick? Even Alexandria . . . Anything.'

A whistle was blown, sounding absurdly thin against the artillery noise, and there was some incomprehensible shouting. Then John heard Sergeant Thom's voice: 'Right lads! Up you get! We're moving in!' and closer, Gordon Rennie, repeating the order: 'Come on lads! We're on our way! Spread out! Don't bunch! And keep moving!'

John and Hughie clambered upright. John heaved the Bren-gun on to his shoulder and they began to plod forward towards the town. It was a kind of relief to be moving. While lying still you had nothing to do except be frightened. You became possessed by, drenched in, terror. Even the act of walking and keeping your balance on the rough ground you were covering provided some small distraction. The Spandaus continued firing in regular bursts. John was aware of the whisper of bullets in the darkness but now he was able to clamp down on the knowledge that at any moment he might be pierced by one. This was a skill he had learnt in past actions. It was like a metaphysical grimace; you shut tight your inner eyes and clamped your teeth, screwing up the mind against the obscene possibilities of being wounded or killed. They stumbled forward. John knew that on either side of them were hundreds of other men going on towards possible death or mutilation, at best a prolongation of misery, privation and fear, yet he was possessed by a deep, hollow loneliness and he guessed that every man was feeling the same. Even the closeness of Hughie, whom he could hear grunting and occasionally swearing, did little to mitigate that sense of being alone.

A clump of mortar-bombs from a Nebelwerfer landed close and when the din of the explosions faded John heard the pitiful, shocking noise of the wounded crying out in shameless, naked fear and agony and then the hoarse, almost despairing appeal, 'Stretcher-bearers! Stretcher-bearers!' The sweet, burnt smell of cordite was strong in his nostrils and throat and the noise of the wounded men's moans and cries were somehow part of the stink and taste, as if his senses had been so shocked by the assault upon them that they had become confused. Again he clamped tight his defences against the horrors around and ahead of him and tramped on. He could hear Hughie now swearing incessant- ly, a rhythmic chant of repetitive obscenities and then he saw, over on their left flank, a brilliant white flare suddenly blossom in the sky and hang glittering there for a few moments before it disintegrated to be almost instantly replaced by a green one.

Gordon Rennie shouted, 'That's D Company! They've taken their position! Jerry must be pulling out!'

'Who's firing them fucking guns then?' Hughie grunted, but in fact the German resistance did seem to be easing a little.

'Come on lads!' Gordon called to those of his section within earshot, 'We'll soon have our heads down! Keep going!'

The Nebelwerfers seemed to have lost their range and their bombs were exploding at a relatively safe distance now, and the Spandaus' fire was growing more sporadic. After another ten minutes John and the other members of B Company were on the outskirts of the village. He could see the irregular, broken silhouettes of the buildings dimly against the sky and, as the company broke their way through the hedges and fences of the fields they had been crossing, they were brought, section by section, into the road which led to the centre of the village.

There they were ordered to keep well apart and to take what cover they could while waiting for further orders. Machine-gun fire still rattled from time to time and the heavy stuff was still landing too close for anyone's ease of mind but, for the time being it seemed, the worst part of the attack was over.

★   ★   ★   ★   ★

For the next two days B Company took up positions in and around a farmhouse on the outskirts of the other side of the village. Captain Urquhart established Company Headquarters in the cellar of the house. John and Hughie dug in with their section in a field with the walled farmyard just behind them. They had been told to expect a counter-attack. Mortar fire and shelling kept up an incessant pounding though the bombardments varied in intensity; to leave the slit-trench, even for the brief time needed for relieving bladder or bowels, was a hazardous exercise, delayed for as long as was bearable. Their positions looked out over level farmland to an extensive wooded area from which the artillery and mortar fire was coming.

'They've got us in their fucking sights,' Hughie said. 'It's no' right to keep us here. It's all right for Urquhart in his fucking cellar.'

It was the late afternoon of a sunless day of occasional showers. John sat hunched in the trench, waiting for the next delivery of mortar-bombs from the woods. Earlier, just after mid-day, the company cooks, working in the cellar, had produced a meal of hot stew and potatoes and one man from each slit-trench had been ordered to take mess-tins for both himself and his partner and, whenever there was a lull in the enemy's fire, make his way to the house and collect two rations. John had undertaken the expedition and when he had reached the cellar he had witnessed something which had shaken him in a way that was more difficult to contend with than anything else that had so far happened since landing in Normandy. He had gone down to the spacious farm cellar, one end of which had been taken over by the cooks while, at the other, Captain

Urquhart and CSM Maclean were fiddling with a field-telephone which evidently was not functioning properly. Curled on the floor close to one wall was a huddled figure whose face was hidden and whose sobbing and choking voice was unrecognisable. One of the company pipers, who also acted as a stretcher-bearer, was bending over him and John's first thought was that the man had been wounded and was being tended by the piper until an ambulance could be summoned.

John was collecting the rations of stew when he was startled by a sudden activity and an increase in noise from the man on the floor whose voice had now risen to a howl, and he looked over to see that it was Denham who had half risen to his feet and was being restrained by the piper. But the smart, keen young soldier was now transformed into something that was at once pitiful and disgusting. The neatly-shaped, alert features had melted and blurred, the mouth was sagging and the whole face, dirty and stubbled, seemed swollen and was smeared with tears and snot. He was making wordless, bleating sounds from which every now and then an identifiable phrase would surface and when this happened the words were recognised as a frightened infant's cry for its mother.

The cook who was filling John's mess-tins raised his eyebrows. 'I know what I'd do to the fucker,' he said, 'and it wouldn't be send him back to Blighty.'

Now, three hours or so later, John could not forget the sight and sound of Denham's collapse nor could he fully understand why he had been so sickened and shocked. His reactions had been bewilderingly complex: he wanted to look away from the spectacle of the quivering and sobbing wreck yet he was, at the same time, compelled to watch and listen. He felt, too, a faint but positive echo of the cook's unequivocal contempt and vicious dismissiveness, even a stab of sadistic hatred, and yet he was aware of a kind of envy of the boy's shameless surrender to his terror, and an intolerable suspicion that he was witnessing something of himself, that he was somehow implicated and had been forced to accept the shame that Denham had moved beyond. He said to Hughie nothing of what he had seen because he knew that his friend's response would be similar to the cook's brutal contempt and rejection, and he would not be able to concur without insupportable hypocrisy.

Hughie said, 'What I can never understand is how those fuckers never run out of fucking ammunition. They've been throwing all kinds of shit at us for forty-eight hours or more and they're still at it, the bastards.'

John grunted.

'You all right, Johnny? You never finished your chuck. You feeling okay?'

'Yeah. I'm all right.'

'Hey, listen. Give us your mess-tin. I'll away over to the farmyard and clean them. There's a tap there.'

'No. We'll rub them out with grass. It's not worth risking your neck.'

'Come on. We need water for the bottles too. Hand it over. And your bottle.'

John unbuckled his water-bottle and passed it, with his mess-tin, to Hughie.

'I'll see if I can get a drop of that hooch while I'm there. What's it called? Callow doss or something.'

'Calvados.'

'Aye. That's what I said. See you bah-deen.'

John watched the squat figure, bent into a crouch as Hughie ran towards the farmyard and disappeared round the end of the wall, heading for the gate which was out of sight of the platoon's positions. The Moaning Minnies seemed to be taking a break, though every few seconds a shell whistled over and exploded behind the farmhouse where no doubt the German observation-post had spotted some kind of movement of men or transport. John turned to face the distant woods towards which his Bren-gun was pointed. He could see no evidence of occupation and he reflected that the only Germans he had seen since landing in France had been prisoners or corpses. Not that he felt the least desire to see any at that moment or ever. He found and lit a cigarette and waited for Hughie to return.

Then with that suddenness that was part of its malevolence

the barrage started again; the Moaning Minnies filthied the air with their mechanical howling and then the bombs were exploding in their dozens. John took a look towards the farm and with a sickening lurch of the heart he saw that Hughie was on his way back to the trench. Another cluster of mortar-bombs shrieked down and exploded, great dry geysers of earth soared up into the sky, scattering rubble and stones around and the white-hot whirring of jagged steel sliced through the shocked air. Involuntarily John ducked low in the trench, hunched and clenched against the assault. He began a rapid litany of prayers and obscenities: 'Christ help us, oh fuck, oh shit, oh God in heaven, Christ Almighty, fucking hell . . .' and on and on he muttered as the bombs composed their own fiendish accompaniment in the air above.

The barrage went on for what seemed a very long time and when the pause after the last explosions lengthened into an interval of respite John looked out over the parapet and saw that Hughie was lying face-down on the ground about twenty yards away. As John climbed out of the trench he saw Gordon Rennie emerge from his position and they reached Hughie together. They both knelt by his side and Gordon extended one hand and gently shook the still shoulder. There was no response. Gordon then using both hands, turned Hughie first on to his side and then right over on to his back.

'Jesus Christ!' Gordon said.

John looked down and saw that the front of Hughie's battle-dress had disappeared. It had been driven inwards into his chest so that there was a great dark cave of blood and slivers of bone and, had John possessed the stomach to look more carefully, no doubt he would have seen something of the human engines that only a few minutes earlier had sustained life. But he did not look at the wound for more than a second, though he did direct one quick glance at Hughie's face before he stood up and headed back to his trench. The face looked like the face of all the dead. The eyelids were not shut but the pupils had swivelled up beneath them so that the eyes looked like those of a blind man. Hughie's mouth was open in a kind of frozen coo.

Gordon called to John as he walked away, but the words were lifeless noises. John dropped into his trench and slumped into his end of it and stared across at the space where Hughie should have been. The sound of gun and mortar fire had not stopped but moved away; the howling of the Nebelwerfers was derisive and celebratory now rather than threatening. He suddenly expelled a long sigh and realised that he had been holding his breath since leaving Hughie's body. What he felt was not grief. Perhaps he would be capable of that later. His body and mind, his entire being, were drained and exhausted as if his own life were leaking away. For those few moments he was beyond fear as he was beyond hope or love, anger or sadness. He was substance without spirit, or as close to that as a man can become while still breathing.

He did not know how long he had been alone in the trench when Gordon joined him, dropping down into what had been Hughie's place.

'It was quick, Johnny. He wouldna felt a thing. If you got to go that's the best way.'

Gordon had placed Hughie's webbing pouches with the spare Bren magazines on the lip of the trench. He was holding a mess-tin and the contents of Hughie's pockets.

He said, 'I've got his AB64s. Here's some fags and a couple of letters. You'd best take them Johnny. I've left one of his discs on him. We're moving out tonight, once it's dark. Sarnt Thom told me just before they Minnies started up. I'll get a couple of lads to put him under the ground. We'll mark the grave. And I'll send Alec over. He can be your number two. I can put somebody else on the mortar. Okay Johnny? And put your mess-tin away in your pack. We'll be well out of this fucking place.' Gordon waited for a moment and when John did not speak he touched him once on the arm and said 'He was a good lad, Hughie. One of the best. But don't let it get you down. He didna suffer, Johnny, remember that. He's all right where he's gone. Okay son?'

Gordon's grimy face with the flat nose and the broadly spaced cheek-bones still held a hint of cheerfulness behind the concern in his eyes.

John felt a small but indubitable flicker of affection and gratitude. He said, 'Okay Gordon,' and watched the relief and cheerfulness break out quite openly.

A few minutes later Alec joined John in the trench. He picked up the ammunition pouches gingerly and put them down again on the parapet. They were soaked in blood.

He said, 'I'd better try and wash some of this off.'

John heaved himself to his feet. 'I'll take them.'

'No. You stay here.'

But John was already climbing out of the trench. He picked up the pouches, opened them and removed the magazines.

'I'll be back in a minute.'

He walked across the open ground pausing for only a moment to look down at Hughie's body which was still lying staring blindly up at the sky. In the farmyard he ran the tap which was on the wall of the cowshed, so that the water flowed over the webbing, falling in a pink stream to the cobbles. When the pouches were thoroughly soaked and the water dripping from them was no longer tinted with blood he shook them a few times in the air and then returned to the slit-trench. When he passed Hughie's body this time he did not look at it at all.

An hour or so later, as the light began to fade towards dusk, Alec said, 'They're putting him in the ground, Johnny. Gordon's got Smith and Webby doing it.'

John acknowledged the information with a nod and a grunt but he did not look out at the operation.

'God rest his soul,' Alec said.

That night the battalion withdrew from Touffréville under heavy fire from mortars, artillery and machine-guns. Private Victor Denham had left earlier in an ambulance, suffering from anxiety neurosis and hysteria. Private Hughie Black and five other soldiers holding various ranks were left behind in shallow graves, each having made his personal armistice. Sixteen men had been wounded at least badly enough to be sent back to the Casualty Clearing Station near the beach-head. 'The lucky bastards,' Alec said. Then he added, 'It's a funny old world where you call somebody lucky because they've had their foot blown off.'

The battalion marched through most of the night and dug in as dawn was beginning to dilute the darkness to a translucent grey. Their positions were in fields on either side of a country road. They had passed some dead German soldiers on the road, six or seven of them, probably members of an ambushed patrol, and a little farther back, near a shattered cross-roads signpost, a dispatch-rider who was still astride his capsized motor-cycle and still gripping the handlebars. There were bloated carcasses of cattle in the fields and the wind was ripe with the smell of putrefaction.

Alec and John sat in their trench. John lit a cigarette and grimaced at the harsh taste of it in his dry mouth.

Alec said, 'D'you reckon anybody knows where we are?'

'Christ knows.'

'Aye. But apart from him.'

'I don't know. Action's always the same. I've never had the faintest idea where I am or where the fucking enemy is or anything else. I bet the civvies back home know more about it than we do.'

Alec laughed. 'Aye. I never thought of that. I think you're right too. I've often wondered where the papers get all their griff from. I've never laid eyes on a war-correspondent, and I don't know anybody that has. D'you reckon they make it –' He stopped abruptly, paused, then said, 'Listen! What's that noise?'

They both listened. At first John heard only the faint and intermittent rattle of machine-gun fire and the muffled thudding of distant guns but then another sound began softly to drill at the silence.

He said. 'It's engines. Transport? Carriers?'

'Could be tanks.'

'Sounds more like trucks.'

'Let's hope they're ours, whatever they are.'

They stared through the thin veils of mist towards the road which was concealed from them by low hedges. Slowly the noise grew louder and then they saw, fluttering above the top of the hedgerow, a Red Cross pennant and, when they stood upright, they could just see the jeeps which had been adapted for carrying the wounded on stretchers secured above the drivers' heads. A dozen or so of these passed by and then they were followed by about half that number of conventional ambulances, lurching slowly along the cratered road.

'More lucky bastards,' Alec said.

'I'm not so sure.'

'No. I know. It's just something you say.'

John slumped back into his end of the trench. 'Can you stay awake if I have a kip for half an hour? I'm so fucking tired. I fell asleep last night on the march. I was out on my feet. I woke up when Gordon halted us and I bumped into the bloke in front of me.'

'Aye. Sure. You have a kip. I'll give you a shake if I feel myself dropping off.'

But Alec did not get his turn to sleep for, while John was still unconscious, Sergeant Thom came round the positions with the order to get back on to the road and, five minutes later, the battalion was on the move again, marching in single file, each company and each platoon section keeping a good distance from the one in front and moving on opposite sides of the road. John plodded mechanically forward, but he had not fully emerged from sleep and his impressions of the journey were like images in dreams. In the pale misty light he saw an abandoned Bren-carrier on its side, half way through a hedge at the side of the road, and just beyond it a signpost bearing a square board which had painted upon it the black skull and crossbones and the 'Achtung Minen' warning of the presence of mines in the field. An RAF fighter-bomber roared overhead and was soon out of sight and soon afterwards he heard anti-aircraft gunfire and the explosions of the bombs coming from some wooded country ahead of them. Every now and then the columns were halted and a jeep from Battalion Headquarters traversed the line of march. The platoon commanders would go forward for consultation with the company commander and then the march would continue.

They had been moving for about three hours when there was

another and protracted halt. John and Alec drank some water from their bottles and ate a couple of biscuits from their compo packs.

'What would I no' give for a mug of cha,' Alec said.

They sat with the rest of the section in the dry ditch at the side of the road. The jeep drove past them again and five minutes later came back heading towards the front of the column. John lit a cigarette, took a few drags on it, then nipped off the burning end and stored the tab away to be relit later. He leaned with his back against the small bank where the hedge grew and, at once, his eyes closed, his head fell forward and he slept again.

He was awakened by Alec shaking his arm and, with a groan, he struggled to his feet, picked up the Bren-gun and heaved it on to his shoulder.

'The word is we're digging in again,' Alec said.

'Whereabouts?'

'In the fields over there. They reckon there's going to be a big Jerry attack on Escoville. Wherever that is.'

'I wonder if Jerry knows about it.'

'I don't give a fuck what happens as long as I can get my head down for a couple of hours.'

Again the company left the road, crossed a cornfield and the platoons were allocated their position in the adjoining meadow, and again they started to dig their slit-trenches.

Gordon encouraged his section: 'We'll be able to get a bit of rest here, lads. There's a wee town up the road a bit. D Company's sending out a patrol. If there's no Jerries we move forward and set-up BHQ there. So get as much rest as you can while things is quiet.'

They did not move again until the following morning. During the night the heavy shelling and mortar fire again kept its distance and, taking it in turns to keep awake, John and Alec were able to sleep for quite long spells. In the morning they heated water on a tommy-cooker and made a kind of porridge with the dehydrated oatmeal cubes from their compo packs.

Alec said, 'One thing about this life it makes you appreciate simple things. I'll never take bacon and eggs for granted as long as . . . when I get . . .'

John knew why Alec's sentence had disintegrated into that mumbled irresolution. He had been about to say, 'as long as I live,' and then, fearing this presumption would be an irresistible temptation to fate he had tried to change the words, only to find himself making the equally bold and provocative assumption of 'when I get back'.

John said, 'I know what you mean.'

After a pause Alec said, 'It's funny. The other day – I don't know, maybe two or three days back – when we were getting a lot of shit thrown at us, I thought this is fucking crazy. How the fuck can sensible grown-ups let this kind of thing happen? And then I thought I'd never known misery as bad as this could happen to anybody. And then – and here's the odd part, Johnny – I suddenly thought words like misery or happy or anything like that don't mean anything any more. You can't talk about being unhappy or happy. They don't mean a fucking thing because what they're supposed to mean – what they *used* to mean – doesna exist any more. There isn't any being happy or unhappy. There's only being dead or alive. See what I mean?'

John nodded. 'Yeah. I just wish to fuck I wasn't here.'

'Aye, me too.'

There was a silence that was suddenly awkward and vibrant with things unsaid and unsayable, and John knew that they were both thinking of Hughie who, less than forty-eight hours ago, had been alive. He looked across the narrow space of the slit-trench at his companion and he saw the dark stains on the ammunition pouches that Alec was wearing. Then he heard voices and soon Gordon was telling them to get themselves ready to move because the battalion was going to occupy the town.

B Company was posted in a field behind a church, with headquarters in the church itself. The town was entirely empty of civilians and there were few buildings which had not been at least partly damaged by shells and bombs. The population would be sheltering, either with families or in camps in the relatively safe areas close to the beaches. The first twenty-four hours in the new positions were unusually peaceful. The skies were clear and the sun was warm. Everyone was able to wash and shave and the only signs of warfare were some exchanges of gunfire between allied and enemy tanks a mile or so away in the bocage on the right flank and the occasional appearance of RAF fighter-bombers on their way over to strafe the ridge of heavily wooded country about two miles ahead of B Company's positions.

It was in the evening of the third day of B Company's occupation of the area close to the church that the German barrage began with that shocking suddenness and intensity for which any kind of preparation must be impossible. Alec had left the trench for a piss and a couple of seconds after the first shells whistled over from the wooded slope, to explode in and around the churchyard, he came diving for cover, one booted foot striking John on the chin. He quickly regained his more conventional sitting position opposite John and they exchanged stares of almost comical terror as the earth around them was gashed and torn and the shrapnel hissed through the air not far above their helmeted heads. Then the Moaning Minnies opened up and their demoniac howling and the percussion of thirty bombs exploding at roughly the same time in a small area were added to the din. The fury of artillery is a cold, mechanical fury but its intent is personal. When you are under its fire you are the sole target. All of that shrieking, whining venom is directed at you and at no one else. You hunch in your hole in the ground, reduce yourself into as small a thing as you can become, and you harden your muscles in a pitiful attempt at defying the jagged, burning teeth of the shrapnel. Involuntarily you curl up into the foetal position except that your hands go down to protect your genitalia. This instinct to defend the place of generation against the forces of annihilation was universal, a pathetic and symbolic gesture, a feeble protest against the uses that man had been put to by his rulers. John had once, in North Africa, amused Hughie

Black by saying, 'Montgomery doesn't protect his privates, but by Christ, I protect mine.'

All normal sense of time is shattered under a barrage. A minute is forever. You pray and curse and dare not hope that it will stop because you know that hopes are always mocked by the vindictive nature of war. Alec and John crouched in their trench and muttered their almost identically profane litanies which faltered and stopped when they heard a high, almost feminine scream that came from one of the trenches quite close to theirs. It went on; a shrill ululation, the shocking and shameful noise of unbearable pain and terror. Then it stopped, as abruptly as a radio being switched off, and the suddenness of this was almost as unnerving as the sound had been.

When the barrage at last began to ease a little and the Nebelwerfers, at least for the time being, were silent, Gordon Rennie scurried across and dropped into the trench with Alec and John.

He said, 'We're pulling out. Mr Mitchell's killed and Smith's wounded pretty bad. There's a few more casualties in the other platoons. Sarnt Thom's taken over the platoon. We're going to get back to the church. See what happens from there. They think Jerry's going to attack any time now. So keep a look out. We're going two at a time. Gray and Burns'll carry Smithy first. Once they're out of sight into the churchyard you two follow. Right?'

'Right.'

Alec said, 'Was that Mitchell we heard yelling?'

Gordon nodded. 'Aye. He was hit bad. Thom had to finish him off.'

'Fucky Nell,' John said.

Gordon looked back at him as he climbed out of the trench and grinned. 'You sound like Hughie,' he said.

B Company was able in the gathering darkness to assemble with their wounded inside the church where Captain Urquhart told them, 'I'm going to have the whole company inside the churchyard. I'll give platoon commanders their exact positions in a moment. The worst of the barrage is over, we hope, and you'll be better off behind the walls of the yard in case of an attack. They'll give you a fair amount of cover. I want all the Brens up on the West wall facing those woods where the attack'll come from. I've been on the line to the CO and it seems BHQ got off lightly. There wasn't all that much landing on the town centre. In fact we got the worst of it. The CO's been on to brigade and they're going to get the RAF to prang those woods with rockets. Keep wide awake tonight. The slightest movement between you and those woods and you blaze away at it. Platoon commanders, get your men dug in but post your Bren-gunners right away. Stretcher-bearers, get the wounded to BHQ as quick as you can. Carry on, Sarnt-Major.'

So B Company dug in where many excavations had been made in the past, among the stone crosses and tablets and angels, many of which had been disfigured and, in some cases, toppled or reduced to rubble by high explosives. Crude jokes were made about occupying the graveyard but John could sense the real uneasiness behind the pleasantries.

Alec said, 'You'd better get the Bren up on that wall Johnny. I'll get cracking on the digging.' The graveyard walls had been considerably damaged yet they still offered useful cover.

No concentrated infantry attack came from the Germans that night. There was a lot of nervous firing from B Company at targets, imagined or real, and on three occasions these bursts elicited a return of fire so it was known that the enemy had ventured out of their positions in the woods, though only in small numbers. John fired his Bren-gun once when there was a rattle of a Spandau in the darkness in front of him and he was startled by the whine of bullets perilously close to his head.

Alec came from the trench to relieve him and said, 'Did I hear you fire a few minutes ago?'

'You did.'

'You hit anything?'

'Hope not.'

Alec chuckled. 'You go and get some kip. I'll be fine now till the morning. Where'd you put the spare mags?'

'There, look. Down at your feet.'

'Okay. Sleep tight.'

John left Alec in charge of the Bren-gun and made his way to the slit-trench. It was luxury to have the whole space to himself but when he fell asleep he was in the curled position at the end of the trench that he would have adopted if Alec had been sharing it with him.

It was in the grizzled dawn twilight that John was awakened by Alec with the unwelcome news that their section had been detailed by Sergeant Thom to form a patrol for the purpose of investigating the wooded area to find out the strength of the enemy presence. John rinsed his mouth from his water-bottle and found a cigarette and lit it.

He said, 'We might just as well blow our own heads off here and now. He must be fucking mad to send nine men over there.'

'It's Urquhart's idea, not his. Thom's going to lead us himself.'

'Oh, that makes all the difference! Sergeant Thom, the scourge of the Wehrmacht's coming to get you, Fritzie. They'll all run like fucking rabbits I suppose.'

'Cheer up,' Alec said, 'we might get a blighty.'

John was still grumbling when Gordon Rennie came across to their trench.

'Get ready lads,' he said. 'You'll be taking the Bren, Johnny. Make sure the mags are all filled, Alec.'

'What kind of patrol's it supposed to be?' John asked him. 'You can't send a fighting-patrol out there. It's almost daylight. They'll see us coming a mile away. It's fucking suicide.'

'No, no. It's no' so bad. We're going out the other way into the road first, cut round to the field over on the right there. There's hedges all the way along. We'll keep down close to them. If we come under fire we scarper back. But Captain Urquhart thinks Jerry might have pulled out. They canna have much infantry or he'd have put in a big attack last night. Everything's been quiet since the barrage, so maybe the big stuff's been pulled out too. Anyway, we've got to try and find out. Okay?'

Five minutes later the patrol left the churchyard, moving in single file along the narrow road to the fields that they were to cross towards the wooded slope. Sergeant Thom was in front with Gordon behind him, both carrying Sten-guns. Alec and John were at the rear with only one rifleman behind them. He was the 'getaway man' whose job was to get back to Company HQ with details should the patrol encounter the enemy. In the field they all moved along the shallow ditch close to the hedgerow, crouching so that their heads were out of sight. John carried the Bren-gun in readiness to fire from the waist. The mist hung its thin grey veils over the field and hedgerows and the grass was as wet as from a recent shower of rain.

When they reached the end of the field they were faced by another hedgerow with no fence or other access to the next field at the intersection. The patrol halted and waited while Gordon and Sergeant Thom conferred. They spoke in whispers although no one in the still distant woods could possibly have been able to hear them. The message was passed back from the leaders: Sergeant Thom was going to use his wire-cutters on the hedge and make a hole big enough for them to get through. This way they would be much less likely to be spotted than if they scrambled over the top. John crouched low with the others in the ditch while in front Sergeant Thom worked at cutting through the hedge.

'How you feeling?' Alec said.

John looked back over his shoulder. 'Don't feel anything much. What about you?'

'Dunno. Too late to worry. It seems like a daft dream. Not real somehow.'

John knew what he meant. He too had been moving for the past few minutes in an increasingly trance-like state that he took to be partly a consequence of stress and exhaustion and partly the result of that surrender of all choice that must be made in this kind of circumstance. When, a few minutes later, the signal to advance was given from the front of the patrol he moved forward with a sense of effortlessness, almost of floating, and the misty light of early morning seemed to be a projection of this subjective condition as much as an external phenomenon. They squeezed and wriggled through the hedge and proceeded along the ditch under cover of the hedge in the field they had entered and when they reached the next corner it was again necessary to cut their way through.

John was on one knee, his gun held as if ready for action but his mind detached and dreamily unprepared, when there was a kind of hissing, whispered shout from Sergeant Thom: 'Jesus Christ!' This was followed immediately by a burst from his Sten-gun. Before the stutter of his firing had stopped there was an answering rattle of automatic fire from behind the hedge that they were attempting to breach. At the same time shouts exploded from both sides of the hedge, in German and English, and Gordon's voice, oddly high-pitched but recognisably his, 'It's a Jerry patrol!'

John did not move. He felt that he was the frozen axis of all the noise and activity swirling around him. Then he saw the German helmet rise, quite slowly it seemed, above the hedge leading to the next field and he looked straight into the eyes of its wearer. He heard Alec's voice behind him screaming 'For fuck's sake Johnny shoot! Shoot the fucker!' as the German raised his Schmeisser machine-pistol – again it seemed that the movement was accomplished with hypnotic slowness – and aimed it at John's stomach. The knowledge that he was about to be shot flared suddenly in John's consciousness and in one instinctive movement he raised the barrel of the Bren, pointed it at the German's head and pressed the trigger. The gun did not respond. It was a dead lump of metal and wood. But there was a crack like a circus master's whip from behind him and a frantic metal jabbering ahead. He was rising from his kneeling position as he felt a blow like a kick from a heavy boot knock one leg from under him so that he fell sprawling into the ditch. Alec dived on top of him and grabbed the Bren-gun which became alive and blazed away, the rounds ripping through the hedge. All of this activity was over within about a minute. Then the weapons and the voices were silent. Sergeant Thom was heading at a gallop along the ditch in the direction from which his patrol had come and the others started to follow. John tried to get to his feet but his right leg instantly melted beneath him in a slur of pain and he fell on to his side. He heard Alec shout, 'Hey Gordon! Johnny's been hit! Gie's a hand!' and then he was being lifted with an arm pulled about the shoulders of each of his friends and they were dragging him along after the rest of the patrol.

The flight back to Company Headquarters was agonising for John and it could not have been much easier for his rescuers who, after the first few yards, were panting from their exertions and these gasps for breath soon became louder and more painful until they were tortured sobs. The pain in John's leg was increasing all the time. All the hurt that he had ever experienced or imagined was now concentrated in a burning, gnawing, piercing frenzy of anguish in the limb that was being dragged along the rough ground. Somewhere behind them a Spandau started to fire in spaced bursts. John was swearing, an uninterrupted stream of repetitive obscenities. This was the only way to prevent himself from howling with the pain. Gordon and Alec had no breath for swearing. They choked and gasped and stumbled along until they reached the intersecting hedge where Sergeant Thom had cut a hole. Here they had to push and pull John through before continuing their purgatorial journey.

When at last they came out of the field into the road leading to the churchyard Gordon and Alec dropped John on to the ground and both of them fell to their knees and took great choking bites at the air as they struggled to fill their lungs. John kept up his non-stop recitation of profanities. By now he had become the wound itself. It was not a part of his body that was suffering pain. It was all of him. He had become a pierced and pulsing wound. Then, down the road from Company Headquarters, came two figures carrying a stretcher. The bearers lifted him on to it and set off towards the town centre and the Regimental Aid Post. Alec and Gordon, now partly recovered, followed and each took a corner of the stretcher. John, through his own incessant swearing heard Gordon's voice trying to reassure him and he tried to answer it and to convey his gratitude to his friends for rescuing him but the pain would not allow him to utter anything except his mindless rosary of obscenities.

★   ★   ★   ★   ★

At Battalion Headquarters the medical officer's orderly cut away John's right trouser leg and put a field-dressing on the wound. Then he gave him an injection of morphine which eased the pain with miraculous rapidity so that, within half a minute, it was no more than a quite bearable discomfort. Gordon had returned to his section but had told Alec to wait with John until the ambulance came to take him to the Casualty Clearing Station. The Aid Post had been established in a large ground-floor room in the house commandeered by Battalion Headquarters. Both John and Alec had been given mugs of tea by the medical orderly and John was smoking a cigarette. Alec squatted down by the side of the stretcher which had been placed on the floor. His usually cheerful face looked dispirited, the eyes were dull with a look of apprehension and, it seemed to John, appeal or perhaps reproach.

Alec said, 'Well, you got the blighty one, Johnny.'

John thought: 'That's it. He's going to be left on his own. I've betrayed him. I'm leaving him to face things.' He said, 'Thank Gordon for me, won't you. And you. I'd have had my lot if you two hadn't got me out.'

Alec attempted a grin but it did not much relieve the general gloom of his expression. 'You're a terrible weight, man.'

John said, 'I still don't really know what happened. The fucking Bren wouldn't fire.'

'Of course it wouldn't. You had the bloody safety-catch on.'

As soon as Alec spoke John knew that what he said was true yet he felt compelled to deny it.

'Never! Of course I didn't!'

'You fucking did. It was still on when I got hold of it.'

'Christ, what a bloody fool I am.'

'You're a lucky one.'

'What happened to the Jerry? The one with the Schmeisser?'

'One of us got him. We all had a go. Bill Gray had a shot at him with his rifle. Gordon and Thom were spraying the whole hedge with their Stens. But the Jerry must have let go a burst with the Schmeisser before he went down. That's what you copped. The rest of the Jerry patrol pissed off back to their positions in the woods. Like us. I think we got two of them. Gordon says Thom got one with his Sten.'

As Alec was speaking John became aware his left foot felt unnaturally warm as if the boot was slowly filling with hot water.

He called to the orderly: 'Corporal! My left foot feels hot. Could you have a look at it?'

The orderly, who had been writing his casualty report, came across and bent over the foot of the stretcher, removed John's webbing gaiter and started to untie the bootlace. As soon as the lace was loosened blood began to ooze out of the boot. The orderly pulled it off and more blood poured from it as he threw it to one side. He pulled off the saturated sock and called to Alec: 'Bring that bowl over will you? And you'll see some dressings on the table over there . . . That's right. Bring one of them as well . . . thanks.'

He began to clean the wound in John's ankle. Then he looked up. 'Didn't you feel this one going in?' he said. 'It must have missed the bone. You're a lucky sod.' He began to apply the dressing. 'It's gone through your foot, just behind the ankle bone.'

Alec said, 'I'd better get back to the platoon.'

'I wish you were coming with me.'

'Aye . . . well, all the best Johnny.'

'Aren't you going to wait till the ambulance comes?'

'I'd better get back.'

John felt guilt and sadness infecting his sense of joy and relief as he watched Alec turn away and move towards the door. He called, 'Good luck Alec.'

His friend looked back from the door. The smile on his face was still touched with melancholy. He raised one hand, then turned and went out.

'Your mate didn't look too happy,' the orderly said. 'He'll have to find somebody else to dig in with.'

John nodded. The feeling of guilt was still quite strong but the prospect of being taken to the Casualty Clearing Station near the beaches and from there by air or sea to England, cleanliness, comfort and safety, engendered an exhilaration that swept away all despondency. This euphoria was modified only by the fear that, even now, he might still be killed by a mine or shell. He dared not offer thanks until he was on English soil.

Half an hour later the ambulance arrived and John was driven slowly along the cratered roads to the Casualty Clearing Station where he was carried into a large tent and his stretcher was laid on the ground with the dozens of other casualties and a captain in the Medical Corps examined both of his wounds.

'If you've got to get hit,' the captain said, 'that's the way to do it. Nice clean wounds. Straight through. That one in the right leg's fractured the tib and fib by the looks of it. The other one in the ankle's not going to cause you a lot of trouble I shouldn't think. We'll get these cleaned and dressed properly and get a splint on the right leg, and you should be away home in a couple of days.'

The captain's forecast proved too optimistic. In the evening of the day that John was carried into the CCS a great storm began. The wind howled and the canvas of the tent bulged and flapped. The noise was so great that it drowned the sounds of gunfire. John lay in the gloom of the tent and listened to the wind and to the moans and cries of the more severely wounded around him and his earlier feeling of triumphant euphoria became steadily more darkened by a growing sense of unease and guilt. He was still glad to be on his way back to safety yet the knowledge that his friends had been left behind to go on enduring the fear and misery and privation from which he had escaped nagged at his composure like a broken tooth. And, try as he would to dismiss it, guilt remained. Gordon and Alec, the better men, had been left to suffer and perhaps to die as Hughie had died, with that capricious, obscene suddenness that reduced all human aspiration to an absurdity.

Four days later the great wind had abated sufficiently for the seas to be calm enough to allow the wounded to be evacuated. John was taken on his stretcher to the beach where he was carried out on an amphibious vehicle to an American Tank

Landing Craft which, once it had discharged its cargo of tanks, could be used as an improvised hospital-ship. Early on the same evening he was in England. Normandy and the war, Alec and Gordon, the Moaning Minnies and the Spandaus, the mines and the shells, all seemed a long way off in another and unthinkably horrible world. He had survived.

Part IV

HOSPITAL BLUES

THE EMERGENCY MILITARY Hospital at Winwick near Warrington in Cheshire had been, before the war, a mental institution and it retained much of the gloomy and forbidding aspect of a Victorian penal rather than sanatory establishment, but it offered to John a cleanliness, comfort and safety that seemed, at least during the first few days of his admission, almost celestial. The bliss of wearing pyjamas and lying between clean sheets, of being looked after by young and sometimes pretty nurses, was quite sufficient to obliterate for a time the less agreeable experiences that were part of life in a military hospital. But gradually these began to disturb his contentment. The ward was large and every bit of available space had been utilized so that, instead of the two rows of beds, one on each side of the long room, as originally intended, there was a third row in the centre and this meant that there were forty-two patients in a ward intended to hold a maximum number of twenty-eight. Some of these men were still suffering considerable pain despite all medical efforts to minimise it and the nights were loud not only with healthy snores but moans and cries of distress and fairly frequent flurries of activity when moments of crisis occurred.

John's neighbours – a dispatch-rider with a broken femur, in the bed on his left, and a sapper who had had one foot blown off by a mine, on his right – were amiable enough companions but their conversation was limited to little else but talk of girls they had enjoyed or were intending to enjoy and the comparative merits of various makes of motor-cycles. Since their exchanges were conducted across John's bed he found they hampered his concentration on whatever he was trying to read. And here, with this matter of reading, came the most disturbing and unexpected problem that his being a hospital patient was to present. Of all the pleasures that he looked forward to on his return from

Normandy the opportunity to spend almost unlimited time with
the literature of his choice was among the most exciting and he
was determined to get his hands on at least some of the novels
and the poetry that he had heard of, but never had the chance to
read, as well as reacquaint himself with works he already knew.
Getting hold of reading-matter proved less difficult than he had
anticipated. A member of the Women's Voluntary Service
visited the ward once a fortnight with books from the local
branch of the public library and she was pleased to do her best to
satisfy his request for particular titles and authors. On her
second visit she brought the *Oxford Book of English Verse*, the
Selected Poems of T S Eliot, Faulkner's *The Sound and the
Fury*, *Moby Dick*, and Evelyn Waugh's *Put Out More Flags*. The
delight with which John received these books soon changed to
irritable frustration when he found that he could not keep his
attention fixed on the pages for more than about half an hour.
His immediate neighbours' chatter was not the only cause of his
inability to concentrate, indeed this was easier to ignore than the
less identifiable distraction of the whole atmosphere of the ward
and, more troublesome still, his own restless, nervous, unfocused excitement, the sense of waiting for something momen-
tous to occur.

For the first four weeks of his stay in Winwick Hospital both
of his legs were in plaster casts, the left one stopping below the
knee but the right one covering the whole of his leg to the top of
the thigh. When the cast covering the wound in his left ankle
was removed he was able with the help of crutches to move about
and he was issued with a suit of hospital blues which consisted of
a jacket and trousers of rough blue woollen material, cut in a style
that was institutional, redolent of the Victorian poor-house.
With this suit was worn a white cotton shirt and a skimpy red
tie. When a patient was allowed out of the hospital grounds he
wore his regimental headgear and badge, the only part of his
apparel that was recognisably military. The lower part of John's
right trouser-leg had to be split to allow the entry of the plaster
cast. At first he found the crutches both difficult and tiring to
manipulate but after a few days' practice he was able to move

around with relative ease and speed. It was on a Thursday mid-morning after ward inspection that he applied to the administrative office for a pass to go into Warrington. Permission was granted and he returned to his ward to collect his glengarry cap before leaving the hospital for the first time since his arrival more than a month ago.

Peter Davidson, the dispatch-rider, said, 'Where you going mate?'

John thought for a moment. 'I don't know. Warrington I suppose. That's the nearest town, isn't it? I don't really mind as long as I can get a pint.'

'You can forget Warrington then. Isn't that right, Fred?'

Fred Lee, the occupant of the bed on John's right, said 'That's right chum. You won't be able to get a drink in Warrington. All the pubs is out of bounds to swaddies in hospital blues.'

John's pay had accumulated to what, by his standards, was a substantial amount of money during the period in action, when of course he had spent nothing at all, and the weeks in hospital when his only expenditure had been on cigarettes. In the pocket of his blue jacket he had three pound notes and some silver, more than enough for some carefree drinking.

He said, 'Do you mean to say nobody from Winwick can get a drink anywhere?'

'Not in Warrington you can't,' Peter assured him. 'It's been like that some time now. Some of the boys used to go into town and get pissed and fall down and bust their stitches an' all sorts. So orders went out no pubs was to serve anybody in blues. That's how it is. You've got to go to Liverpool or Manchester if you want a drink.'

'Which is the nearest?'

'Nothing in it. Maybe Liverpool's a bit closer. They're both about twenty mile from Warrington.'

'I think I'll go to Manchester. I used to live near there when I was a kid.'

'You want to get a move on then. You've got to be back here by 8.30 tonight. Don't give you all that much time what with train journeys and all that.'

'I'll worry about that when the time comes.'

'Don't do anything I wouldn't do,' Fred called as John left the ward and made for the exit from the hospital.

It was a warm day in early August. The sky had that fresh, rinsed blueness that belonged to childhood and the few clouds were small and snowy clusters like blossoms. The touch of the sun was a caress which seemed to hint at undisclosed promises of adventure. He caught a bus into Warrington and there he was directed by the conductress to the railway station where he bought a return ticket to Manchester and sat on a platform seat with his crutches at his side and his plaster-covered right leg stretched out in front of him. He did not have long to wait before the train arrived and he settled himself in an otherwise empty compartment and lit a cigarette as the engine with its slowly spaced grunts of exertion started to move out of the station and gradually increased its speed until it was galloping along to its steady dactylic rhythm.

Excitement hummed along the wires of his nerves and tingled on the flesh. His sense of freedom was intoxicating and even the drab institutional blue suit seemed to be colluding with the feeling that he was no longer a part of the military machine, that he had been resurrected, if not as a civilian then as a species that was evolving towards that state. He thought: 'I'm on my way out. They'll never get me again. I'll never be shot at or shouted at or fucked around by brainless, big-mouthed NCOs or pissed on by public school prefects with one pip. I've got the army by the short hairs. I can do what I like. They can't send a one-legged man to the glasshouse.'

The train arrived in Manchester shortly after twelve o'clock and John swung along on his crutches into the brilliant, busy streets of the city. It was true that he had lived in Eccles, a few miles away, when he was a child but he had left there at the age of eight and excursions to Manchester had been infrequent so he had no memory of the geography of the place. He moved along the pavements enjoying the warmth of the sun and the sight of women who had blossomed like flowers with their butterfly-wing dresses, and the slender bare stems of their limbs.

From the open entrance to a pub drifted the yeasty smell of beer mixed with tobacco-smoke and this brought back memories from his stay in Eccles when his uncle had taken him and the Alsatian, Major, out for a Sunday morning's walk and they had stopped at the *Cross Keys* where he and Major had waited outside the saloon bar with potato-crisps and lemonade, sniffing the magical, grown-up scent that floated from within. It excited him then and it excited him now as he left the bright street and went into the voluble and pungent gloom of the bar. At once he was greeted by a big, muscular young man wearing a coarse woollen shirt with no collar and blue serge trousers held up by a broad leather belt.

'Hey! Come over here soldier. Here's a seat for you. Come and sit down.'

John was led to a table at which sat three other young men and he was welcomed by them with the same warmth that the fourth member of the group had shown. He sat down and his crutches were taken from him and placed against the wall.

'Now what you going to have?'

The four men were Irish stevedores working on the Manchester Ship Canal and they were enjoying their annual holiday. They were drinking pints of Guinness and the same drink was given to John. When he offered to buy a round he was told to keep his money in his pocket and he then realised that what he was receiving was a kind of hero's welcome. The Irishmen drank at a pace which, after his third pint, John found quite difficult to sustain but whenever a fresh round was bought his attempts at refusal were ignored and soon he found that he had acquired a kind of second wind and was able to match their rate of consumption. Because of his glengarry and Gordon Highlander badge they assumed that he was a Scotsman and they addressed him with ever increasing affection as 'Jock'. They sang songs, sentimental and patriotic and then demanded a solo from John. By this time the Guinness had drowned most of his natural reserve and he obliged with a rendition of Loch Lomond which was received with loud applause from the stevedores if not from the other occupants of the bar.

At closing-time John parted with his Irish friends on the pavement outside the pub. They invited him more than once to accompany them to the greyhound track which was their next destination but he declined with gratitude and after many hand-shakes and repetitive exchanges of goodwill they made their rather unsteady departure. John was feeling quite drunk but using his crutches compelled him to concentrate his attention on his manoeuvres and exercise caution in a way that probably disguised some of his unsteadiness. The sun still bathed the city in its warmth and flashed its signals from windscreen and chrome of passing traffic. A girl in a yellow dress passed him and her perfume trailed in the air behind her like an invisible and delicately tinted scarf.

He felt very hungry and when he came to a small workman's café he went in and ate meat pie and beans and chips. After he had eaten he smoked a cigarette over a cup of tea and then returned to the sun-splashed streets. He was beginning to get very tired and hot when he reached a large square with tall, imposing buildings, which might have been government offices, looking down upon a small park. He went into the park and left the gravel path for the neatly-barbered grass and there he dropped his crutches, took off his blue jacket and folded it to make a pillow and lowered himself to the ground. The sun delicately touched his closed eyelids and he could hear the irregular murmur of the traffic. Once he was jolted back from the edge of sleep when a motor-cycle engine stuttered into life, sounding for a moment like a machine-gun, but the stab of alarm was brief and easily dismissed and he was smiling faintly as he drifted from the shallows into the deeper waters of sleep.

When he awoke the sun had lost much of its strength and it was beginning to dip behind the tall buildings so that shadows like stains darkened the grass. He pushed himself up on to one elbow and shivered, feeling a moment of chill which quickly passed as he heaved himself to his feet, put on his jacket and picked up the crutches and began to move quite slowly back on to the path leading out of the park. His mouth was dry and tasted as if he had been sucking pennies. He guessed that his eyes were bloodshot and he felt a loose fitting was rattling about inside his skull. There was only one cure for this condition and that was to drink again. He did not know the time but he guessed that it would be about seven o'clock and certainly the pubs would have reopened. One good thing, he told himself, he was not short of cash. Those Irish stevedores had made sure of that. The thought of them brought a faint smile to his lips and he began to move a little faster. If he could find the same pub he would go there, but he would drink something other than Guinness.

John did not find the pub. After half an hour of moving along various streets trying to locate a familiar landmark he realised that he was lost and that the only hope of finding the place was to return to the railway station and start out again from there. But, before he saw someone who looked like a suitable guide to direct him to the station, he noticed an inn sign in a narrow street that he was passing and he decided that, before he did anything else, he would have a restoring drink.

The pub was quite full although, as John saw from the clock behind the bar, it was only twenty past seven. People made way for him with marked solicitude and the barmaid ignored customers who had been waiting to be served and asked him, with a kind of motherly concern, what she could get for him. He ordered a pint of bitter and when it was placed before him and he had paid for it he looked around to see if there was an unoccupied seat. He could not quite make out what kind of pub it was. Most of the customers looked fairly affluent; the men wore suits and the women were smart in a slightly vulgar style, plenty of lipstick and mascara, high heels and those wide-shouldered jackets that were fashionable at the time. None, he thought, looked under thirty and most of them a good deal older. It was a smarter pub than the one he had visited in the morning but the smartness was meretricious, the kind of tinselly flashiness that he vaguely associated with the lower strata of show business. He found it rather exciting.

Someone at his elbow spoke to him. 'You looking for a place to sit down, lad? Look, there's a seat over there by that big plantpot. Give us your ale. I'll take it over for you.'

The man was short and rather fat. He wore a navy blue pin-stripe suit and his brilliantined but thinning hair was carefully parted slightly off centre. His moustache was a couple of thin dark lines on his upper lip which looked as if they had been applied by an eyebrow pencil. There was something engaging about his shiftiness; the dark bright eyes gleamed with real humour and seemed to say, 'Yes, I know I'm an awful little man but at least I don't pretend to be anything else.'

John said, 'Okay. Thanks,' and followed him to a table at which were already seated two women, one with blonde, lifeless looking hair, which might well have been a wig, and her slightly younger companion who was dark and quite good-looking in a hard-bitten, though not masculine way. John guessed that the blonde would probably be in her forties and the dark one in her late thirties.

The small man put John's pint and his own glass of light ale on the table and said, 'This young man's going to join us . . . here, let's have them crutches.'

The women smiled and nodded at John who said, 'Hullo,' as he lowered himself on to a chair and arranged his right leg so that it would not be in anyone's way.

'What's your name, love?' the blonde said.

The little man joined them at the table.

'Aye. What's your name, lad?'

'John. John Bain.'

'How do John. I'm Eric and this is Connie – looks like Jean Harlow, don't she? – and this is Vi.'

Both women raised their glasses, which also appeared to contain light ale, and John lifted his in salutation. 'All the best,' Connie said.

John nodded. 'Cheers.'

Vi, the dark one, said, 'What you done to your leg then?'

'I got a bullet through it.'

'Where was that, son?' Eric asked.

'Normandy.' John felt curiously embarrassed, as if he were guilty of boasting. 'I'm in hospital at Winwick.'

'Winwick, eh? That's a tidy way,' Connie said.

'That's a Scotch hat, isn't it?' Vi asked. 'You're not a Scotchman, are you?'

'No. Not really. My father's family came from Scotland. He was in a Scottish regiment in the last war.' He sounded, in his own ears, strangely stilted, almost as if he were reading from a poor script. An instinctive need to correct this led him to say, 'I've got a bloody terrible hangover. I had about a dozen pints of Guinness at lunch-time,' but it sounded just as forced and, again, boastful.

'Well I never,' Connie said.

John took a long drink of his bitter.

'You married?' Vi asked.

'No.'

'Got a steady girl-friend? Engaged?'

'No.'

'You're pulling our leg. A good-looking boy like you's bound to have a girl-friend.'

John drank again. His glass was now half emptied.

'He's shy,' Connie said. 'Don't you worry, love. You'll come to no harm with us.'

Eric winked at him. 'Take no notice of them, Johnny. You know women. What was it like over there then?'

'Not too bad. I was lucky. I wasn't there all that long.'

'Not too bad, he says! You hear that Connie? Not too bad! Must a been terrible. We owe you lads a lot and that's a fact. I only wish I'd a been able to be with you. Got a bad ticker. Otherwise I'd a gone. I tried, but they wouldn't have me.'

'The Sally Army wouldn't have you,' Connie said. 'Fred Karno's Army wouldn't. You? A soldier?' She laughed, a humourless, contemptuous noise.

Eric did not seem to be offended. He smiled at her quite amiably as if they were sharing a joke.

Vi said, 'Where you from then, Johnny?'

'Place called Aylesbury. I wasn't born there but that's where I was when I joined up.' Then he added: 'I used to live in Eccles when I was a little kid.'

'You never did!' Connie exclaimed, not in disbelief but feigned amazement. 'Whereabouts, love?'

'Bardsley Street.'

'Eh, well I never. I've got a cousin used to live there before she got married. Polly Turner that was. She'd be Polly somebody else now. I've forgot her married name.'

'I was only eight or nine when I left there. I don't remember much about it.'

'Eh, it's a small world.'

John finished his pint. 'What you going to have?' he said. 'Drink up.'

'Just a tick,' Eric said and for a moment John thought that he was going to insist on buying the drinks himself but this misconception was soon corrected. 'You can't manage with your leg. Give me the money and I'll go up and get them. What's it to be then girls?'

Connie reflected: 'I don't know really. I'd like a change from this stuff. Have they got any gin?'

'I'll ask Freda. I bet she's got some under the counter. What about you Vi?'

'I'll have the same as Connie if that's all right with Johnny.'

While Eric had gone to the bar with one of John's pound notes Connie said, 'It's terrible in pubs these days. Sometimes they don't have no spirits at all. Or so they reckon. But Eric'll get us some if there's any to be had.'

When Eric came back he was carrying a tray which held John's pint of bitter, a bottle of light ale and two small wine glasses full of dark red liquid.

'No gin, girls,' he said, 'but I got you a drop of port. Here's your change, Johnny.'

He handed the money over as if he were bestowing a gift and John found himself receiving it with gratitude.

'I bet she's got gin under the counter,' Connie said.

Vi raised her glass of port. 'Good health, Johnny love.'

John said to her, 'Do you live in Manchester?'

'Yes. Well, very near. Salford really. Me and her lives in same house.'

'Are you married?'

Connie laughed. 'No darlin', but we're still hoping.'

Vi said, 'I was but I'm not now.'

John drank more beer. He thought Vi was really rather attractive in her tough, worldly way. He brought out a packet of cigarettes and passed it round. They all took one and Eric lit them.

'Players,' Connie said. 'This is a real treat, Johnny. You can't get a good smoke anywhere these days 'less you're in the know. It's all black market. The only ones I could get this morning was Tenners and we all know what they're made of. But she'd got plenty under counter. If I was back home I'd be all right. My sister's man's got an off-licence. Sells fags too. I'd be well away there.'

'Where's home?' John said.

'Rochdale, love, where our Gracie comes from.'

'And Jock MacAvoy,' Eric said.

'You interested in boxing?' John asked him.

'Interested. Meat and drink to me, lad, meat and drink. I love it. The greatest game in the world.' He cocked his head slightly to one side and regarded John with eyes narrowed a little in appraisal. 'Aye. Come to look at you, I reckon you've done a bit. Am I right?'

'A bit.'

'Light-heavy?'

'Middle.'

'You're a big middle. Good shoulders. Carry your weight on top. That's the best way. Aye, I can tell now, looking at you, that you've had 'em on.'

'What are you two on about?' Vi asked.

'Boxing,' Eric told her, 'the greatest game in the world. I knew Johnny here'd done a bit soon as I laid eyes on him.'

'He don't look like a boxer to me,' Connie said. 'He's too good-looking. Boxers has got squashed noses and cauliflower ears an' all that. Johnny don't look that that.'

'Shows he's a good 'un,' Eric said. 'Noble art of self defence. You hit the other fellow. He doesn't hit you. That's the game,

Connie. It's the mugs get thick ears and broken noses, not the good 'uns.'

'Jackie Brown's got a thick ear. He looks like a tram's hit him,' Vi said. 'I saw him in a pub once. He looked something awful.'

'Ah, Jackie went on a bit too long. That's the trouble. They never know when to pack it in. He was great was Jackie, at his best.'

Connie finished her port. 'Well, I think it's daft, two lads trying to knock each other's heads off. What about another drink?'

Eric said, 'Right. Good idea. Drink up Johnny. You can manage another.'

John finished his pint and realised that he was beginning to feel slightly drunk. It seemed that the two drinks he had swallowed had reactivated the alcohol he had swallowed with the Irishmen, for his sensation of unfocused well-being and friendliness could not have been caused by a couple of pints of bitter. He hardly noticed that Eric had left his seat and was bending over to whisper into Vi's ear and that Vi, after muttering something that sounded as if she was displeased, opened and delved into her handbag and gave Eric a ten shilling note.

After Eric had been to the bar and returned with the next round of drinks John's blurred perceptions and feelings of affection for his companions became mistier and warmer. He told them about the ENSA concert party that had visited the hospital to entertain the patients and how, before the show had ended, the hall was empty except for those unfortunates who had been brought in on stretchers. John explained that his own feelings for the performers had been a mixture of embarrassment, pity and resentment.

'They were terrible,' he said. 'Terrible. You'd have to see it to believe it. Comedians telling jokes I'd heard at school and hadn't laughed at then. A fat old woman singing – if that's what you call it – songs about love in the Rockies or something. Impersonations of Winston Churchill. A ventriloquist. Christ they were pathetic.'

'It's a shame,' Connie said and placed a hand on his arm. She had moved from her seat, exchanging places with Eric so she could be closer to John who wished that it had been Vi who had asked for the swap. But now he was beginning to think Connie didn't look too bad really.

His glass was empty again. 'Let's have another,' he said. 'And see if you can get some fags, Eric.' He handed over more money.

Connie said, 'I think you're a bit of a lad underneath.'

'Underneath what?'

She gave her laugh which did not sound quite so raucous now.

Vi said, 'When you got to be back in hospital, Johnny?'

'I dunno. Any time. Tomorrow. Any time I like. Tomorrow and tomorrow and tomorrow. That's Shakespeare.'

'I think he's a bit of a lad,' Connie said. 'What do you think, Vi?'

'I think he's very nice.'

Eric placed more drinks on the table and a packet of cigarettes. He said, 'I got some Weights. Under the counter. You've got to know your way around.'

The pub was becoming more crowded now. The air was misty with tobacco smoke and loud with laughter and talk. Connie kept returning her hand to John's sleeve and occasionally pressing his arm but Vi was looking across the table at him with a half-smile and a secretive, perhaps conspiratorial look in her eyes and John again wished that it was she who was sitting close to him. They all seemed to be drinking faster now and when their glasses were again empty John bought another round.

While Eric was at the bar he said, 'I think I've got to go to the gents.'

'Can you manage?' Vi asked.

Connie's laugh was loud and coarse. 'He's a big boy, Vi. I bet he can manage very well.'

'I mean his crutches. I'll get them for you, Johnny.'

Vi collected the crutches from where Eric had placed them against the wall near a hat-and-coat stand while John pulled himself upright.

She said, 'Here you are, love. It's over there, look. You going to be all right?'

'Thank you. Yes, I'll be fine.'

He steadied himself, tucked the crutch rests under his armpits and headed for the gents. He was not entirely in control of either the crutches or his own limbs and he collided with a few people and chair-legs on his journey, but everyone was tolerant and friendly and a lance-bombardier in the Royal Artillery, who was bound for the same place, paused at the door to hold it open for him to enter. Inside he stood at the stall with the gunner while they eased their bladders.

'How's tricks, mate?' the gunner said.

'Okay. And you?'

'Not bad. I'd watch out for them brass nails if I was you.'

'What do you mean?'

'Them old tarts you're with. You know they're on the game, don't you?'

John now had to admit that the thought had crossed his mind but he had managed not to confront it. He said, 'I'm only having a drink with them.'

'Yeah. Well, it's none of my business but I just thought I'd warn you.'

When the lance-bombardier had left, John looked in the decaying mirror above the parched and cracked hand-basin and although the image was not very clear he could see that he looked pretty drunk. His glengarry had slipped so that it was almost slantwise across his head and the ribbons hung down over his right ear. There was a smudged look of belligerence about his eyes and jaw and he did not like the face he was looking at. He straightened his glengarry, pulled up the knot of his red tie and tried to look more alert and agreeable. The results were not much more appealing. Maybe the mirror was distorting his appearance. What did it matter, anyway. He went back to Eric and the ladies.

As they continued drinking John tried to dismiss the knowledge given to him by the lance-bombardier and soon he was able almost to convince himself that although Connie might indeed be a prostitute Vi was not. In fact behind the rather tough and shrewd exterior there was a very nice and affectionate girl.

She had probably had a tough life, been pretty badly treated by men so that she'd developed a defensive hardness. But she looked very nice at times, when she smiled, and she was smiling at him quite a lot.

John said, 'Let's have another. Come on, Eric. Do your stuff. You're a better man than I am, Gunga Din.'

'Eh, what a lad!' Eric exclaimed. 'I'n't he a lad, Connie? Okay . . . here, that ten bob'll do . . . that's it . . . Ta, . . . there's a good lad.'

'Gunga bloody Din, the water-carrier,' John said.

'You and your Shakespeare!' Connie squeezed his arm and cackled.

Vi was looking at her wrist-watch. She had done this two or three times during the past half hour or so. She probably did not want the evening to end.

'What time do they close?' He asked Connie.

'Don't worry, love. Another half hour yet. Plenty of time for another. Maybe a couple.'

Eric was back at the table with the fresh drinks.

'Here we are again, happy as can be. Connie . . . Vi . . . and a pint for Johnny. Get that inside you, son and you'll be dancing the Highland Fling.'

John drank only a small amount of his pint, not much more than a sip. He was beginning to feel bloated with beer and he knew that, unless he was careful, he could easily be sick. It was hot in the pub and he could feel the sweat pricking his forehead, damp in his hair. He was just saying to himself that he had better not drink any more when he saw Eric suddenly jump to his feet and wave towards the entrance to the bar. At the same time Vi, who had begun to look rather preoccupied, became visibly excited. Her smile was wide and welcoming and her eyes were bright as she looked eagerly in the direction towards which Eric was enthusiastically signalling. Connie's hand was withdrawn quickly from his arm and she turned and began to wave too.

'Chester!' she called. 'Yoo-hoo! Gary! We're over here!'

John turned and saw two American GIs pushing their way through to the table. One was short, not much taller than Eric,

and thick-set with hair so closely cropped that it was impossible
to tell its colour. His companion was quite tall, a little over six
feet, and rather handsome with black shiny hair and dark lean
jaws and teeth that looked as white as the flesh of a coconut.

'Hi!' the shorter one said as he reached the table.

Eric had left his chair and was bustling around at other
people's tables to collect spare seats for the newcomers.

'Come on, Chester,' he said, 'you sit here next to Vi. Okay.
Gary. Take my chair. I'll find another don't you worry.'

Gary, the tall GI, did not look at all worried as he sat down.

Eric said, 'This is Johnny. We've been having a little chat.
Johnny got wounded in Normandy. This is Gary and Chester.'

Both Americans nodded in John's direction but after that they
ignored him completely. Connie and Vi were not much more
attentive. Vi had become suddenly much more vivacious and
was gazing and smiling at Gary as if she were marvelling at his
wit and beauty. Connie had turned her back on John and was
wearing Chester's cap and reproaching him for being late. Eric
alone remained aware of John's presence. He was on his feet,
hovering like an especially obsequious waiter, and he included
John in his enveloping bonhomie.

'You want me to get you something, gents?' he said. 'What
about the ladies? I'm yours to command.' He winked at John.

'What they got?' Gary asked him. 'I don't want more of that
goddam English beer. They got any scotch.'

''Fraid you're unlucky. Not tonight Josephine.'

'Aw shit. Let's get out a here. We got a couple of bottles in
the jeep. We'll go drink it at Connie's place. Okay Chester?'

'Sure. Let's go.'

John sat lumpily in his chair feeling literally sick and tired and
curiously heavy as if, in the past hour or so, he had put on a great
deal of surplus flesh. He watched the American soldiers stand up
and start for the exit without waiting to see if they were being
followed. They were. Connie and Vi were snatching at their
possessions, matches and cigarettes and handbags, and hurrying
on their chattering high-heels after the GIs. Connie spared a
quick glance and grimace over her shoulder at John and a squeak

of ''Bye Johnny' as she wiggled and tapped after Vi. Eric, too, was following them.

'Abyssinia Johnny!' he called and waved as he set off in pursuit.

John watched them go and then looked down at the table-top with the dirty ashtrays and empty glasses and his own three-quarters' full pint. He reached out and lifted it but replaced it without having taken even a sip. The beer he had already swallowed seemed to be rising from his stomach, up into his throat. He belched uncontrollably and quite loudly. 'Fuck it,' he thought, 'I'd better get out of here.'

It took what seemed a long time to find the resolve and then to accomplish the act of getting on to his feet and when he had managed to do so he stood supporting himself with one hand on the chair-back and the other on the table-top looking over at his crutches against the wall which looked a forbidding distance away. Two middle-aged civilians, each accompanied by a female companion, came over to the table.

'You leaving?' one of the men asked.

John said, 'Yes. If I can get those crutches, over there against the wall.'

The man looked towards the coat-stand. 'Right. Here. Sit down, Charlie. Edie, look after my place while I get this lad's crutches.'

He went away and returned. 'Here you are then, son.' He looked at John more carefully. 'You going to be all right? You've had a jar or two haven't you?'

'I'm all right,' John said and set off for the door.

But he was not all right. The hot abrasive pressure of the undigested beer was increasing in his stomach and throat. The floor was strangely uneven with little dips and hummocks over which he stumbled and twice bumped heavily into standing customers and once against a table, knocking over someone's beer. He did not pause to see how the owner was reacting. He could not see very clearly at all. The tobacco-smoke seemed to be very much thicker and the lights more dazzling. He blundered on towards the door, lurching and stumbling and he was vaguely aware that comments, ribald and sympathetic, were being made. He thought, 'It's like trying to walk on a fairground roundabout. The fucking room's going round,' but he managed at last to get to the door and out on to the pavement where, almost at once, he vomited. The tidal-wave of beer and bile rose into his mouth and burst out in a great rank flood, jetting on to the pavement and splashing over his left boot. Each time it seemed as if the upsurge was abating, it would rush upwards again and there would be another bitter deluge. His chest and stomach-muscles were sore from the repeated seismic assaults when at last it appeared that he had finished vomiting. He was gasping for breath and tears filled his eyes and ran down his face.

After he had recovered his breath he started to move away from the pub in the direction of the busier road off which he had earlier turned. But he could see almost nothing in the black-out. Once he collided with what he took to be a lamp-post and a few moments later one of his crutches skidded off the kerb into the gutter and he lost his balance and, dropping the other crutch so that he could stretch out his arms in the hope of saving himself or at least easing the fall, he keeled over and hit the ground. Since he could not bend his right leg the impact was inevitably sharp but he landed on his right side, jarring his elbow and winding himself but not striking his head. He reached with his left hand for his right elbow and clutched at the pain.

'Fuck 'em all,' he said, and lay back his head and closed his eyes. The evening was warm. There were no shells or Moaning Minnies or Spandaus. He'd slept in worse place than this. So fuck 'em all. He lay there and waited for sleep, which came very soon.

When consciousness returned he was for a bare second in a panicky state of total ignorance of time, place and circumstance. There were voices in the dark. He was no longer lying in the road. He was upright, his back against a wall, his crutches in place, one under each oxter. Then a muddled recollecting of

events began. There was something familiar about one of the
voices, a man's, which was now saying: 'What's Joyce going to
say if we get back with a drunken swaddie?' He spoke with a
South London accent.

A woman's voice answered, 'Well, we can't just leave him
here.'

A second man spoke, 'What about police? Maybe I ought to
get a copper.' Both of these voices were unmistakably Lancashire.

John felt as if the discussion had little or no connection with
him, that he was like an unnoticed onlooker on the fringe of the
crowd at some public accident.

'Copper?' This was the woman. 'You can't do that, George.
You might get lad into trouble.'

'No. We'd better take him back,' the London voice said.

John thought it was time for him to speak. 'I'm all right.'
Even in his own ears the words slurred drunkenly. He tried
again: 'I'll be all right. Thanks. Leave me. Be all right.'

A beam from an electric torch cracked the darkness and made
a pale yellow pool at his feet.

'Can you manage? Our house's only a step or two up road,' the
Lancashire man's voice said.

'Leave me here. Very kind of you. Be all right,' John
mumbled.

'Will you heck be all right. Come on, lad. This way.'

There was a sustaining hand beneath each of his elbows as he
left the support of the wall and swayed before regaining some
balance.

'Here, George, give us torch,' the woman said. 'You two try
and keep him from falling over.'

Their progress along the dark street was accompanied by
grunts, curses and exchanges of tactical advice which sounded
like the dialogue of two furniture-removers handling a particu-
larly difficult burden, but they managed to reach their goal with
John still precariously upright. A door was opened, light gushed
from inside on to the pavement and John was pushed, pulled and
supported through the doorway into the small front room of the

house where he was allowed to collapse on to a sofa. He leaned back, the leg in plaster stretched out, and he blinked up at his rescuers who were now joined by the other occupant of the house, a woman who was uttering exclamations of astonishment and concern. The man with the London accent was the lance-bombardier whom John had earlier encountered in the pub lavatory.

'Hullo Corporal. I mean Bombardier,' John said and again he heard not only the drunkenness but the fatuity in his voice.

George, the civilian, said, 'How you feeling, lad?'

The woman who had been inside the house on their arrival and who subsequently turned out to be George's wife, Joyce, looked anxious but not unwelcoming: 'Eh, look at state of poor lad. What happened to you then? How did you hurt your leg?'

'Bullets,' John pronounced carefully, 'Normandy.'

'You could do with something inside you. I've got a bit of cheese left over from last week's ration. I could toast that for you.'

'No, no,' John protested. 'Certainly not. I mean it's very nice of you but no. I couldn't eat anything.'

George smiled. 'Joyce's got a funny idea that everybody in the forces's got malnutrition.'

'Where you stationed? I mean what hospital you in?' the artillery man asked.

'Winwick.'

'Where's that? Never heard of it.'

'Miles away,' the woman who had held the torch said. 'You think you'd be all right on sofa if we got you a couple of blankets?'

John assured them that he would be perfectly comfortable and that he did not need blankets since the night was so warm. His drunkenness had now taken the form of a kind of veil between him and external objects and events which he could perceive but not with clarity. He looked round the little room and suddenly recognised it as being almost identical to the front room of the little house in Eccles where he had lived with his grandparents.

'Used to live in a house like this,' he said. 'Exactly same. With my granny. Bardsley Street. Eccles.'

He heard Joyce say something about making a nice cup of tea but by then his eyes were closed and he was almost asleep. A little time must have passed before he became aware of tugging at his left foot and he opened his eyes and saw the lance-bombardier kneeling on the carpet to remove the boot.

'You've got a bandage on this leg as well,' the gunner said.

'S'right.'

'Look. I've got you a blanket and my great-coat. I'll put them handy case you get cold. All right, mate?'

'Fine.'

'If you want a piss you'd better go in the sink. That's next door. You'd never find your way out to the privy.'

'I'll be all right.'

'Okay. I'll leave the light on. See you in the morning.'

John said, 'Goodnight. Everybody's been smashing.' He closed his eyes again, heard the door open and close, then footsteps on the stairs and muffled sounds from above his head before he lost consciousness again.

When he awoke he had no idea of the time. His hangover was not too bad. Perhaps being sick on the previous night had helped to get at least some of the alcohol out of his system. He eased himself off the couch and managed to put on and lace up his left boot. Then he took his crutches, which had been left leaning against a chair close to the sofa, and moved over to the window and parted the curtains to see grey, misty twilight in the cobbled street. He rearranged the curtains and went out of the little parlour into the only other downstairs room, the kitchen. The light from the gas mantle in the front room was sufficient to show him the way to the sink into which he discharged a long stream of urine while the tap was turned on and cold water allowed to flow for some time afterwards. Then he saw on the mantelpiece above the cooking-range a brass alarm clock which showed the time to be ten minutes to six.

He had to search for some seconds before he found a piece of paper, a receipt for coal, and on the back of this he wrote with his fountain-pen a message of thanks and apologies for his early departure. Then he counted his money. He found that he had

one pound note and almost fifteen shillings. It could have been
less, he thought. He paused, wondering whether to leave some
money for his Samaritans, but he decided that this would almost
certainly offend them. So he went back into the front room,
turned out the light and let himself quietly out of the house into
the street, carefully closing the door behind him.

The sun had not yet filtered through the early mist but he felt
sure that another brilliant hot day was waiting to announce
itself. He moved towards the main road for which he had been
heading on the previous night and he passed first the pub, which
he saw from the sign was called *The Golden Lion*, and then, a
couple of yards away from the entrance, some squalid evidence
of his sickness. He thought he would look for a place to clean
himself up. In every town of reasonable size there was an all-
night forces' canteen and he was sure that Manchester would
possess at least one YMCA or Church Army establishment
where he would be able to find soap and water. There were a few
traces of dried vomit on his shirt front and lower trouser leg but
not so many that they could not easily be removed by a little
scrubbing. Today was going to be different, he promised
himself. He would not make the mistake of drinking too fast and
too much. He would take it easy. Box clever. Not go crazy. And
not be taken for a ride by con men and old whores. It was going
to be a glorious day.

John found the place he needed but only after a long and
exhausting search which ended when a special constable on his
way home after night-duty directed him to the YMCA in Peter
Street. Although it was still very early, no later than seven
o'clock, the canteen was fairly busy. The black-out screens had
not yet been taken down from the windows and the harsh
electric light showed clearly the debris of the night and the
weariness of the soldiers, sailors and airmen who sat at the tables
littered with loaded ashtrays, mugs, plates and cutlery. Kit-bags,
webbing, rifles and discarded articles of clothing were strewn

about the place. The women serving food and drink from behind
the long counter looked resolutely cheerful.

John swung himself along to the men's lavatories and
washroom, propped his crutches against the wall and removed
his jacket and shirt. Three people were at the wash-basins, a
sailor and two soldiers.

John said to one of the soldiers, a gingery freckled boy of no
more than eighteen or nineteen, 'Borrow your soap, mate?'

The boy was peering into the blistered mirror as he shaved.
He pointed with his left index finger to the tablet of red carbolic
soap as he continued to shave. John took the soap and began to
wash. The boy finished scraping at his face and ran water on to
his razor.

He said, 'Want a lend of this?' He held the razor up.

John looked up from the basin and nodded. 'Thanks. Very
nice of you.' He took the razor.

'Better have this too,' Ginger said, transferring a shaving-
brush and small piece of shaving soap from his own basin ledge
to John's.

John thanked him again and began to lather his face. The
razor-blade had seen some service but it removed the worst of
the stubble and John felt better for having used it.

Ginger said, 'Got a towel?'

'No.'

'You can use this if you like. A bit wet though.'

The towel was very damp and rather grimy but it was better
than nothing.

'How you get that leg broke?' Ginger asked.

'Normandy.'

'Fuck that for a lark. I'm graded, thank Christ. B2. Asthma.'

'What mob are you in?'

'Service Corps. Drive a three-tonner.'

'You on leave?'

'No. On my way up to Scotland with a load. Got to be in
Lossiemouth tonight.'

When Ginger had stored away his shaving gear in his small
pack and left the washroom John did what he could to clean his

shirt and trouser-leg. Then he went back into the canteen and ordered a mug of tea and four slices of toast. The woman behind the counter told him to sit down at one of the tables and she would bring his breakfast to him. He was able to find a table to himself and he put his crutches on the floor at the side of his chair and sat down. The woman brought his tea and toast and told him to call out if he wanted more of anything. She looked at him with a moistly sweet, maternal smile which embarrassed but also gave him an oddly shameful feeling of pleasure. He ate his toast and drank the tea and realised that he was feeling drowsy. He had not had a very long sleep on the previous night and he had covered a considerable distance on his crutches in his search for the YMCA so it was not surprising that he should feel tired.

He had noticed that there was a rest-room next to the canteen so he left the table and found himself an armchair and a copy of a two-day-old newspaper and settled himself to read until sleep overcame him. He had not long to wait. The headlines on the front page spoke of a big advance by the British Second Army in Normandy. John began to read but almost at once his head fell forward, weighted with a suddenly overwhelming weariness, and he sank into sleep.

When he awoke the black-out screens had been taken down from the windows from which sunlight slanted and the blue tobacco-smoke and motes of dust swayed and danced in the golden shafts. He stayed where he was for a few minutes and then he heaved himself out of the chair, picked up his crutches and propelled himself back to the canteen where he ordered another mug of tea which again was brought to him by one of the attendants. He found a cigarette and lit it. The place was now much livelier than when he had first seen it in the early morning. There was a steady murmur of talk and frequent little explosions of laughter from groups of service men and, he noticed, service women. Although the numbers of men exceeded those of the women there were quite a few girls, predominantly in ATS and WAAF uniforms, with a couple of WREN ratings. Looking at these two girls in their jauntily tilted sailor hats John wondered if they were called Able Seawomen and it even occurred to him to ask them, but he was afraid of a rebuff so he sipped his tea, smoked his cigarette and glanced through the newspaper which he had brought with him from the rest-room.

The canteen clock told him it was now just after half-past ten, time for him to move. He stubbed out his cigarette, adjusted his glengarry, picked up his crutches and started for the exit. He emerged from the relative dimness of the entrance-hall on to the top of a small flight of steps leading to the street and he paused, accustoming his eyes to the brilliance of the sun. He was about to descend the steps when a female voice at his side said, 'Excuse me. Is that a Gordon Highlander's badge?'

A small ATS girl was looking up at him from beneath the peak of her cap. 'I hope you don't think I'm being forward,' she said in what he recognised as the soft accents of the North West Scottish Highlands. 'It's just that I'm feeling a wee bit homesick and I thought maybe you're a Scot and . . .' her voice was beginning to falter ' . . . maybe we could have a wee chat about . . .'

John interrupted, 'I'm sorry. You're out of luck. I'm a Sassenach . . . Well, not exactly. Scottish grandparents. My name's Scottish, too. Bain. But I'm a Highlander from Buckinghamshire I'm afraid.'

'Oh. I shouldn't have bothered you. I'm sorry. I hope you don't think . . .'

'Think what?'

She had a plump little face with very dark eyes which managed to look both shy and mischievous. 'I wasn't trying to – you know – get picked up.'

'Pity,' John said.

Her smile broadened. 'You don't mean that.'

Suddenly he knew that this was precisely what her intention had been. He felt flattered, a little excited yet obscurely suspicious.

He said, 'Where are you from?'

'Shall we go back in there and sit down?'

'No. I'd rather go somewhere else.'

'Okay. I was thinking of your leg.'

'I'm all right.' He started to negotiate the steps and she stayed by his side, one hand not touching but hovering close to his elbow, ready to offer support.

They reached the pavement and moved away.

She said, 'I'm from near Dingwall. My dad's got a wee farm. I've been up there on agricultural leave. Three weeks. I just got back yesterday.'

'And where you stationed?'

'Ack-ack site in the suburbs. Near a place called Levenshulme.'

'Sounds cushy. I mean no Jerry raids now.'

'Aye, I suppose you could call it that. But it's boring.'

'I'd rather be bored than bombed.'

They continued along the street for a few yards without speaking. Then she said, 'What happened to your leg?'

'I was shot on patrol in Normandy. Both legs. The other one wasn't so bad. Missed the bone. I was lucky.'

'And where are you in hospital?'

'Place called Winwick. Near Warrington.'

'And what's your name?'

'I told you, Bain.'

'Your first name I mean.'

'John.'

They went on a little further.

'Mine's Maxie. Maxie McCulloch.'

'I thought that was a man's name. There's a boxer. Two in fact. Maxie Rosenbloom and Max Baer. Both ex-world champions.'

'I'm not a boxer.' Another pause. 'It's short for Maxine.'

He said, 'It's nice. I like it.'

'Where are we going?'

'I don't know. Have you got a watch?'

'It's five to eleven.'

John stopped moving forward.

Maxie said, 'Are you tired? It must be hard work on those.'

'No.' He appeared to be in deep thought.

'What is it, John? What are you thinking about? Don't you want me with you?'

'Yes. Yes, of course I want you with me. I was just wondering. I wonder if . . . do you drink? Go into pubs?'

Her frown of concern was changed instantly into a wide and delighted smile. 'Not on my own I don't. But I'm not on my own, am I?'

'No. You're not. Shall we go and have a drink then?'

'I see no reason why not.'

They found a small pub in which they were the first customers of the day.

Maxie said she would like whisky if there was any to be had.

The landlord told them, without much enthusiasm, that they could have one whisky each and that was all.

John said, 'All right. Two whiskies and a pint of bitter.'

Maxie carried the drinks to the table which was farthest away from the bar. They sat down.

'You can have both scotches,' John said. 'I'd just as soon drink bitter.'

'Don't you like whisky?' Her eyes were wide with disbelief that such a thing could be.

'I like it well enough. I like most drinks. But I'm no judge. I'm just as happy with a pint.'

'But you do like whisky,' she insisted. 'You'd drink it if you could get it. I mean if I said I'd got a bottle of malt you'd like to share it with me, wouldn't you?'

'I certainly would.'

She grinned at him mischievous and with a kind of triumph. 'Well I *have* got a bottle of malt. I brought it back from leave. And another thing. I've got plenty of money. So you're not to spend any more.'

'Where's the catch?' John said. 'Come to that, where's the whisky?'

'The whisky's back at my billet. And there's no catch. I just like you.'

'You don't know me.'

'I know you enough.'

She had taken off her cap and she was smiling in her secretive, warm and excited way. Her hair was dark, cut quite short, and straight. She had very clearly-defined dark eyebrows. The whites of her eyes were very clear with a faint hint of blue. He thought she ought to look boyish but she did not. Despite the drab and bulky uniform, the woollen stockings and heavy shoes she was unambiguously feminine.

He said, 'This seems to be my lucky day.'

She shook her head. 'Mine.'

When they had finished their drinks they left the pub and went to another a few yards along the road but, when they were told that there was no whisky, they left and tried the next one where again they were able to obtain two whiskies and a pint of beer for which Maxie insisted on paying. After they had visited two more pubs and been served with what appeared to be the statutory two whiskies they found a restaurant where they ate fish and chips and then Maxie suggested that they should catch a bus to a quiet place she knew near her billet where John could wait while she fetched the whisky.

'What kind of quiet place?' he asked her.

'Wait and see.'

They sat on the lower deck of the bus, and held hands, neither speaking, until Maxie said that they had reached the stop where they were to dismount and they descended to the pavement which seemed to tingle with the heat of the sun.

'It's not far,' Maxie said. 'This way.'

The neighbourhood was a quiet one of semi-detached, prettily curtained respectability. They passed a small park with deserted tennis courts and a little farther on they turned off the main road and made their way along an almost rural lane with hawthorn bushes on either side. This ended at a wicket gate which opened on to the path leading to the porchway of a small church that presided over the stone tablets, crosses and flowers of the graveyard. They went through the gate and passed the church, leaving the pathway to reach a secluded place near the hedge at the far end of the little cemetery.

'Here we are,' she said. 'It's nice and peaceful. You can have a wee sleep while I'm away. I won't be long.'

'Doesn't anyone come here? Isn't there a keeper or a parson or something?'

'I've never seen anyone. And I come here a lot, just to be on my own. What's it matter, anyway? We're doing no harm. We're not disturbing anybody.'

He said, 'You will come back, won't you?'

She looked up at him with a kind of astonishment that he could doubt it and then smiled. 'Twenty minutes at the very most. So don't you go away.'

He watched her walk down the path to the gate. When she had disappeared he dropped his crutches and lowered himself to the cropped grass. The blue sky was cloudless. He could smell the sweetness of cut grass and flowers and, unseen, a bee hummed steadily, stopped, then started again. He looked at the large headstone at the side of which he was sitting and read the inscriptions: *Ada Messiter, beloved wife of Ernest Messiter, died 1906 aged 34 years.* Then below this in more recent lettering: *Ernest Messiter, died 1937, aged 72 years. Reunited in Heaven.*

He took off his glengarry and put it into his pocket then lay back on the grass and closed his eyes listening to the soft voices of summer. Already his meeting with Maxie was beginning to be tinged with a faint shading of unreality. The heat of the sun and perhaps the effects of the comparatively small amount of alcohol added to this feeling. He thought how amazingly lucky he had been, meeting her like that, and how delightful it was to be talking to a girl with no one else around to eavesdrop and to mock. It seemed like years since he had enjoyed the intimate company of a woman.

Suddenly he sat up. She was not going to come back. He was certain of it. For whatever reason she would not return, either because the little escapade had been a joke, or, more likely, since he could not really imagine her acting maliciously, she had been prevented by some kind of military necessity. He lit a cigarette and, leaning on one elbow, looked towards the gate. The heat became oppressive rather than caressing and the little graveyard a place, not of cherishable solitude but vacancy and loneliness, his only company the long sleepers under the ground. No, she would not come back. But he would wait and hope and pray that she would. He finished smoking his cigarette and stubbed out the butt into the ground. Then again he lay back and closed his eyes. A song-thrush sang from somewhere quite close, clean silvery phrases, repeated three times, and he was momentarily tempted to sit up and try to see the bird but he was beginning to feel drowsy and he did not stir.

He was almost asleep when the sound of footsteps on the gravel path brought full consciousness sharply back. He sat up and opened his eyes and saw Maxie leaving the path and coming across the grass towards him.

'I wasn't long, was I?' she said, as she drew close.

She unslung from her shoulder the respirator-haversack she was carrying and sat down by his side.

He said, 'It seemed like a year.'

She looked at her watch. 'Twenty-three minutes exactly. Did you miss me. Or was it this that you were missing.' She opened the haversack and brought out an unopened bottle of malt whisky.

'I missed you. I thought you wouldn't be coming back.'

'Och, you could never have thought that!' She sounded reproachful, not entirely believing him, wondering.

'I was beginning to think I'd dreamt it, meeting you in the YM, coming out here on the bus.'

'This is real enough,' she said, patting the bottle of whisky. She removed her cap and shook her head as if she were shaking long hair into place.

'Did you used to have long hair?' he asked her.

'Yes. Well, longer than this.'

'I'd like to see you in civvies.'

'I was never a great one for fashion,' she said. 'Working on the farm, I didn't have much call to wear smart things.' Then she added, 'That doesn't mean I wouldn't like nice clothes. For you. I'd like to dress up and look maybe a bit glamorous. But I'm too wee and too dumpy for glamour.'

'You look all right to me,' John said, 'more than all right,' and he meant it.

She opened the bottle and was holding it out to John. 'Have first droppie,' she said.

He took a small drink and felt the whisky slide down and explode in his midriff like a little incendiary bomb. He gave a small gasp and handed Maxie the bottle. 'It's good stuff. But I think we'd better go easy on it.'

She said, 'Here's tae us,' and took what seemed to John a longer pull from the bottle than the one he had taken.

'I was looking at that gravestone,' he said, 'while you were away. Wondering what they were like, Ada and Ernest. He lived on for twenty-one years after she died. Didn't remarry it seems.'

'Maybe nobody would have him.'

'Or maybe he was faithful to her memory.'

Maxie said, 'If he'd really loved her he wouldn't have gone on living all those years. D'you know that wee poem:

> *He first deceas'd; she for a little tried*
> *To live without him: lik'd it not, and died.*

Well, that's the way it ought to be. That's true love.'

'Who was that about?' John asked. 'I've read it somewhere but I can't remember who wrote it or who it's about.'

'It's by Sir Henry Wotton. I forget who the wife was. It's called On the death of Sir Somebody's wife. It's in the *Oxford Book of English Verse*.'

John said, 'Do you like poetry?'

'I love it. Always did, even when I was a wee lassie.'

There was a pause. Then she said, 'Do you?'

He nodded. 'I always did, too.'

Maxie sounded excited: 'What poets do you – no, let's have a wee dram first. Then we'll talk. Here you are.'

John took the bottle and drank a little more whisky. Then Maxie drank some before she went on: 'What are your favourites, John? Och I wish I'd thought. I've got a couple of poetry books back at the billet. I could've brought them. I keep them hidden from the other girls. They'd think I'm daft if they saw them. They think I'm a bit weird anyway.'

He said, 'I like Keats but I don't like Shelley much. Except for one or two things.'

'What about Auden? W H Auden. Do you like him?'

'I've only read a few things. I've liked what I've seen. I'm not . . .'

She waited a moment then said, 'What? What were you going to say?'

'I don't know. I'm so bloody ignorant.' He spoke with angry impatience. 'There's so much I want to read, want to know. I've wasted nearly four years. I'm just as ignorant and silly as I was when I joined up. Four years and I've hardly read anything. And now I've lost the knack. I *can't* read. I've tried. In hospital. I can't keep my mind on the words. I read whole pages and then find I haven't taken any of it in. The army's turned me into a bloody vegetable. No, an animal. Vegetables don't feel anything. Here . . . let's have another swig.'

She handed him the bottle and watched him drink. Then she took it back and drank some herself.

'Don't worry, John,' she said. 'The war's going to be over soon. You'll get back to civvy life. You'll be all right. You'll be able to make up for all that lost time. I know you will.'

He took off his jacket and folded it. 'Here. Lie down. Use this as a pillow. And take that bloody tunic off. You must be boiling.'

She unbuttoned the tunic and slipped it off. Then they lay back on the grass together, his left arm cradling her head which rested on his shoulder.

After a while she said, 'Do you get any pain with your legs?' Her voice sounded warm and drowsy.

'No. Well, a bit with the ankle. I have to do physiotherapy. Exercises and things. I've got what they called a dropped foot. I can't flex it upwards if you see what I mean. Just a stiff ankle really.'

'And what about the leg in plaster? When do they take it off? The plaster, I mean. Not the leg.'

'About another couple of weeks.'

Neither of them spoke for a minute or so. John could hear again the purposeful hum of the bee.

Then Maxie said, 'When do you have to be back at the hospital?'

'Any time. Tomorrow. The next day. Never.'

'What do you mean? There must be a time on your pass. What time do you have to be in at night?'

'I was supposed to be in at eight-thirty last night.'

'Last night!'

John felt her head jerk up. He pressed it back into the hollow of his shoulder. 'Don't worry, Maxie. There's nothing they can do. They can't send you to the glasshouse with your leg in plaster. The worst they can do is stop your pay and I'm well in credit at present. I'll go back when I'm ready.'

She moved closer. 'God, you're brave,' she said. 'I'd never have the nerve to treat the army like that.'

'I'm not brave. Anything but. It's just that I've got them where I want them.'

'Of course you're brave! Going over there on D-Day and fighting and getting wounded.'

He was tempted to tell her about Wadi Akarit; perhaps he would one day. But not now.

He said, 'What's it like in the ATS? What are the other girls like?'

'It's all right. I mean I've no right to complain. But I can't say I'm very happy. I got my call-up deferred for eighteen months on account of working on the land. Then my papers came and I was kind of curious. I'd never been further south than Edinburgh before and I thought it'd be a bit of an adventure. And this is where I was posted.'

'I'm glad you were. Or I wouldn't have met you.'

'I'll drink to that.'

They disentangled themselves and sat up. Then they each took a drink of whisky.

John thought, 'I wish this could go on for ever, just like this. The sun, the flowers, the whisky.' He said, 'This is perfection. Perfection.'

Maxie chuckled. 'I think the malt's beginning to work. Perfection!' She mimicked the emphatic plosive and slight slurring of the last syllable.

'No . . . Well, perhaps a little bit. It's not just the whisky though.' He put his arm round her shoulders and lay back again, drawing her down with him. 'Tell me more about the other girls. Have you got a special friend? What do you all talk about?'

'No, I've no real friend, but they're all right. Mostly quite nice but . . . I don't know. They treat me like a bairn or a wee puppy or something. As if I'm not grown-up like them.'

'So you get lonely.'

'Aye. I do a bit.'

He closed his eyes. Her hair was faintly scented. Her shoulder and upper arm felt firm and plump.

She said, 'I know why they treat me like that.'

'Like what? Who?'

'The other girls. I told you. They treat me like a baby.'

'Oh yes. Why?'

'Because I'm not the same as them.'

'No. I don't suppose you are.'

'I mean in a special way.'

He waited for her to elaborate.

She said, 'All they're interested in is men.'

'Go on.'

'It's all they talk about. Think about. Even the married ones. Two of them are married. In fact they're the worst. They all go out with men. GIs mostly. When they go to a dance it's just for one reason really.'

'And what's that?'

'You know.'

'No I don't. I've never been in the ATS. Go on. Tell me.'

'Of course you know. They go to get a man.'

'Well, that's what men go for. I mean to get a woman.'

'Did you?'

'Did I what?'

'Go to dances to get a woman?'

John gave a little snort of laughter. 'I'd be unlucky,' he said. 'I can't dance a step. I've no idea.'

Maxie said, 'I don't go to dances either.'

They lay in silence for a time. Then John said, 'Let's try another little swig of that nectar.'

When they had each taken a drink John lit a cigarette and they stayed sitting up.

Maxie said, 'I'm really trying to tell you something, John, but it's very hard to say.' Her head was turned slightly away from him and she was looking down at her left hand on the grass.

'Just tell me,' he said.

She stayed silent, her head still turned away from him.

He said, 'You mean you've got a bloke somewhere? You're engaged or married or something?'

She shook her head.

An idea which had been slowly taking shape in John's mind seemed to click into focus. 'You're not – I mean you don't prefer other women. Do you?'

She turned her face towards him and her eyes were puzzled. 'What do you mean?'

'Nothing. I just thought. Nothing really.'

She continued to look straight into his face and her expression took on a slightly challenging look. Then she said, 'I'm a virgin.' She continued to stare at him for three or four seconds, her face suddenly dark with embarrassment, and then she turned her head away again.

John just managed to suppress the impulse to grin. Then he said, 'You say that as if you're confessing a crime or something. It'll all right, Maxie. Good for you. I mean I'm glad. And you needn't worry about me. I'm not going to try to – well, I don't suppose I could even if I wanted to with this thing on my leg, not unless . . . but I don't. I mean I like you very much. I don't want to do anything you wouldn't want me to do.'

She was looking at him again, her face now pink. She seemed to take a deep breath and then, still staring solemnly into his face, she said, 'But I don't want to be a virgin.'

'Oh . . .' John found that he was now avoiding her gaze. 'Well, it's not all that difficult to not be one, if you see what I mean.'

She said, 'All the other girls, they've all done it. Lots of times, most of them. I'm the only one. I'm the only virgin. I hate it.

They all talk about what they've done and what their boy-friends do and they all know I don't know anything about it and they treat me like a child or an idiot or something and I hate it! I don't want to be a virgin. But I don't want to do what they do either. I don't want to go with GIs and sell myself for a pair of nylons and a few packs of Lucky Strikes. I wouldn't know how to go about it anyway. I don't talk like the other girls. Wisecracks and Yankee talk. I can't dance. I'm not glamorous. I don't use make-up, don't know how to. I'm not slim and tall and blonde and pretty. They wouldn't want me anyway.'

When she stopped speaking the silence seemed startled. John was disconcerted by the bitterness of her self-deprecation and unhappiness.

He said, 'Of course they would want you. Anybody'd want you. I can imagine the other girls. Lots of make-up and peroxide hair. They're cheap. I bet they're envious of your looks, Maxie. You don't need paint and powder. You've got a lovely complexion and lovely eyes. First thing I noticed as soon as I saw you. Don't you think of wasting yourself on a Yank. You're intelligent. You're good to be with. Anybody'd be happy – proud – to have you for a girl-friend.'

'Would *you* be happy?' she said. 'Would *you* be happy to have me as your girl-friend.'

'I certainly would,' he said without hesitation and, as he realised with a pinprick of surprise that the words were true, he repeated, 'I most certainly would.'

They looked into each other's eyes with wonder and discovery.

She said, 'I want to be. I want to be your girl.'

'Good. That's what I want, too.'

'You haven't kissed me yet.'

'No.'

They kissed. It was not a very satisfactory kiss. Their mouths did not seem to fit properly and her lips were dry and unyield-ing. He came up for air, then tried again. This time it was much better. The third kiss was better still: her mouth now seemed soft and pliant, it opened and their tongues investigated one another. They drew apart. They were both breathing more quickly and Maxie was smiling.

She said, 'I still don't want to be.'

'We can't do much about that just now.'

'Can we later? When it gets dark.'

'Yes. No. I don't know.'

'You're not a – can men be virgins? You're not one, are you?'

'No. No, I'm not.'

'Good. I'm glad. You'll be able to show me what to do, won't you?'

'I don't know. I mean it might be a bit difficult with this leg and you not being . . . well, you know. You not having . . . you being a virgin. And in any case I haven't got any, you know . . .'

'Any what?'

'Things. You know. To stop you having a baby.'

'Oh. I'd forgotten about that.'

'Course, there're ways of doing it without using anything but it's a bit risky.'

'I don't mind the risk.'

'No. Well . . . I tell you what. Let's have another drink and then see what happens.'

They had another drink and John observed that about half of the whisky had gone. He noticed, too, that his swigs were becoming deeper with each visit to the bottle. They talked for a time about their lives before the army had claimed them and Maxie was persistent in questioning him about his experiences with girls, which were considerably more limited than he allowed her to assume. He guessed that she interpreted his evasiveness as modesty or an honourable resolve to preserve the secrecy of his liaisons. The sun was by now declining behind the tips of the churchyard cypresses and the day-time sounds of birds and other creatures were fading to a few last, tired chirrups. They took another drink and then lay back with Maxie snuggling close and, between kisses, they talked about the past and about their hopes for the future and they exchanged compliments and endearments with the old, mad egoism and solipsism of early love and increasing drunkenness.

When the evening had faded to a smoky, cobwebby twilight and a few stars had appeared, bright pin-heads on the darkening blue of the sky, and the whisky bottle was almost empty, Maxie said, 'I know what we'll do, John. I've been thinking and I've got the answer. Listen. There're only three other girls in my hut. I'll go first and see if they're there. Even if there's just one of them I'll ask her to sleep in one of the other huts – there's plenty of spare beds – and if the others are out I'll leave a note pinned on the door telling them to go to Number Three Hut. They'll do it. That's one thing about them. They'll do anything for you. They'll never let anyone down.'

John said, 'Let's sleep here. I don't think I can stand up anyway. What's wrong with sleeping here. I've slept out often enough. Not like this though. Not like this . . . *I got my love to keep me warm . . .*' The last words were meant to be sung but they emerged as an unmelodious, muted bellow. The whisky had done its work. John felt decidedly drunk. Quite pleasantly so, but indubitably drunk.

Maxie said, 'I've got to go back. There's a roll-call at ten-fifteen. Once that's over nobody bothers you till reveille. We can sneak you out just before it gets light. I know a way in and out of the site where you don't have to go past the picket on the gate. It'll be all right, John.'

Despite his fuddled mind and warmly optimistic feelings of well-being John was not convinced of the practicability of Maxie's scheme, as far as he was able to understand it. The talk of pickets and roll-calls did not inspire confidence.

He said, 'Are you feeling drunk, Maxie?'

'No. Well, maybe a wee bit. But I know what I'm talking about. We'll be all right. I'll take you to the site and leave you outside while I go and check in and fix it so's we can have the hut to ourselves. Then I'll sneak out under the wire behind the cookhouse. That's where I'll leave you to wait for me. I won't leave you long. Fifteen minutes at the most. You'll be able to get under the wire. There's bags of room. Even with your leg.'

'Okay,' John said. 'You're the boss, boss. Let's just finish off this little drop in the bottom.'

They emptied the whisky bottle and Maxie went away to hide it in the hedge. When she came back John was almost asleep.

'Come on,' she said. 'We'd better be moving.'

★   ★   ★   ★   ★

It was not easy to get him upright. The first time they succeeded he fell over while Maxie was picking up his crutches. The fall did not hurt him. It seemed that he toppled over quite slowly, like a falling tower filmed in slow motion. Giggles rose in him like bubbles which had to be released and Maxie's initial concern turned quickly to impatience.

'Come on, John! Try again. Stop laughing. I mustn't be late for roll-call. Here, put your arm round my neck.'

She was, for such a small girl, amazingly strong and she managed to get him to stand again and this time she was able to see that he was propped up by his crutches.

'Take it steady,' she said as they began to move away, 'and hang on to me if you lose your balance. It's not very far.'

Once they were moving he made surprisingly rapid progress. Events and surroundings began to take on the dream-like quality that he recognised as peculiar to the Kingdom of the Drunk. A tree lurched into him and he begged it not to apologise. He looked up at the sky. The stars were brighter and more plentiful now. He could hear them very faintly sizzling. He could hear, too, Maxie's voice but he could not quite make out what she was saying and the sounds seemed to be coming from far below him.

'I am the King of Drunkdom,' he said. Then he went on: 'I've lost my Queen. Where's my little Highland Queen? Where are you, Maxie? *Listen to the stars. Listen. The bright boroughs, the quivering citadels. The grey lawns cold where quake – quaking –* sounds like an old duck, quake-quake! *– where quaking gold-dust – no, gold-dew – where quaking gold-dew lies.* Who the hell wrote that? Can't remember. You know who wrote that, Maxie? *The bright boroughs, the quivering citadels. Look at the stars!* That's how it begins.'

'John! John! Please! Listen to me! John!'

Her voice reached him then and he heard something of the anxious appeal in it. He stopped on the pavement and peered down and could see her pale face in the gloom looking up at him. He tried hard to concentrate on what she was saying.

'Listen John, we're getting close to the site. Keep quiet now, please. The chap on picket'll hear us if we make any noise now. Please, please keep quiet!'

'I shall be silent,' John said. 'Hush, hush. Silent as Ada Messiter in the deep dark grave.'

'Come on darling. And don't say anything at all. Please. The place where we go under the wire isn't far along here.'

'The wire? If you want to find the sergeant-major I know –'

'John! If you don't shut up I'll just leave you. I will. You're going to spoil everything. Please. Please darling. Don't make me leave you.'

'Right,' he said. 'Not another whisper. Lead on.'

Apart from one rather noisy belch and a single expletive when one of his crutches slipped and he almost fell John kept quiet until they reached the place in the perimeter fence where the lower strands of barbed wire were loose.

Maxie whispered, 'I'm going in now, John. You stay here. Sit down if you like. I don't think anyone'll come along here. It's too early for people who want to avoid the picket. Let me help you to sit down.' She took his crutches and hung on to his right arm while he lowered himself to the ground. They seemed to be in a fairly narrow lane.

He started to speak in a normally loud voice but immediately stopped and then whispered, 'Any traffic come along here?'

'No. It's a dead end. Just leads into a field. You'll be all right. But don't smoke. You can have a smoke once we get into the hut. Okay?'

'Sah!'

'All right, darling. I'll see you soon.'

She kissed him quickly on the lips and a few seconds later he heard her give a tiny grunt of exertion as she began her serpentine entry into the ack-ack site.

He wished that she had not mentioned smoking because her

warning had promptly caused him to yearn for the comfort of nicotine but he dismissed the temptation to light up and settled down to wait for Maxie's return. The journey from the churchyard had been timeless and almost effortless. His crutches had seemed to function independently and carry him swiftly and smoothly forward. They were lying on the ground by his side where Maxie had left them. He reached out and patted them. Good old crutches. They had served him well tonight.

He could not see the wire fence but he thought he could make out against the sky the outline of the roof of a building on what must be the other side of the wire. This was probably the cookhouse that Maxie had mentioned. He felt the ground around where he was sitting and decided that, from its unevenness, he was on some kind of cart-track. It would not be a very comfortable place to sleep if Maxie did not return. He had not fully understood her plans for the night. The idea of spending it in an ATS billet alone with her was very appealing but he was not convinced that to accomplish this would be nearly as simple as Maxie seemed to believe. Whatever happened he hoped she would not get into serious trouble. Did ATS girls do CB? Detention? No. There couldn't be a special glasshouse for girls, surely? No. It was unthinkable.

He lay back with clasped hands behind his head. The night was very still and dark and quite warm. He tried to remember who wrote the poem from which he had recited a few lines to Maxie: *Look at the stars* . . . something about *fire-folk sitting in the air* . . . he didn't like that at all. But there were other bits he liked very much. It was one of those poems with terrific lines in it but spoilt by a few feebler or silly ones. Or so it seemed to him . . . but he couldn't remember for the life of him who wrote the bloody thing. He closed his eyes and almost instantly felt himself drifting into unconsciousness. He did not try to resist but sank into the dark.

He was awakened by Maxie's whispered voice and warm breath close to his ear: 'Wake up John! Shush! Don't talk . . . Come on. We mustn't make any noise. You don't want to stand up. If you can manage to crawl on your side . . . do you think

you can? It's just over there, only two or three yards. I'll be able
to hold the bottom wire up while you go under it. Do you think
you can do it?'

John, half asleep and half drunk, allowed himself to be coaxed
and prodded towards the fence. It was not difficult to drag
himself along on his left side.

'Now, careful,' Maxie whispered. 'I'm holding the wire up.
Here, reach up here and feel it . . . You got it? You know you've
got to keep under that. Don't lift your head or you'll get an awful
scratch.'

John dragged himself forward. He knew that his head was
underneath the wire. He wriggled on. Then he heard rather than
felt the tearing of his jacket shoulder as it was caught on one of
the barbs. He tugged and it ripped again.

'I'm stuck,' he gasped. 'Hanging on the wire. Like the
sergeant-major.'

He heard Maxie, behind him, 'Shush! I'll get the coat free.
Don't move!'

Then he was aware of sounds other than those made by him
and Maxie: a rustling, an unidentifiable tampering with the
silence in the darkness in front of him, inside the site.

He began to whisper, 'Hey, Maxie! I can hear some–' when an
icy brilliance of dazzle slashed at his eyes and he heard a voice,
masculine and gruffly authoritative, 'What's this then! What the
hell do you think you're on?'

Both he and Maxie were revealed in the bright light of the
electric torch, he half-way through and she still on the other side
of the fence.

'Fucky Nell,' John said and closed his eyes.

He heard the man's voice say, 'You, McCulloch. Go and report
to Sergeant Weston, at the double. I'll look after your boy-
friend, here.'

The light went out and John was dragged violently through
into the compound with more tearing of his coat. He heard
Maxie wailing, 'Leave him alone! Don't hurt him! He's
wounded! Be careful! John! John! Don't let them hurt you! I'll
kill them if they do!'

There was another man with the torch-bearer and together they hauled John upright.

The second man spoke: 'Christ. Look at his fucking leg Sarge. It's in plaster.'

John said, 'Get my fucking crutches. They're there somewhere.'

Maxie was still imploring and threatening from the other side of the fence.

The sergeant said, 'Shut up and piss off, Maxie. Push them crutches through. Go on, that's an order.'

The torch had been switched on again and John saw Maxie pushing the crutches under the bottom wire where they were collected by the sergeant's subordinate. Then he saw that she was crawling under the wire in defiance of the sergeant's orders. He was given the crutches and the sergeant said, 'Let's get the bastard to the guardroom. Keep a hold of him. I'll shine the way: you bugger off, Maxie, and for Christ's sake stop that yelling.'

Then from the darkness beyond the beam of light another woman's voice, more mature and altogether unlike Maxie's shouted, 'Are you there, McCulloch? Sergeant! Is that silly girl with you?'

He called back, 'Yes, Sarnt Weston, she's here! Come and get her! I'm taking the bloke to the guardroom.'

By this time John was concentrating on handling his crutches and the clamour of voices had no meaning for him. Vaguely he was aware that Maxie's protestations had been silenced by the female sergeant, and he hoped, but not with much passion, that she would not be punished too severely. He was too fuddled and weary to feel strongly about anything except the prospect of peaceful silence and sleep.

When they reached the guardroom he saw that the sergeant was a red-faced man of about thirty with little blue eyes and pale vestigial lashes. He looked like a pork-butcher who had come to resemble the creatures he dismembered and purveyed. The other man was small and dark with a melancholy expression. The guardroom was in a Nissen hut and it was lit by two bare electric bulbs. It smelled of stale tobacco-smoke and sweaty socks. It seemed that Sergeant Weston, the ATS NCO, had taken Maxie away.

John's captor said, 'You can sit on that bench if you like.' He pointed to one of two benches on either side of a trestle table and when John had lowered himself on to the seat the sergeant took the bench opposite him, with the table between them, and said, 'Right, lad. Let's see what we can find out about you. Got your AB64?'

John's head was beginning to ache and his eyelids were drooping with tiredness. He felt in his pocket and found his paybook and dropped it on to the table. The short-period pass that he had been given two days earlier at the hospital was between its pages.

The sergeant found it, glanced at it and said, 'You're a bit overdue aren't you, lad?' Then he turned to the little dark man. 'Simpson. Nip over to Lieutenant Clough's quarters and tell him we've got a prisoner here. Bloke trying to get into the ATS billets. Drunk by the look of him. In hospital blues. Absent without leave from his hospital. What we got to do with him. Hand him over to the redcaps or what. You got that? Off you go then . . . Oh, and tell him the bloke's got one leg in plaster!'

The sergeant pushed the paybook and pass back across the table to John.

'It looks as if you've dropped a bollock, lad,' he said.

★   ★   ★   ★   ★

Later that night John was taken back to Winwick by two military policemen in a fifteen hundredweight truck, arriving at the hospital at about one o'clock in the morning. A sleepy and angry sergeant of hospital administration and discipline was summoned from his bed to accept delivery of the redcaps' prisoner and, after various formalities and exchanges of documents, John was at last sent to his ward and to his voluptuously welcome bed. The procedures of justice were delayed for a couple of days because the wound in John's left ankle was found to be infected and he had to have a small operation under anaesthetic for an incision to be made and the area sterilized. When he was brought before the hospital commandant, a pouchily dyspeptic major, he was reprimanded in a bored, mechanical way and awarded fourteen days' CB and a week's stoppage of pay. The sergeant whose sleep had been disturbed by John's arrival in the custody of the redcaps said, when they had left the major's office, 'You'll report to me at five-thirty this evening and I'll see you're kept busy with spud-bashing or some other interesting occupation. And don't be late.'

For the next two days John attended his physiotherapy sessions each morning and spent the rest of the day reading in the hospital grounds and reporting for fatigue-duties after tea. He thought much about the meeting with Maxie and that strange day in the churchyard which was already beginning to assume the gauzy, insubstantial quality of something delightful that had happened so long ago that only its essence and a few imprecise and disconnected images remained. He could remember her eyes, dark and luminous, smiling with an enchanting mixture of mischief, secrecy and innocence, her soft mouth, the generosity, the vulnerability. He remembered the purring heat of the sun, the singing of birds, the bee's hum among the flowers, the intermingling of summer's fragrances that could not be separated and exactly identified, all of which seemed to be properties of Maxie herself; but of the sudden end of their little idyll he could recall only the darkness split by the electric beam of the torch, the harsh voices of authority and his being bundled off to the guardroom where drunkenness and sleepiness had protected him from a full knowledge of his humiliation. He preferred not to think of this but to savour only the leisurely, fragrant lyric of that afternoon and early evening. The possibility of his seeing Maxie again would occasionally press itself forward to claim recognition and consideration but John managed to turn aside from it for he felt, at some shadowy level of consciousness, that a second meeting might break the spell and drain the remembered day of its magic. Or that is how he felt until Maxie's letter was delivered to him and then the change was immediate and extreme.

The post orderly had left the letter lying on his bed, where John found it when he returned to the ward from physiotherapy on a Wednesday morning. He picked up the envelope which was addressed to *Private John Bain, The Military Hospital, Winwick, Near Warrington, Cheshire* in a square, strong hand with no curlicues. He put the letter into his pocket and went out into the grounds to the garden seat on which he was accustomed to sit for his daily sessions of reading. He tore open the envelope and extracted the two sheets of pale blue note-paper and saw, as he had already guessed, that the letter was from Maxie. It was headed with her Army Number, and the address of the gun-site. She wrote:

> *Dear John,*
> *I have been dreadfully worried about you since you were taken away that terrible night and I feel responsible for what happened. It was all my fault giving you all that drink and then trying to take you back to the billet. I can't tell you how sorry I am and I only hope that I haven't forfeited any feeling you might have felt for me. I do hope they haven't punished you too severely. I remember you said you were not worried about what they could do to you for being absent without leave. Oh John darling, I think about you all the time and I pray that you are well and happy. I was not put on a charge, though Sergeant Weston, the ATS NCO in charge of us girls was very angry. She is not really as fierce as she pretends to be. All I worry about is you, and I hope and pray that we will meet again. I am free on Friday and at 6 pm I shall go to the YMCA where we first met. I shall wait there and pray that you can come and meet me. I hope this letter reaches you safely. I did not know your Army Number or Ward Number but I thought it should reach you if I put your name and regiment. I do hope it will. I shall be in the YM at 6 o'clock on Friday. Please, please, try to be there.*
>
> *Love,*
Maxie.
> *P.S. I miss you and love you. xxx*

This simple and not especially eloquent letter had a powerful and surprising effect on John. The mood of indolent dreaminess in which he had been bathing and mistily reconstructing and idealising that afternoon in the graveyard and the growing acceptance of its being irrecoverably in the past were exploded and at once replaced by a feverish need to see her. Friday was two whole days away and during that time she could easily meet another man who would have no scruples at all about changing her virgin state. It had been little short of a miracle that one of the very few, perhaps the only, virgin in the ATS, should offer her maidenhood to him and he, having failed, through over-indulgence in alcohol and feeble irresolution to accept the prize, could not reasonably expect a second chance. Yet that was exactly what he wanted and the thought of being forestalled by some smooth Brylcreem Boy or a GI with a Clark Gable moustache and a wallet that bulged almost as much as his trouser fly was almost too agonizing to contemplate. Maxie was his. She loved him. She had just declared it in her letter. He would write to her at once and tell her that he returned her love, that he, too, missed her and longed to be with her again, and he would see her in the Manchester YMCA at six o'clock on Friday evening. To hell with being on CB. He would be there to see his beloved and this time he would not drink himself silly. He would show her that her instinct in choosing him for her lover had not been misguided. He would be strong and wise and tender and ardent. So roll on Friday. He would be there. Nothing would stop him. Nothing.

The fine weather continued but the warmth of the evening was sultry and a little oppressive when, at ten minutes past six, John swung himself up the stone steps of the YMCA and went into the crowded canteen. He paused just inside and looked round, his eyes at once picking out the ATS uniforms at the tables or queueing in line at the food counter. But Maxie was not there. He looked again, more carefully and still failed to see her. This was something that he had not for a moment considered as a possibility. Disbelief was followed by a body-blow of disappointment and then, even more quickly, by outrage. The bitch! She had said that she would be here at six o'clock. She would wait for him. She loved him. He had defied the army to be here to meet her. He had broken out of being on CB and gone absent without leave. He had risked a great deal. And, incredibly, she had not turned up.

He could not have made a mistake about the hour or day. He had read the letter half a dozen times. All the same he decided to make sure, and he was reaching for the pocket of his new blues jacket which had been issued by the hospital stores in place of his old torn one, when a breathless voice behind him arrested his action. Maxie had arrived.

She said, 'Oh John, I'm awful sorry. Have you been waiting long? The bus was terribly late. I don't know why. I left in plenty of time. What did you think? Oh love, I'm glad you waited!'

He looked down at her, and relief came almost simultaneously with disappointment. She had obviously been running and her face was flustered and anxious, her service cap was slightly askew. But this was not the face that he had found so poignantly disturbing in his many reconstructions of that idyllic day they spent in the cemetery. It was as if those lovely features had been faithfully copied by a competent but uninspired artist who had been unable to capture the elusive magical quality of the original.

'Are you cross with me?' she said.

'What? . . . No. No, of course not. It's all right. What shall we do?'

She looked dumpier, too, he thought, almost a cartoonist's version of an ATS private, unshapely, unfeminine.

'Shall we have a cup of tea?'

He said, 'I'd rather have a drink.'

He knew that he sounded ungracious but Maxie did not seem to mind.

She said, 'Shall we go to that pub we went to the first time? The first one. Remember?'

'If you like.'

They left the YMCA and started off for the pub.

Maxie said, 'You *are* cross with me, aren't you, John? It really wasn't my fault.'

'No I'm not.' He heard the impatience in his own voice and felt a twinge of remorse. 'I'm sorry,' he said, 'I've been feeling a bit depressed. I'll be all right when we've had a drink.'

And this last casual statement proved to be prophetic though in fact it took three drinks before he began to feel positively cheerful and before he noticed that Maxie had lost her drab plainness and was looking much more like the vivacious and attractive girl he had been so eager to see again. The landlord said that he had no whisky but could offer Maxie sherry which she accepted. John drank bitter and they stayed there for a little over an hour before going to the next pub. Here they were permitted one whisky each, both of which Maxie drank while John kept to pints of bitter. By this time the initial feelings of disappointment with Maxie's appearance had completely dissolved though they had not been entirely forgotten. He looked now at her bright and gentle features, the confiding, warm smile and eyes whose candour and trust touched his heart and he felt angry with himself for having been, however briefly, blind to her exceptional qualities.

He said, 'You look lovely, Maxie.'

He must have spoken more loudly than he intended for an elderly civilian couple sitting at the next table looked across at them, the woman with an indulgent smile, the man with a small, lop-sided, smirk that could well have been sceptical.

Maxie shook her head. 'I know I'm not very pretty. And I look awful in uniform. But I can look all right when I'm dressed properly. Now you – well, you'd look handsome in any kind of clothes. Even that funny blue suit.'

John looked quickly to see if the civilians were listening but saw with relief that they appeared to have withdrawn their attention.

'Okay,' he said. 'We're a couple of smashers. What are we going to do about it?'

She had already told him that she had been given a pass until noon on the following day and, rather than cause her anxiety with the truth, he had said that he had not to be back at the hospital until the following evening.

'But I don't think we'll go back to my billet,' Maxie said.

John grinned. 'A pity to disappoint them. I hope they haven't gone to a lot of trouble . . . I tell you what we'll do. Find another pub and see if we can get you another scotch. Have another couple of drinks and then see what happens. How's that sound?'

'Sounds fine.'

He thought, as they left, that this was another wonderful thing about Maxie: she wasn't like most girls he had known who would firmly reject the suggestion of a pub-crawl as an evening's entertainment and expect to be taken to a cinema or theatre. Maxie was not only a lovely girl but as pleasant a drinking-companion as anyone he had known.

They found a pub which, though it was not serving scotch, was able to offer a couple of liqueur glasses of Drambuie and they secured seats in a quiet corner and John again drank beer while Maxie drank the liqueurs. The pub was beginning to become crowded and there were probably as many service men among the customers as civilians. Two American soldiers were standing at the bar and one of them, while paying, with occasional nods, formal attention to his companions' talk, was clearly more interested in Maxie towards whom his gaze continually strayed. John soon became aware of this and felt both angry and jealously concerned that Maxie might be covertly returning his glances.

When he could no longer conceal his annoyance and anxiety, he said, 'That Yank seems very interested in you, Maxie. The fat-faced one with all the medals. He must be very brave.'

Maxie glanced quickly across to the bar and when she saw the GI that John was talking about she gave a little snort of laughter and turned back to John. 'Maybe I remind him of his girl back home or something. Soft-looking laddie isn't he? You know about all those medals they wear? They get them for things like passing proficiency tests on the rifle-range, things like that. One of the girls told me her Yankee boy-friend had got the Purple

Heart – that's a medal for getting wounded – and he told her he'd got hit by a bit of a doodlebug when he was on leave in London. She said it was only a scratch really but he had to have a couple of stitches or something and that was enough. Wounded on active service.'

John said, 'That one'd better stop gawping at you or he'll be next for a Purple Heart.'

'Take no notice of him. I didn't know he was there till you mentioned him.'

John took a pull from his pint. Then he said, 'Yes. You're right. I shouldn't take any notice. He's the one to be jealous, not me.'

'Jealous!' Maxie's eyes were wide with amazement. 'You weren't jealous, were you? I can't believe it. As if I could see anybody else while I'm with you.'

John's reaction to this was a perplexing confusion of pleasure, embarrassment, and some guilt, as if he had deliberately set out to deceive her as to his true nature; and there was something else there too, a kind of fear for her vulnerability, a sudden passion of protectiveness.

He said, 'Let's get out when we've finished these, shall we?'

'Where to? Where shall we go?'

'I don't know . . . Are you sure you . . . you know . . . want to . . .'

'What? Want to what?'

'Well. You know. Stay out all night. With me.'

Her smile was joyous and without any hint of reservation or guile: 'Of course I do! I want that more than anything in the world. Why? Don't you want to? Don't you want me?' The smile dimmed, began to fade away.

John took her hand quickly in his, 'Yes. Of course I want you. I just can't believe my luck. You wanting me. And I'm a bit afraid you might have regrets. After.'

Her bright, trusting smile returned at once. 'Shall we try and get a room in a hotel?'

'We could, I suppose,' John said without total conviction.

'You seem doubtful.'

'It's just . . . well, one thing I've only got about four bob left.'

'That's all right. I've got nearly three pounds. It won't cost more than that, will it?'

'No. I don't know. I shouldn't think so. But we haven't got any luggage and both of us being in uniform, in the ranks. You know. Be different if I was a major or something. Or a Yank.'

Maxie clearly had not thought of this but she seemed quite undaunted: 'If we've got the money they can't turn us away. Just let them try!'

'Do you know any hotels in Manchester?'

'No. Well, I've seen that big one, the Piccadilly. It's not far from here.'

'Big one?' John said doubtfully. 'Don't you think we ought to try somewhere a bit smaller, out of the way? I mean we don't look exactly like members of the smart set, do we?'

'We look like what we are, members of His Majesty's Forces, and we've as much right as anybody to stay in whatever hotel we choose.'

John was impressed by her spirit though not wholly convinced that her confidence was justified but he did not want to cause her anxiety by confessing that he was absent without leave and would prefer to avoid making himself conspicuous by seeking accommodation in a place that would almost certainly be full of officers and even possibly be out-of-bounds to other-ranks.

He said, 'Okay, Maxie. Let's have another couple of drinks somewhere else and then we'll storm the Piccadilly Hotel.'

When they went out into the street the light had faded to a smoky blue, tinged strangely and faintly with crimson. The air was very still and warm.

'It's going to rain,' John said. 'A storm. I can feel it.'

'We'll go this way and we can turn up Portland Street. That leads to Piccadilly. There's bound to be a pub on the way.'

'Right.' John looked up into the sky and as he did so a single heavy drop of rain fell on to the bridge of his nose and a second later thunder growled in the distance, a dark stertorous rumbling like the noise made by a lion whose sleep has been disturbed. 'We'd better hurry.'

He swung along quickly on his crutches and Maxie trotted to keep up with him. The pavement was now blotched with huge rain-spots. Then the warm air seemed momentarily chilled as lightning flicked at the darkening sky and another louder, angrier roar of thunder sounded more closely and the pavements were suddenly drenched by sizzling, bouncing torrents of rain-drops.

It took Maxie and John only a couple of minutes to reach the shelter of another pub but it was quite long enough for them to receive a thorough soaking. Inside the bar they shook themselves and gasped from the exertion of their flight. The landlord was amused and sympathetic and when John asked if he had any whisky he said that, since it was for medicinal purposes, he could hardly refuse to supply it. The pub was small, a single bar with long seats against the wall and old marble-topped tables on legs of wrought-iron and there were only four other customers in the place, two middle-aged civilian couples. John and Maxie sat side by side, their backs to the wall, facing the bar. He took a sip of one of the whiskies but otherwise continued to drink beer.

Sitting at the table next to them the couple or, rather, the man, presumably the husband, immediately attracted John's attention. He nodded and smiled at John and Maxie as they sat down and there was something faintly disturbing and familiar about his appearance, the neat head set on a short powerful-looking neck, the flat, pugnacious face and the little blue eyes, challenging and sceptical, the sharp transformation of the smile from guarded belligerence to sudden warmth, merriment and mockery. His wife was thin, worn down to the bone by hard work and anxiety, yet her eyes possessed a kind of melancholy beauty.

The man, aware of John's scrutiny, returned his gaze, grinned and said, 'I see you're a cocky wee Gordon. I was in the fifty-first myself in the first lot, the war to end wars. Where d'ye come frae, son?'

The unmistakable accents of Glasgow at once made John aware of what it was that had seemed familiar about the man: in spite of the considerable difference in age he bore a distinct resemblance to Hughie Black.

John said, 'I'm afraid I'm from England, though I'm sort of half Scottish. My girl-friend's a Scot though. She's from Dingwall.'

'Is she so? Ah well, you canna help no' being Scotch.'

'My name's Bain,' John said. 'That's Scottish enough.' He was suddenly excited by the man's resemblance to Hughie which seemed to become more marked as they conversed and the wild and curiously thrilling notion that the man was related to his dead friend, was perhaps his father, began to grow strong.

'What are you doing down here in Lancashire?' Maxie asked.

The Glaswegian shrugged. 'Nae choice. We came down over ten years ago. I got a job here. I was lucky. I'd been on the b'reau for nearly three years. Hard days in Scotland then.'

They conversed for a little longer before John felt compelled to say, 'What's your name? I know somebody that looked very much like you. I wondered . . .'

'My name's Watson. Joe Watson.'

'Oh.'

'It doesna strike a bell?'

'No. No. The person I knew was called Black. Hughie Black. He was from Glasgow. Looked a bit like you. I thought . . . well, I suppose it's unlikely really. Too much of a coincidence.'

John and Maxie stayed in the pub for rather longer than they had intended for Joe Watson insisted on buying them drinks and John was just as insistent that they should have a drink with him. It was quite dark when they left the pub and the storm seemed to have passed over though rain still came down steadily and rivulets swirled and gurgled in the gutters.

'Be careful on the pavements,' Maxie said. 'They'll be slippery.'

John was silent as they started off towards Piccadilly.

'Are you all right, John?'

He said he was fine.

A little later she said, 'You're very quiet. You're sure you're feeling all right.'

'I'm okay.'

'Don't you want to go to the Piccadilly?'

'Yes. Of course . . . I was thinking about . . . that little bloke, Joe. He was very like somebody I know. It was a bit odd.'

'Yes. You said . . . John . . .'

'What?'

'Who was this person? What was his name? Hughie?'

'Hughie Black. Just a friend.'

'In the Gordons.'

'Yes.' Then he added. 'He was killed.' And, a few moments later, as if the words had suddenly surfaced from a source deep below the level of consciousness to find involuntary utterance, he said almost inaudibly and with a sad, helpless recognition of the truth, 'It should have been me.'

★　★　★　★　★

As John had feared, and to some degree *because* he feared, he and Maxie were not welcome at the reception desk of the Piccadilly Hotel. The receptionist who, as John afterwards remarked, looked more like a prison wardress, listened to his request for a double room with both suspicion and disdain though she did not at once refuse it. Instead she said, 'Just one moment please while I check,' and she went into what was evidently the manager's office to return after a few seconds. 'I'm sorry. There is no room available.'

John had already turned and was moving away when Maxie began her tirade: 'What do you mean not available? Do you mean to say all the rooms are booked? I don't believe it. Or do you mean not available to *us* because you think we're not high class enough. Well let me tell you something. We're as good and a damn sight better . . .'

By now John had paused and looking back he called, 'Come on Maxie! Don't make a scene. Let's go!'

But Maxie was only beginning to get into her stride: ' . . . My man's been wounded fighting for the likes of you and I gave up a comfortable home . . .'

'Maxie!' John rapped her name out. 'For Christ's sake come on. I'm going,' and he began to swing himself rapidly towards the exit.

He heard her call, 'Wait for me John! Just a minute!' but he took no notice and headed out into the dark rain-slick streets where he paused briefly before moving slowly away. Maxie's display of anger had surprised him and he felt admiration for her refusal to be intimidated, but the admiration was tainted with resentment and shame. He knew that he should have been the one to protest and her adopting the role that he should have played and adopting it with such conviction reduced him in his own estimation if not in hers.

He heard her calling his name, then the tapping of her footsteps as she ran to catch up with him.

'John, are you all right?' she said. 'I'm sorry I made a fuss like that but that woman made me feel mad. Snooty bitch. Of course they had rooms. I'm sure they did.'

He said, 'You shouldn't have kicked up a fuss,' but he knew that she had been right to protest and it was only timidity that had prevented him from supporting her.

Her silence, he guessed, was caused by surprise.

He went on, 'Look, Maxie. I should have told you. I haven't got a pass. What's more I was on CB so the last thing I want is trouble. You were quite right to give that woman a piece of your mind. I'd have done the same myself but I was afraid somebody might call the police or redcaps and then I'd be in trouble. Sorry I left you to it but that's the reason why.'

She touched his arm. 'Oh, I'm the one should be sorry. I shouldn't have lost my temper. I'm sorry, John.'

'No. You were quite right to tell her off. I just wanted you to understand why I left you to it. It was instinct really. Get the hell away from there before the coppers arrived.'

'You should have told me about not having a pass.'

'I didn't want you to worry.'

'Oh well. Nobody seems to be chasing us. It looks as if we've got away with it. So what shall we do now?'

'I don't know. Get out of the rain as soon as we can. Maybe look for one of those little private hotels. You know the kind. What do they call them? Commercial or temperance hotels or something. And talking of temperance, what time is it? Are the pubs shut yet?'

'It's just past ten. I think we've had it.'

John grunted.

They walked on in silence for some minutes before she said, 'You're disappointed, aren't you, John?'

'What? The pubs being shut?' He knew that she did not mean this so he added, 'It's just bad luck. The storm and . . . well, the hotel being like that and everything.'

'Do you really want to find somewhere? For us to stay together?'

'Yes.' He knew that he sounded less than enthusiastic. 'Of course I do. Sooner the better.'

She said, 'We'll have to get further away from the city. If we carry along here I don't think we have to go far before we get to a more residential part.'

The drink John had swallowed had created a slight sensation of blurring and had made him feel more tired than exhilarated. By now they were both sodden by the rain. He tried, not entirely successfully, to extinguish the treacherous desire for the comfort of his hospital bed.

Guilt caused him to affect a cheery note: 'Don't worry, Maxie. We'll find somewhere soon.'

They moved along the blacked-out pavements as the rain continued to fall.

He said, 'Oh well. We can't get any wetter now. Let it come down.'

'I'm sorry.'

'For Christ's sake, it's not your fault!' he heard his own anger and impatience. Then he said, 'Listen, Maxie. Why don't you go back to your billet? It doesn't look as if we're going to find anywhere and if we did they probably wouldn't have us, the state we're in and no luggage and everything. You go back to the billet and I'll go back to the YM. I'll be able to get dried out there.'

She stopped walking and he, too, halted. He could see the whiteness of her raised face and just make out the dark glitter of her eyes.

She said, 'John . . . you . . . do you want to get rid of me?'

Tears were not far away, he thought; pain, but not reproach.

'No. Of course I don't. It's not that, Maxie. I just thought it'd be best for you. Better than plodding all round Manchester in the rain. Of course I don't want to get rid of you!'

'But I don't mind the rain! I don't care what happens as long as we're together!'

They stood still in the weeping darkness, she peering up at him and he looking down.

She said, 'You haven't kissed me yet.'

He bent, tilting his head to one side to avoid the peak of her cap, and she reached up to clasp her hands about his neck and she stood on tip-toes as she drew his face down to hers. John found the kiss wet and uncomfortable but after it he felt, rather to his surprise, more cheerful and almost careless of the malice of the rain.

'That's better,' Maxie said. 'Come on. Let's find somewhere to stay.'

They had moved on for only a few minutes when they reached an intersecting street on their left and here John suddenly stopped and said, 'Wait! Listen!' and they both stood still.

Maxie began to speak but he shushed her to silence, at the same time seizing one of her hands and holding it tight. 'Listen!' he whispered again.

Then the sound coming from the side-street became clearly identifiable: what John had heard like a ghostly echo of his own progress along the pavement was the rhythmic tap and following thud of someone moving on crutches. They waited another few seconds and then they could see in silhouette the pyramidic shape of someone on crutches drawing close. The figure stopped and John and Maxie could make out the head jutting forward to peer at them. Then a man's voice spoke: 'Hello. What you two doing in rain? You must be soaking wet.' It was a thin, unused voice, reaching uncertainly for a kind of gentility.

John answered, 'We're looking for somewhere to stay for the night. Do you know of any little hotels close by?'

'Somewhere to spend night, eh? You'll not find any hotels

round here lad. I see you're like me. On crutches. How did that happen then? You're a soldier aren't you? You been wounded?'

'That's right. Normandy.'

'What about young lady? Who's she then?'

'I'm his wife,' Maxie said, 'if it's any business of yours.'

The man's tone changed, became conciliatory, almost obsequious: 'I didn't mean no offence, love. I just wondered what two young people in forces is doing wandering about in rain at this time of night. Maybe I can help you.'

John could just make out the pale blur of the man's face under the brim of a trilby hat but could see nothing more than the dark smudges of eyes and mouth.

'How?' he said. 'How can you help us?'

There was what seemed like a long and calculated pause before the man answered: 'You sound like nice respectable young people. I thought maybe I could offer you shelter. In my humble abode. You *are* married, you say?'

Maxie said, 'I told you quite distinctly we're married.'

John thought she sounded ungratefully sharp, even aggressive. He said, 'It's very kind of you to suggest it. But I think we'll carry on and look for a hotel.'

'But you'll catch your death. You want to get them wet things off quick or you'll both be getting pneumonia. I don't live more'n a few yards away, just back there, where I come from. Come on. I'll fix you both up nice and comfy for the night. How about that then?' He suddenly sounded quite anxious for them to accept his invitation.

John said, 'Well . . . Maxie? What do you think?' He felt embarrassed to be so hesitant in the face of the man's generosity.

Maxie said, 'Whatever you say, darling.'

John thought that it would be foolish to refuse the offer of accommodation for the night yet an unfocused but quite positive uneasiness persisted. But he had to give an answer quickly so he said, 'Okay. Thank you very much. It's very nice of you.'

Maxie said, 'Yes. Thank you.' She sounded rather grudging.

'That's champion,' the man said. 'Come on then. Keep close behind. You can't see a bloomin' thing in this black-out.'

John said, as he followed, 'Haven't we stopped you going somewhere? Where were you off to when we met you?'

'Not important, lad. Post a letter. It'll do just as well in morning. I wouldn't have gone out if I'd known it was still raining as heavy as this.'

As far as John could make out they were in a street of small terrace houses, and after they had covered about thirty yards the man stopped and said, 'Here we are then. Home sweet home.' There was a rattle and click of key in lock. 'Wait there a tick while I put light on.'

Maxie and John stood just outside the open door. Then the light of a gas mantle filled the small front room and their host was beckoning them in. They went into the little parlour and squinted in the sudden brightness as the man shut and locked the door.

He was of rather less than medium height, aged about fifty and, as Maxie and John saw when he took off his hat, almost completely bald. His face was bony and pale, with a thin almost colourless mouth, but the eyes were startling. They were bloodshot, so much so that it seemed that all the colouring missing from his other features had concentrated itself in those painfully inflamed eyes. He wore a dark suit, that looked old but carefully looked after, a starched shirt collar that was more yellow than the white it had once been, and a thin black tie with a tie-pin. His left leg had been amputated just above the knee. John was impressed by the speed and ease with which he moved around the room on his crutches. The room was furnished with a shiny black horsehair sofa and one armchair, a sideboard on which stood a small bronze Cupid and two framed photographs of a stern-looking man with mutton-chop whiskers and a woman who, though whiskerless, looked almost as forbidding and masculine as her partner. The only decoration on the walls was a large and elaborate framed scroll proclaiming that Herbert James Spicer was a member of The Royal and Ancient Order of Buffaloes.

'My father was a buffalo,' the one-legged man said, seeing that John was looking at the scroll.

Maxie who evidently had not noticed the framed certificate gave a little gasp of amazement. 'He was . . . *what?*'

'Ancient Order of the Buffaloes. He was very high up in it. Teetotaller and non-smoker all his life. Like me . . . Now, you'd best get them wet things off. I'll show you where you're going to sleep. The good room. Where my mam and dad slept. Where I was born. Just a tick while I get a candle. The mantle's gone in the bedroom but you'll manage, I expect, with a candle.'

He went into the next room which John knew, from the type of house, was the kitchen and came back with a lighted candle fixed into a holder with an enamel dish to catch any overflow of melted wax.

'Follow me then,' and, as they went through the kitchen to the staircase, he said, 'My name's Harold by the way.'

Maxie said, 'We're John and Maxie. He's John and I'm Maxie.'

'Maxie?'

'That's right.'

'Funny name for a girl.'

'I know. I didn't choose it.'

They followed Harold up the narrow staircase and into the front bedroom where they saw in the nervous yellow light of the candle a large brass-railed bed. The room smelled of age and dust and dead nightmares. The window was covered by a black-out screen. Harold put the candle down on a marble-topped wash-stand which held a large china bowl and jug.

'I'll go and find you a towel so's you can dry yourselves.'

He swung nimbly away on his crutches and came back with a rough but perfectly clean towel which he threw on to the bed.

'Now you get them wet things off and give yourselves a good rub and get into bed. I'll go and make a nice cup of cocoa.'

'No,' John said. 'No thanks. Not for us. Thanks all the same. We don't drink cocoa.'

'It'll do you good. I won't be a tick.' He swung out of the room and they heard him descending the stairs.

'He's nifty on those crutches,' John said in a whisper as he closed the bedroom door.

'Yes. And his dad was a buffalo. I wonder what his mother was!'

They both began to giggle.

'Christ! We must stop!' John gasped. He picked up the towel. 'Come on, Maxie. Get your clothes off and dry yourself. And stop laughing.'

She took the towel and removed her service cap and rubbed at her hair. 'I'm not going to take off anything more than my cap while Harold's around.'

'What do you make of him?' They were both whispering.

'I don't know. A bit peculiar. Those eyes!'

John pulled back the eiderdown and the top sheet. 'The bed looks clean enough.'

'Yes . . . I can hear him moving about down there.'

'I think we're going to get cocoa whether we like it or not.'

John was right. They heard Harold on the stairs and the small rattle of cups and saucers. There was a tap on the door and John opened it. Harold had somehow managed to climb the stairs with the help of only one crutch while carrying a tray bearing two cups of cocoa.

John took the tray from him and put it on the wash-stand. 'It's very kind of you, Harold. You shouldn't have bothered. We'll be fine now thank you.'

But Harold was inside the bedroom. 'Not in bed yet? Come on. We don't want you getting poorly do we.'

'Right . . . Well, thanks again,' John said, waiting for Harold to leave.

But Harold had no intention of leaving. He said, 'Hurry up and get into bed before your cocoa gets cold.'

Maxie said, 'I'm not getting undressed while you're in the room. So do you mind leaving?'

Harold stayed where he was. 'You're not shy, are you? Don't mind me, love. I'm just a harmless cripple. I'm only concerned about your comfort. I'll just see you both tucked in and then I'll say goodnight.'

'Tell him to go, John,' Maxie said. 'He might take some notice of you.'

John could not summon up real anger. Harold, after all, had brought them in from the rain and offered them hospitality. He said, 'Come on, Harold. Off you go. We're all right now. Or we will be when we can get our clothes off and get to bed. So you go now and we'll see you in the morning. Okay?'

John took him by the elbow and turned him towards the open door.

Harold said, 'All right. I just wanted to make sure you was comfortable. That's all. So sleep well.'

John and Maxie heard him descend the stairs to the kitchen.

'What's he up to now I wonder,' John said.

'I wish he'd go to bed.'

'Perhaps he's sleeping downstairs. Do you think he usually sleeps in here?'

'I hope not,' Maxie said, 'I don't fancy sleeping in a bed he's been in somehow. He looks like an undertaker, don't you think?'

'More like somebody who keeps the undertaker in business.'

Maxie's eyes widened. 'You mean . . .?'

'Well he does doesn't he? Look like a murderer I mean. I imagine Crippen looked something like Harold.'

'Oh John! You don't really think so do you? You don't really think he'd murder us?'

'Maybe not. But I don't think we'll drink that cocoa.'

They began to giggle again. Then John said, 'To hell with Harold. I'm going to bed,' and placed his crutches against the wall and began to undress. He had taken off his jacket and shirt and was sitting on the bed and bending forward to untie the laces of his left boot when they heard the sound of Harold ascending the stairs again. Maxie, who had removed her tunic and was standing at the foot of the bed, whispered, 'It's him! He's coming up here again!'

They both waited in silence as the sound of Harold's progress came closer, reached the landing outside the bedroom, paused for a moment and then went on a couple of paces. A door opened and shut. He had gone into the other bedroom.

'He's gone to bed,' John whispered. 'We'll be all right now,' and he finished undressing, pulled the upper bedclothes farther down so that he could heave his plastered leg between the sheets and settled himself in the bed to wait for Maxie to join him.

She stayed where she was and made no move to continue undressing. Her short hair was disordered from the towelling and it seemed that she was crowned with a coronal of dark leaves or petals.

John said, 'You look like a chrysanthemum. Hurry up and get into bed.'

'You don't think he'll come in again, do you?'

'No. Why should he?'

She took off her khaki tie, but that was all, and John suddenly suspected that she was indeed shy.

He said, 'Would you like me to blow the candle out?'

'No!' she said quickly and emphatically. 'No. Let's keep it on.'

'I won't look if you feel shy. I'll close my eyes. Promise.'

'It's not that . . . well, it is in a way. I'm afraid you're going to be disappointed.'

'I won't be. Come on sweetheart. Don't be shy and don't be afraid. There's no need to be. I promise I won't do anything to hurt you or anything you don't want me to do. So come on.'

Reassured, Maxie undressed and hung her clothes and his, which he had left in a pile on the floor, over the bedrail and then she came towards him her arms crossed over her breasts and, in the soft light of the candle, her skin looked white and flawless and he saw the startling blackness of her pubic hair, a neat triangle like a Van Dyck beard. She climbed into bed and he put his arms about her and held her tightly to him and kissed the top of her still damp head. Her skin felt smooth, like cool velvet. 'Christ, Maxie,' he said, 'you're beautiful!'

Muffled against his chest, her voice was just audible: 'So are you.'

They kissed.

'Here,' he whispered, 'give me your hand . . . here . . . yes . . . that's right . . . that's . . . Oh my God, that's lovely! Oh darling! Oh love! . . .'

There was a knocking on the door and they jerked away from each other.

John sat up. 'What do you want?' he called.

The door opened and Harold came in on his one crutch, carrying a large chamber-pot. He was still fully dressed.

'I suddenly thought,' he said. 'You might need this in night. One or other of you. You'd be in a right pickle, wouldn't you?'

Maxie's head had disappeared beneath the bedclothes from where John heard a muffled exclamation. He said, 'All right. Put it down. And for Christ's sake go to bed and leave us alone.'

'There's no need to take the Lord's name in vain,' Harold reproached. 'I was only thinking of your comfort.'

'Yes. Well, thank you. But please. Let's all settle down for the night. Okay?'

'Shall I put it under bed?'

'Just put it on the floor. There. Anywhere. And goodnight.'

'I'd best put it under bed then you'll know where to find it if you have to get up in night.' He approached Maxie's side of the bed and bent down to push the chamber-pot into place. 'Is little lady all right?' he said as he slowly straightened up.

'She's fine.'

'Good. That's good. You'll be nice and comfy now. I'd best be off to my own bed. So sleep tight.'

'Goodnight,' John said.

Harold paused at the door for a last long look at the little hump under the eiderdown that was all he could see of Maxie. His thin, almost lipless, mouth was fixed in a kind of smile but those awful red eyes showed only a mournful hunger and reproach. 'You never drank your cocoa,' he said. Then he swung himself out of the room and closed the door quite gently. A few seconds later John heard the sound of the other bedroom door open and close.

He said, 'You can come out now, Maxie.'

Her head emerged, cheeks flushed and eyes bright with amazement, indignation and incredulous laughter. 'What will he think of next!'

'Let's hope he's run out of ideas. I wonder if I could block the door somehow, just in case.'

'I shouldn't think he'd have the nerve to come in again.'

John was not sure about that but he did not voice his doubts. 'Shall I keep the candle burning or blow it out?'

'Keep it going for the time being. I want to be able to see you.'

They kissed again. Then he pulled the bed-clothes down so that he could look at her nakedness. She seemed to have lost all shyness.

He said, 'Come here darling. Here, on top of me . . . No . . . Like this . . . that's better . . . that's marvellous . . . you've got lovely breasts . . .'

She was sitting astride him but he was not inside her. He lifted his face from her breasts and she brought her lips down to his and they stayed like that for some seconds in a long, luxurious exploratory kiss. When she lifted her face from his she shifted back a little and looked down.

'It's . . . so big!' Her voice sounded awed rather than alarmed. 'Oh darling, will it . . .? I don't think it'll go in me . . . will it?'

John sounded a little breathless. 'I hope so . . . we'll have to take it easy . . . oh sweetheart . . . here, let me feel you . . . ooh . . . ah, yes . . . oh lovely . . . Yes! You hold me . . . like that . . . oh yes, like that . . . Oh God . . .!'

Maxie's voice joined his in a small sonata of cries and answering cries, intermingling moans and gasps and sighs.

Then John seized both of her busy hands and panted, 'Just a minute . . .! Let me get my breath . . . Now darling. . . ease up . . . that's it, like that . . . go very gently and see if you can . . . yes, that's right, put it there. Work it very gently inside if you can . . . no hurry . . . oh my God . . ! Oh dear! Oh Maxie, love, I can't stop it! I'm coming!'

His shout of ecstatic, despairing release was joined by quite a shrill squeak from Maxie.

'What . . .? Oh love! Oh darling! Why? . . . What's happen– Oh John it's all over me . . . oh . . . it's lovely . . . oh darling what have we done?'

Neither of them saw or heard the door open. The first inkling

John had of Harold's presence was when he heard a kind of
throaty grunt that sounded like a cruel parody of their love cries
and he sat up and looked over Maxie's shoulder to see Harold,
still dressed except that he had removed his collar and tie,
standing just inside the doorway. John pulled Maxie off him and
hauled the bedclothes up to cover them both. 'What the bloody
hell do you want?' he roared.

Maxie again disappeared beneath the blankets.

'I heard a funny noise. A shout. I thought something had
happened. One of you was ill or something. How was I to know?
You might have been fighting. All that noise. It's my house after
all.'

'Get the fuck out of this room,' John shouted, 'or I'll pull your
good leg off!'

'Now just a minute. What right have you got –'

'Out! I'm not kidding. I'll do you if you come in here again. I
don't give a fuck whose house it is. Get out and stay out. We'll
leave as soon as it gets light so just you keep out of here till then.
You understand?'

'I've a good mind to get the police, threatening me like –'

'Piss off! Go on. Out!' John started to heave himself out of bed
and Harold, at last persuaded that he was in real danger, went
out of the room, shouting as he closed the door, 'You're not
married neither! You can't fool me!'

John waited until he heard Harold's bedroom door close
before he lay back and drew Maxie from her hiding place.

She sounded frightened. 'What's he doing, John? Why does he
keep coming in here? He couldn't have thought we were
fighting. What does he want?'

'He's a dirty old man. A Peeping Tom. If he comes in again
I'll put one on his whiskers, cripple or not.'

'Oh no, you mustn't hit him, John. I don't want you to. Please.
Will you promise you won't hurt him?'

'Yes, I promise. I don't suppose I would anyway. Let's hope
I've scared him off for the rest of the night.'

They lay close in each other's arms and kissed a few times
before Maxie whispered: 'I'm still a virgin, darling.'

'You're a lovely virgin.'

'But not a happy one.' Then she quickly added, 'I don't mean I'm not happy, like this, with you. 'Course I'm happy. But I won't be truly and completely happy till I'm not a virgin any more.'

As she was speaking John felt drowsiness become suddenly importunate, its soft pressure on eyelids, its warmth blurring Maxie's voice.

He mumbled, 'Let's sleep for a while . . . a couple of hours . . . I'm so tired, suddenly so tired . . . we'll go to sleep . . . and . . . when we wake up . . . we'll . . . make love . . . love . . .'

If Maxie was disappointed she showed no evidence of her feelings. He was aware, briefly, of her kissing him on the mouth and nose and chin and murmuring endearments as he let himself be drawn down into the insensible dark.

His awakening was like a small explosion of consciousness, a bewildering sense of dislocation and echoes of fear, lasting for only a mote of time, and then he realised that Maxie was sitting upright with the bedclothes clutched to her chin and that it was her cry of alarm which had awakened him. The candle was still alight but was guttering very low in its holder. Shadows on the wall and ceiling rippled and swayed and there was another, motionless shadow at the foot of the bed. Then he saw that this was not a shadow. Harold was back in the room. John struggled upright at Maxie's side.

She said, 'John! Thank God you're awake! It's him! Tell him to go away! Please! Please! Go away!'

John could now see that Harold was still wearing his dark suit and was propped up on the single crutch.

'What the . . . what do you think you're doing now?' John demanded. 'Get out of here!'

Harold remained silent and he did not move.

'You'd better get out or I'll throw you out.'

Then Harold said, 'I'm not doing any harm. It's my house, I can go in any room I like.'

'You're not staying in here.' John started to move out of the bed.

Harold stayed where he was.

Maxie said, 'Don't hurt him, John! Please! Don't hit him.'

John was now sitting on the edge of the bed. He said, 'What time is it?'

Maxie peered closely at her wrist-watch in the tired light of the expiring candle. 'It's . . . I think it's . . . yes. Twenty to four.'

'Okay. I think we should go. Old Harold here's not going to leave us in peace so we'll get moving. What do you think?' He reached for his clothes from the end of the bed and began to dress.

Harold said, 'You're ungrateful. Both of you. I brought you in out of the rain. I give you the best bedroom. You never even drunk the cocoa. The waste. In wartime too.'

John pulled on his trousers and then pushed himself upright. 'Out you go, Harold. We're going to get dressed. So piss off for a couple of minutes and then you've got the whole house to yourself. Go on. Outside.'

Harold did not move.

John picked up his crutches and swung himself to the foot of the bed. 'Come on, Harold. Give us five minutes. You can't stay here. Just five minutes and it's all yours.'

'You can't talk to me like that. Giving me orders. In my own house.'

John was reminded of a dog that cannot be coaxed away from an especially compelling scent but can be removed only by force. He reached out with his left hand and pushed his host towards the door. Harold did not move but remained staring at Maxie's head which was all that could be seen of her. John pushed again, with more vigour, and Harold almost lost his balance but, in regaining complete control of it, he moved back towards the door. John followed him and, for a moment, he thought that Harold was going to raise his crutch and use it as a weapon but then the older man turned away and with lowered head and some incomprehensible muttering went out of the bedroom and again there seemed to be something canine about his cowed and resentful retreat.

'Come on, Maxie,' John said, throwing her clothes to her. 'Get up and get dressed. I'll stay near the door in case he tries to come in again. You all right?'

'I'll be all right when we're out of here.' She threw back the bed coverings and began quickly to get dressed.

John waited until she had on enough clothing to cool the interest of the voyeur before he finished dressing himself.

'You take the candle,' he said, 'what there is left of it. It'll just about see us down the stairs.'

She led the way out of the bedroom, clutching the candle-holder in which little more of the candle remained than the still lighted wick and a dish of melted tallow. The light it afforded was timid and faltering and John could smell the religious sweetness of its dying. They were half way down the stairs when the small petal of flame was extinguished.

John heard Maxie from the darkness in front and below him: 'Are you all right, John? Can you manage?'

He said, 'Stop a second. I'll get my matches . . . Here . . . Can you feel them?' He held the box at arm's length, downwards, in front of him. 'Can you take them,' he said, shaking the box so that she would hear the rattle of the matches.

He knew that she was reaching into the darkness. He rattled the matchbox again and felt her touch, first on his wrist and then moving to fumble for and finally grasp the box. Another few moments of dark immobility and then the scratch of the match and the sudden spurt of the tiny flame and they were able to move down a couple of steps before the darkness surged back. Maxie struck another match and they moved downwards again, this time reaching the foot of the stairs leading to the kitchen before the flame was again extinguished.

He said, 'Good girl. We'll be out of here in a second.'

Then, from the darkness behind them at the top of the stairs, they heard Harold's voice, raised to a thin whine, which carried more sorrow than anger, ushering them from his house with valedictory objurgations: 'Good riddance, that's what I say! Ungrateful, wicked, dirty pair that you are! I know you're not married! I know what you've been up to! I know! Sinful, that's what I call it. God's been watching you! Don't think you'll get away with it! God sees everything! You'll be punished! Just you wait and see . . .'

By this time John and Maxie had reached the front door. The key was in the lock. Maxie turned it and a moment later they were out of the house and moving away along the dark, faintly gleaming street, still wet although the rain had stopped. When they reached the turning on to the main road they stopped.

Maxie said, 'Oh dear. It was terrible, wasn't it?'

He drew her close to him. 'Never mind. We're all right now.' Then he said, 'We had our moments, didn't we?'

'But . . . I was no good. I couldn't do it.'

'You were lovely. Anyway, how the hell could we make love with old Harold hopping in and out of the bedroom all the time.'

'And God watching us.'

'The great Peeping Tom in the sky.'

They began to laugh.

'That's why he's got those red eyes,' Maxie said.

'Who? God?'

'No. Harold. Peeping through draughty keyholes.'

'Come on,' John said. 'We'll go to the YM. It's open all night. We'll get a cup of tea and something to eat. Thank God it's stopped raining.'

The journey to the YMCA took almost an hour and when they arrived they found the canteen crowded with the usual weary itinerant servicemen and a few members of the women's forces. They found seats at a table which they had to share with two aircraftsmen and Maxie went to the counter and returned with two mugs of tea and four slices of toast. There was a low buzz and mutter of talk in the smoky room but many of its occupants were either asleep or too tired to say very much. The airmen, who were waiting for a train to London, soon left and Maxie and John had the table to themselves. They drank their tea and ate some of the toast and John lit a cigarette.

Maxie yawned. 'God, I'm tired,' she said.

'There might be a couple of armchairs in the rest-room. Shall we go and look?'

'No. You stay here. We don't want to lose these seats if there aren't any armchairs. I'll go and look.'

She went away and came back shaking her head.

'It's crowded. There're even some sailors sleeping on the floor.'

John cleared a space on the table and said, 'Rest your head on your arms on the table there. You might be able to get a bit of sleep.'

She took off her cap and did as John suggested, folding her arms and resting her head on the rough pillow they afforded. Once she looked up at him with a drowsy smile and then her head fell back on to her cradling arms and she slept. He looked at her as he smoked his cigarette and suddenly he was aware of a brief, breath-catching surge of tenderness. The small, sleeping dark head seemed both vulnerable and trusting and he reflected, with gratitude, on his great good fortune in having met her. He promised himself that he would in future be much more considerate and gentle to her for she deserved all the solicitude and love and protection that he could offer. She was someone rare and precious and he must never take her for granted. He would perhaps try to tell her something of this when she awoke.

Then the two military policemen came into the canteen. It seemed that John sensed danger a second before he actually saw them. Something in the atmosphere changed. Perhaps it was only a current of air from the opening door but it seemed like something more metaphysical, a scent of threat, a sudden watchfulness, among the occupants of the canteen.

John watched the two redcaps begin their tour of inspection during which they stopped at each occupied table demanding to see passes. Had he not been handicapped by his plaster-cast and crutches he would have attempted to find an escape route, perhaps through the washroom and lavatories, but as things were he knew that his only chance of not being apprehended was to say that he had lost his pass and hope that his wearing hospital blues would make it seem unlikely that he would be on the run. The redcaps were drawing closer. John decided that it would be better to waken Maxie than wait for the military police to do so. He reached out and touched her head.

'Maxie!' he said. 'Wake up, Maxie!'

She did not move.

'Come on, love! Wake up!' He gave her a gentle shake and she stirred and moaned softly.

'Maxie!'

She raised her head and for a moment her eyes were unfocused and hazy with sleep. Then she smiled as full consciousness returned.

He said, 'Look. Over there. Redcaps. They'll be here in a minute. I thought I'd better wake you.'

Instantly her eyes filled with alarm. 'What will you do? You haven't got a pass. What will you say, John?'

'Don't worry. I'll say I've lost it. If the worst happens they'll send me back to Winwick. There's nothing to worry about. I'll write to you, Maxie. So don't worry.'

But as the redcaps drew close to their table Maxie's look of apprehension did not diminish. One of the military policemen was a sergeant, the other a corporal. They were now standing above Maxie, looking down at her, each with the same smirk that registered their contempt for the notion of female soldiers.

The sergeant spoke. 'You're up late for a little girl, or I suppose I ought to say early. I take it you have a pass?'

Maxie produced her pass without speaking. The sergeant examined it and handed it back to her. Meanwhile John was going through a pretence of searching his pockets.

The sergeant said, 'Well, Jock. You having a bit of trouble?'

'I thought it was in my paybook. That's where I put it.'

'And now it's disappeared?'

'Looks like it.'

'I see.' The sergeant looked sceptical. 'Are you on leave?'

'No. Just a twenty-four hour pass. I'm due back tomorrow – I mean this evening.'

'Back where? What hospital you in?'

'Winwick. Near Warrington.'

'You're a long way from there, aren't you?'

'I came to Manchester to see my girl-friend. Fiancée.' John nodded towards Maxie.

'Fiancée eh? How long you known her?'

Maxie broke in: 'That's nothing to do with you, how long we've known each other.'

'Just taking an interest,' the sergeant said equably. 'Nothing to get upset about. What you done to your leg?'

'Gunshot wounds. Normandy.'

'That so? Still, I'm afraid you'll have to come along with us if you can't show us a pass. You understand that, don't you?'

John shrugged.

Maxie said, 'He had a pass. He showed it me. I saw it. He must have dropped it.'

'Yes. Well perhaps he did and perhaps he didn't. Thing is, he hasn't got one now and that's what matters. Corporal, take him out to the truck while I just check that little bunch over there.'

'Come on, lad,' the corporal said. 'Let's have you.'

'No!' Maxie wailed. 'You can't take him away! Leave him alone!'

John stood and took up his crutches. 'Maxie,' he said, 'I told you everything's going to be all right. I'll write and you write to me. Okay? We'll see each other again soon. You stay there. Please. Don't make a fuss, love. It won't do any good. I'll see you soon. And write to me.'

He turned away and followed the corporal to the exit from the canteen. At the door he looked back and saw Maxie standing near the table at which they had been sitting. Her face was twisted in misery and though he could not see the tears he knew that she was crying. In her bulky uniform she looked small but stocky, almost squat, and her short dark hair was untidy. She looked pathetic, yet also comic. He felt, irrationally, a stab of guilt as he went out of the building to the parked truck and then he was assailed by a sense of loss although he did not then know that he would never see Maxie again.

★   ★   ★   ★   ★

The hospital commandant looked up from behind his desk at John and sighed. Then he looked down again at the papers he had been consulting and said, 'You've had the plaster removed, I see. I suppose you think that means you'll find it even easier to clear off to the flesh-pots of Manchester where, incidentally, the Corps of Military Police are getting a little browned off with you. But let me tell you this. I've got a little surprise for you. You'll be going from here into close confinement. This hospital, as I expect you know, used to be a loony bin. That means there are padded cells available. And that's where you are going. Into a cell. I don't like doing it but it's your own fault. And another thing. I'm going to get you out of this hospital as quickly as I can. Normally you'd spend quite a few weeks on physiotherapy before being discharged but I'm going to get rid of you in a hurry. Back to your depot. What happens to you from there is not my worry. I expect your MO will send you to a convalescent depot. All I'm concerned with is getting you out of my hospital. You're a Bolshie. A trouble-maker. Right, Sarnt. Take him over to the cells and lock him up. You let him out only once a day for physiotherapy and then under escort. Otherwise he's to be kept locked up at all times. With luck we should be rid of him in a week or two. Carry on, Sarnt!'

So John was put in a padded cell where he spent the next fortnight before being sent to his regimental depot. During that time he wrote two letters to Maxie but received no reply. He suspected that the provost-sergeant was not posting his letters and that Maxie's letters to him were being intercepted. He decided that he would write again when he was free to post the letter himself. But he did not fulfil this intention. Once he was out of hospital blues and back into khaki he seemed to put on, with the uniform, a change or reversion of personality. He was drawn back into the harsh and brutalising ambience of barrack-room and camp. Hospital life soon seemed as remote and idyllic as his civilian existence and he felt the tough rind of deliberate insensitivity rapidly growing over the areas of feeling which had begun to reawaken while he was in Winwick. He spent what little money he received on drink and tobacco and he often became violent when he was drunk.

From the depot he was sent, as the hospital commandant had

predicted, to a convalescent depot in Hamilton. This establishment, which was housed in the old Cameronian barracks, was far more military in its character than medical. Remedial exercises were carried out under the supervision of physical training instructors and the parades and picket duties were little different from those of the depot from which he had been posted. John's right leg, which had been fractured, soon lost its stiffness and seemed little affected by the injury but his left ankle caused more trouble. He found it almost impossible to flex the foot up and down and the routine of exercises did not cause any improvement. The handicap was not severe but it was enough to prevent his being discharged and returned to an active service unit, so he was still in Hamilton when the Germans surrendered in May, 1945. As far as John was concerned, his war was over. He packed his small kit, shaving-gear, towel and toothbrush in his haversack and walked out of the barracks, heading South. Private John Vernon Bain was on the run once more. He was walking away from the army before it dehumanised him completely. It was going to be a long journey.